D0463447

TEACH YOURSELF BOOKS

GERMAN GRAMMAR

The difficulty in learning a language lies not in understanding the grammar and learning the rules, but in storing up in the memory a huge number of sentence patterns appropriate for a large number of situations and having them at the tip of the tongue ready to roll off whenever you want them. This book aims to help you to build up that reservoir of sentence patterns. It is a complete grammar of the German language.

This is a praiseworthy attempt to clarify in a practical way what is to most a rather forbidding subject.

The Times Educational Supplement

TEACH YOURSELF BOOKS

GERMAN GRAMMAR

P. G. WILSON, M.Sc.

TEACH YOURSELF BOOKS
ST. PAUL'S HOUSE WARWICK LANE LONDON EC4

First printed 1950
This impression 1971

ISBN 0 340 05790 4

Printed in Great Britain for The English Universities Press, Ltd., by Richard Clay (The Chaucer Press), Ltd., Bungay, Suffolk

CONTENTS

FOREWORD

People are generally prone to look upon grammar as a dreary, dry-as-dust study fit only for the intelligentsia, the highbrows and the quidnuncs, and beyond the grasp of the normal average brain. Its jargon of technical words, such as Subjunctive Mood, Copulative Verb, Accusative Case, Passive Voice and all the rest of it, is often quite enough to turn the enquirer away from any further dalliance with the subject.

And yet grammar is within us all, embedded deep in our mind, guiding our speech willy-nilly at every moment of our waking life. You *do* know grammar even if you have never been to school nor even learnt to read and write. Let me prove that assertion. You speak your native language so that other natives understand you, and hence you speak it according to a pattern which is familiar to those who hear you, pattern being merely a homely word for grammar. If you did not follow this native pattern you would not be understood. Of course you may not always follow the pattern in every particular: you may, for instance, say "You was", "I come home late yesterday", "I seen him". That merely means that you do not in certain respects conform to what has been accepted as correct by a certain socially important section of the community; your pattern is slightly different from the accepted form. Nevertheless your language as a whole is governed by the national pattern—that is to say, that it conforms to the national grammar. Like Molière's Monsieur Jourdain, who was amazed to learn that when he said to his servant Nicole: "Bring me my slippers", he was speaking prose, you may be surprised to learn that when you say "I could have done it", you are using the Subjunctive. You cannot get away from the fact that you have a whole system of grammar in your head; all that the grammarian has to do is to make this unconscious grammar conscious knowledge.

Your unconscious grammar has even sorted out the parts of speech for you. How do I know that? Because people suffering from aphasia, or disease of the memory, may find that they cannot use one part of speech at all. Thus cases have been known of patients who, although uneducated, have had all the adjectives blotted out, or all the nouns. This is, I understand, a medically attested fact. Grammar consists of bringing into conscious knowledge what is all arranged in the unconscious mind. There is no abracadabra about it, but just plain commonsense. Let us agree not to be frightened of grammar.

There is another point I should like to put before you. Language was not made by grammarians, philologists, philosophers, poets and other great minds, but by humble people like you and me and the farmer's boy. It is the most democratic thing created by man. Hence all the ideas underlying grammar are simple, and well within the grasp of anybody who will take the trouble to think. There is nothing difficult about the Subjunctive and the Indicative Mood; it is just horse-sense. The difficulty of learning a language lies not in understanding the grammar and learning the rules, but in building up in the memory a huge number of sentence patterns appropriate for a large number of situations and having them at the tip of the tongue ready to roll off whenever you want them. It is not a high order of intelligence that is wanted, but perseverance and unremitting practice.

The method followed in this book is to discuss first the idea that lies behind a grammatical phenomenon (e.g., the Subjunctive) and illustrate it by English examples, then to attack the German angle and back that up by numerous examples which, if learnt by heart, will build up that reservoir of sentence patterns that will in the end constitute the only knowledge worth retaining. Of course much of grammar consists of lists of words, exceptions, irregularities, etc., with which all languages abound, and which have little to do with grammar proper. Thus, besides being a reasoned grammar, this book is also a work of reference which supplements the dictionary. It is, I think, a pretty complete grammar of the German language.

Remember that its title is "Teach Yourself German Grammar"; it can help you to teach yourself, but YOU must do the learning.

P. G. Wilson.

CHAPTER I

THE VOCABULARY

Polonius : What do you read, my lord ?
Hamlet : Words, words, words.

Before proceeding to deal with German grammar proper in orderly sequence, let us cast a rapid glance at the language as a whole, so as to see where the difficulties lie and how they may be tackled.

PRONUNCIATION AND SPELLING

The pronünciation and spelling of both English and French are a very great stumbling-block to the foreigner, especially the elderly one, who wishes to learn these languages. Nothing can, of course, be done about the pronunciation of either French or English or any other language, but spelling is a purely man-made difficulty of which we could rid ourselves at any time with a little intelligent planning.

German sounds are not difficult for an English-speaker, especially if he comes from the North or from Scotland, Wales or Ireland, since in those parts the vowels are kept pure and do not, as in the South, start on one sound and gradually shift into another : Northern " no ", Southern " nou ". Moreover, the " r " is rolled and the guttural " ch " in " loch " has the same value as the German " ch ". The guidance given in Appendix B will prove sufficient to put you on the right lines, especially if you supplement it by studying gramophone records of German texts and by listening in to radio stations using the German language or giving German lessons.

There is no rigid " standard " German, the dialects being

still alive, and influencing the speech of even the educated more than is the case in England, where Southern English tends to oust all others. It is true that an artificial standard pronunciation exists, called **Bühnendeutsch**—stage German—which is adopted by actors and taught in the schools, but it is not generally spoken in everyday life.

German spelling is beautifully regular, and if you know the pronunciation of the individual letters you can pronounce any German word correctly, thus being spared the misery of such phonetic horrors as plough, enough, cough, hiccough, which dumbfound the foreigner. The German word **Knöpfe**—buttons—is pronounced **k-n-ö-p-f-e**, exactly as it is spelt, all the letters being sounded. This spares you a great deal of useless drudgery and allows you to concentrate on more important aspects of the language.

German, like English, has a strong stress on the root syllable of a word: forGIVing, **verGEBend**; forGIVeness, **VerGEBung**; LOVely, **LIEBlich**. As you see, the root takes the strong stress, while the prefix for-, **ver-**, and the suffixes -ness, **-ung**, -ly, **-lich**, and the inflexions -ing, **-end** have a weaker accent. This makes German words much more easy to pronounce and remember than French words, with their delicate shifting stress so unfamiliar to our linguistic habits.

German sounds, spelling and word-stress all combine to make the learner's task comparatively easy for the English-speaker; but what about the German alphabet? The beginner is always inclined to boggle over this unfamiliar type, but its terrors are largely imaginary. You can learn the alphabet in a few days, and become quite expert at reading it in a few weeks. After all, the German is only a slight modification of the Roman, and presents no real difficulty; but the written script takes longer to learn to read and write, and the question arises: is it worth while to learn it? You need yourself never write the script, and you will need to be able to read it only if you have to deal with letters written by older Germans; my advice is to practise the script only if you have time, but not to worry about it otherwise. Personally I tackled it, and found it amusing to use, and was glad I could read the script when I had to read many hundreds of German letters during the late war.

THE GERMAN VOCABULARY

Let us examine the German vocabulary—**der Wortschatz** = word treasure—with some care, as there are important points connected with it. In English you learn the word " vocabulary " as a block, swallowing it whole and attaching to it the meaning of " list of words "; you do not pick it to pieces to see what makes it tick. In German, on the other hand, it pays you to do just that, as I shall show.

French, as you know, has very many words so like English that you can recognize them at once: *arriver, rivière, table, possible, honneur, avantage, prospérité, satisfaction, horrible, compassion, sympathie,* etc., etc. These are a great encouragement to the beginner, whose memory they help considerably by reducing the load it has to bear.

German has not nearly so many familiar words of this type, but it has nevertheless a large number of homely, everyday, basic words connected with the family, the home, the simple activities of life: **Vater, Mutter, Schwester, Bruder, Sohn, Tochter**; **Knie, Arm, Finger, Daumen** (thumb), **Zunge** (tongue); **Haus, Garten, Gras**; **Kuh, Ochs, Schaf, Kalb**; **Milch, Wasser**; **Land, See, Schiff, Boot** (boat); **springen, singen, fischen, lieben** (love), **sagen** (say), and so on. There is something very comforting to find that you are on familiar ground when, in the first lesson, you learn: " **Was ist das? Das ist ein Buch.**" It encourages you to go on with a language which is so like your own, and encouragement is what a language student needs above all things if he or she is to succeed. What you think is easy, *is* easy!

Then there is another large class of words which are not quite so readily recognized, but which are only thinly disguised. It is worth your while to be on the look-out for them, because they will more easily take a grip on your memory if you can associate them with the English sister-word, even if the meanings are no longer quite the same in the two languages. Thus **Knabe**—boy—is our " knave ", which once meant a youth, then a servant, then a thief; **Knecht**—man-servant—is our " Knight ", once a youth, then the squire of a lord. **Wald**—wood, forest—is our " wold " of the North and our " weald " of the South. **Dicht**—compact, dense—is our " tight ", and **wasserdicht** means " watertight ". **Sehr**—very—is our English " sore ", as in " he was sore afraid ". **Zimmer**—room—is our " timber ", of which rooms used to be made. **Zaun**—hedge—is our " town ", first meaning a hedge, then what is within the hedge, " garden ", then what is in the garden, the Scottish " toon ", a house, and finally " town ", a collection of houses. **Ritzen**—to scratch—and **reiszen**—to tear—are both cognate with our " write ", writing being originally scratching the surface. The German **schreiben**—to write—comes from the same Latin word that gave us " scribe ". You will find the study of such words not only useful to you in learning German, but most interesting in itself.

Now, in English we have built up a large part of our vocabulary by adopting French, Latin and Greek words, especially those which express abstract ideas. German, on the other hand, although it has quite a considerable number of such words, has built up its vocabulary from its own native materials. There was a time, in the seventeenth and eighteenth centuries, when German was threatened by too great an influx of foreign words, but the language reacted vigorously, and ever since the days of the philosopher Leibniz there has been a movement to keep German free from them. Thus German had no native word for " consciousness " until Christian Wolff germanized the idea by inventing the word **Bewusstsein**, " consciousness " being the Latin for " knowingness " and **Bewusstsein** being the German for " being in a state of knowing ".

I hope you do not think I am getting too highbrow and erudite; you will see shortly that I am being severely practical. Let us examine a group of words we have adopted from French, Latin and Greek, and see how they are expressed in German. Here they are: compassion, sympathy, conscience, circumstance, accident, dialogue, suicide, ineffable, hæmorrhage (or hemorrhage), constellation, equilibrium. They are mostly bookish words which would be used only by persons of a certain degree of education. We shall find that in German they would be familiar to any German of any degree of education.

" Compassion " is Latin for " with-suffering ", and " sympathy " is Greek for exactly the same; the German word is **Mitleid**, which on the face of it means " with-suffering ": any German child understands it as soon as he sees or hears it. " Conscience " is the Latin for " with-knowing "; the German **Gewissen** means the same, **ge-** being a collective prefix and **wissen**—our " to wit " and " God wot "—meaning " to know ". " Constellation " is a collection of stars in Latin; **Gestirn** says exactly that, but in German, **Stern** being " a star ". " Circumstance " is Latin for " around-standing "; **Umstand** says it in German. " Accident " means a " to-falling " in Latin; **Zufall** translates it into German. " Dialogue " is Greek for " two-speech "; **Zwiegespräch** keeps to German. " Suicide " is Latin for " self-killing "; **Selbstmord** is " self-murder ". " Ineffable " means " unspeakable, inexpressible "; the German is **unaussprechlich**, " un-out-speakly ". " Hæmorrhage " is a technical medical word from the Greek meaning " blood-burst "; **Blutsturz** means " blood-gush " in German; a German child can understand—and spell—it without help. Do you know what " autotoxin " means? It is Greek for

" self-poison "—poison that creates itself in the body; the German **Selbstgift** is self-explanatory, **Gift**, originally our " gift ", something given, is " poison ". " Equilibrium " is Latin for " equal-balance "; **Gleichgewicht** is German for " equal-weight ".

The moral of all this is that when you have learnt your basic German words you can get at the meaning of many technical and abstract words by simply breaking them down, though you may not be able to translate them into good English without a dictionary. And there is a further lesson in this German building-up of words from purely native elements: you can group German words into families all derived from the same root, and thus get a grip on the thread that leads you through the maze. This is not possible in English, or only partly possible—and then only if you have studied the etymology of the language. Thus there is nothing in English to connect the following group of words: pronounce, acquit, promise, contradict, telephone, intercessor, language, conversation, monologue, all of which in German have the root **sprech-** as their basic element. Pronounce is **aussprechen**, to out-speak; acquit is **freisprechen**, to free-speak; promise is **versprechen**, to away-speak; contradict is **widersprechen**, to against-speak; telephone is **Fernsprecher**, far-speaker; intercessor is **Fürsprecher**, for-speaker; language is **Sprache**, speech; conversation is **Gespräch**, with-speech; monologue is **Selbstgespräch**, self-speech. Duden in his *Grammatik* gives a list of 127 words formed from this root alone! You should learn to make little lists of word-families of this kind, and you will find the lists of prefixes and suffixes in this book of use to you in your studies in **Wortbildung**, word-formation.

That last word leads us to a German characteristic which it shares with English in a somewhat exaggerated form—viz., the tendency to build up words by putting them together, steamship and **Dampfschiff** both being written as one word. German, however, is not afraid of very long compound words written in one block (and known humorously as **Schlangenwörter,** snake-words), as for instance this monstrosity which I extract from Sütterlin's *Die deutsche Sprache der Gegenwart*—" The German Language of the Present Day " : **Dampfschiffahrtsgesellschafts-direktorsstellvertretersgemahlin.** If you break it down into its component parts you get : steam-navigation-company's-manager's-deputy's-wife. **Gemahlin** is a typically German word ; it is our " consort ", and illustrates the German tendency to delight in titles. If you happened to be the manager of a company, your employees and your visitors would bombard you with your title : " **Ja, Herr Direktor. Nein, Herr Direktor. Guten Tag, Herr Direktor** ". And there would be a little stiff bow with every **Herr Direktor.** *Autres pays, autres mœurs !*

CHAPTER II

GRAMMAR

Grammar's a master whose harsh sway
E'en kings, like schoolboys, must obey.
(Molière, " Les Femmes savantes ".)

We have cast a rapid glance over the words of the German language ; let us now survey its grammar—in other words, let us see how words behave in speech.

You are used to the English language pattern, in which the position of a word plays an important grammatical rôle. You will have to get used to the German language pattern, in which the rôle of a word is shown very largely by its form. In other words, German is more highly inflected than English. I will explain what I mean by discussing an example or two.

THE ENGLISH PATTERN

Here is a very simple sentence which any little child might pronounce :

A poor man once saw a little boy and a lovely lady.

Let us pick it to pieces to show the grammatical pattern it follows. First of all, " a " is attached to " man ", " boy " and " lady ". There is nothing in the word " a " to show that " man " and " boy " are males and " lady " female ; nor does it show that " man " is the subject of the verb and " boy " and " lady " the objects.

Next let us examine the adjectives " poor ", " little " and " lovely ". Here again there is nothing except position that shows that " poor " is attached to " man ", " little " to " boy " and " lovely " to " lady ". We could switch round these adjectives and say: "little man", "lovely boy" and "poor lady", and still the sentence would be perfect grammatically, though the meaning would have been altered.

The three nouns could also be switched round—e.g. "A poor boy once saw a little man and a lovely lady"—but the meaning is considerably altered, the "boy" now doing the "seeing". The only reason why we know that it is the "man" who saw is the fact that "man" stands in front of "saw", and likewise the only reason we know that "boy" and "lady" are the objects of the man's seeing is that they stand behind the verb "saw". Position, you see, has a grammatical function of great importance in English.

THE GERMAN PATTERN

Now how would a German child make the same statement? It would, without any effort and without knowing that it was doing what to us seem difficult grammatical tricks, say:

Ein armer Mann sah einmal einen kleinen Jungen und eine schöne Dame.

Our English "a" has blossomed into **ein** for **Mann**, **einen** for **Jungen** and **eine** for **Dame.** Why? Because **Mann** is masculine gender and the subject of the verb; **Jungen** is masculine gender and the object of the verb; **Dame** is feminine gender and the object of the verb—though it would still be **eine** for the subject in the feminine.

Now take the adjectives: **arm-er, klein-en, schön-e.** "Poor" is the German **arm**; "little" is **klein**; "lovely" is **schön**, but now we have inflections added to show grammatical function. The **-er** of **armer** shows that **Mann** is the masculine subject of the verb; the **-en** of **kleinen** shows that **Jungen** is the masculine object of the verb; the **-e** of **schöne** shows that **Dame** is the feminine object of the verb (though it would still be **-e** for the feminine subject). In

German, then, each adjective shows by its form the grammatical rôle of the noun it qualifies. We cannot possibly switch the adjectives and say, for instance, as we could in English: **Ein kleinen Mann sah einmal einen schöne Jungen und eine armer Dame.** It would be utterly ungrammatical and ridiculous German—a sort of broken German.

Now for the nouns. **Mann** does not show by its form whether it is subject or object, nor does **Dame**; but **Jungen** is marked out as the object by the **-n**, the subject-form being **Junge.** We cannot switch the nouns as we could in English without making chaos of the grammar.

Thus **ein** + **arm-er** + **Mann** are grammatically linked together by their inflections to show the masculine subject; **ein-en** + **klein-en** + **Junge-n** are similarly linked together to show the masculine object; **ein-e** + **schön-e** + **Dame** are also linked together to show the feminine object (though in this case the feminine subject would also be **ein-e** + **schön-e** + **Dame**).

Note that the task of showing gender and case falls mainly on the article and the adjective, not on the noun—an important point. It means that you must learn thoroughly the declension of the articles and suchlike words (e.g. the, this, that, which, etc.) and the declension of the adjective. The declension of the definite article "the" (= **der, die, das**) is the basis for all the declensions, and you must know it so that the correct form springs automatically to your mind. That is your first task in German grammar.

GENDER AND CASE

Next you must know the gender of the nouns. How are you to do that? Well, most male creatures are masculine; most female creatures are feminine, but not all; inanimate objects may be either masculine, feminine or neuter. You will find rules on p. 23 for spotting the genders, but your golden rule must be to learn the definite article with the noun. Thus **Tisch** (= table) is masculine, **Tinte** (= ink) is feminine, **Glas** (= glass) is neuter. Do not try to memorize: **Tisch,** m.; **Tinte,** f.; **Glas,** n. Learn, by saying ALOUD and FIRMLY the word-blocks **DER-Tisch**; **DIE-Tinte**; **DAS-Glas.** That will stick in your memory because you have used the natural channels to it—viz., the ear, the muscles of the organs of speech and also the eye. Write out the words, too, and you will add the memory of the muscles of your fingers and arms plus your eye memory.

I said above that the nouns do not, on the whole, show the case, that task being put upon the articles and adjectives. This is broadly true. To encourage you let me state the position as simply as possible, omitting all exceptions and one or two fairly large groups.

A. Feminine nouns are not inflected for case in the singular:
Nom. **Frau.** Acc. **Frau.** Gen. **Frau.** Dat. **Frau.**

B. Feminine nouns add **-n** or **-en** to make the plural and all the cases end in **-n** or **-en**: thus the plural is Nom. **Frauen.** Acc. **Frauen.** Gen. **Frauen.** Dat. **Frauen.**

C. Masculines and Neuters have, in general, only one case ending in the singular; they add **-s** or **-es** for the Genitive (though some MAY add **-e** for the Dative; this **-e** is, however, dying in modern German and is not so often used in the spoken language):
Nom. **König.** Acc. **König.** Gen. **Königs.** Dat. **König(e).**
In the plural the Nominative, Accusative and Genitive have the same ending and the Dative always ends in **-n** or **-en**:
Nom. **Könige.** Acc. **Könige.** Gen. **Könige.** Dat. **Königen.**

The plural of nouns in English is simple: add -s to the singular. In German it is more complicated, but I will not go into that matter now; you will find it fully treated on p. 26. A good way of learning the plural is to learn it with the singular—e.g. learn aloud **DER-Tisch + DIE-Tische**; **DIE-Tinte + DIE-Tinten**; **DAS-Glas + DIE-Gläser.**

Well, the above sets out your first headache in German grammar. It sounds very complicated, but it will soon sort itself out if you give your mind to it, and PRACTISE, PRACTISE, PRACTISE.

THE CASES EXPLAINED

We have talked about "cases" without explaining what we mean; we had better tackle this problem. English has cases, as, for example, the interrogative "who?":

	English.	German.
Nom.	who?	**wer?**
Acc.	whom?	**wen?**
Gen.	whose?	**wes?** or **wessen?** *
Dat.	whom?	**wem?**

Examples in both languages are:

Nom.	Who saw him?	**wer sah ihn?**
Acc.	Whom did he see?	**wen sah er?**
Gen.	Whose book is that?	**wessen Buch ist das?**
Dat.	To whom did you give the book?	**wem gaben Sie das Buch?**

The only difference in the cases is that the German has a special form for the Dative. Let us rapidly run over the use of the cases.

The Nominative is used in German only for the doer of the action, the subject of the verb. It cannot be used for any other purpose, except for calling—the Vocative—as in "Father, just look!" = **Vater, sieh mal!** But the Nomina-

* **wes** is the old form, replaced by **wessen** in modern German.

tive is used with the verb "to be", "to become", etc., as: he is my father; he became a doctor.

The Accusative is used for the object of the verb: "I love my father" = **Ich liebe meinen Vater.** Since the Nominative is restricted to the subject of the verb, we must use another case in sentences like: "He remained one day in Berlin", where "one day" is a measure of time; "It weighs one grain", where "one grain" is a measure of weight; "the box is one foot long", where "one foot" is a measure of length. The Accusative is the case used: **Er blieb einen Tag in Berlin; Es wiegt einen Gran; Die Kiste ist einen Fuss lang.**

Certain prepositions also govern the Accusative.

The Genitive is used to show the relationship of one noun to another, often a sort of "possessive" relationship, as in English: "Father's book" = **Das Buch des Vaters** (or, more poetically, **des Vaters Buch**); "the tree's colour" (or, more naturally, "the colour of the tree") = **die Farbe des Baumes**; "the king's subjects" = **die Untertanen des Königs.**

Certain prepositions and verbs also govern the Genitive.

The Dative is used to mark out the indirect object of the verb (generally a person): "He gives the man the book" = **er gibt dem Mann das Buch.** It may also show the person indirectly interested or affected by the action: **Der Dieb stahl dem Bauer das Geld** = The thief stole the money from the peasant.

Certain prepositions and verbs govern the Dative.

The German verb is easy to conjugate, and we shall not trouble about it here. Your difficulty will be mainly with the use of the Subjunctive and the Passive Voice, which you will find on p. 113 and p. 134. The Adverb is easy, and so are the Personal Pronouns and the Relatives, once you have mastered the declension of the Definite Articles and the uses of the cases.

WORD ORDER

We saw above that in German the nouns are marked out to show their function; hence it does not matter much where you put them in the sentence, it will still have the same meaning. In English you alter the meaning if you alter the position of the noun.

Take this statement in English:

A poor man once saw a little boy.

We can ring the changes on it in a very limited way:

Once a poor man saw a little boy.

We can hardly say:

Saw a poor man once a little boy or
A poor man a little boy once saw.

If we want to turn it into a question, we still keep in English the order " man : seeing ", by using the verb " to do " as a sort of interrogative introducer:

Did a poor man once see a little boy?

We just cannot afford to play about with that " subject : verbal idea " order in English, because we should produce chaos if we did.

Now let us take a look at the German. We could say:

1. **Ein armer Mann sah einmal einen kleinen Jungen.**
2. **Sah einmal ein armer Mann einen kleinen Jungen?**
3. **Einmal sah ein armer Mann einen kleinen Jungen.**
4. **Einen kleinen Jungen sah einmal ein armer Mann.**
5. **(Dass) ein armer Mann einmal einen kleinen Jungen sah.**

All these are possible, and all mean the same thing. No. 1 is the normal statement, " A poor man once saw a little boy." No. 2 is the question form, the interrogative, " Did a poor man once see a little boy? " No. 3 begins with a word which is not the subject of the sentence, and therefore the verb holds the second place and is immediately followed by the subject. No. 4 shifts the emphasis as in the English, " It was a little boy that a poor man once saw." As it begins with what is not the subject, the verb holds the second place and is immediately followed by the subject. No. 5 is a subordinate sentence, **dass** meaning " that ", as in " I know that a poor man once saw a little boy." Now, in German—I am sorry to have to tell you all this so soon, but you had better face it like a man, or woman—in subordinate clauses the finite verb always falls to the end of the sentence, and that is why **sah** is where it is. Do not worry unduly about this; practice makes perfect or, as the Germans put it, " **Übung macht den Meister** ", practice makes the master.

THE MORAL

That concludes our rapid and superficial survey of German grammar; it has shown you where your main difficulties will lie and how you may surmount them. Remember that this book can only set out in as clear a fashion as possible the principles of grammar; it cannot teach you grammar or teach you German: you must do that yourself. The title of this book is " Teach Yourself German Grammar ". It is an honest title, and this is an honest book. Teach yourself by studying the explanations given and by learning the rules and the examples; then turn these rules into the living language by reading and learning texts, both prose and poetry, by listening to wireless talks in German and gramophone records, and by speaking German whenever you have an opportunity. Lord Avonmore said of Blackstone that " he found the law a skeleton, and clothed it with life, colour, and complexion ". This grammar is a skeleton; it is up to you to clothe it with life, colour and complexion.

CHAPTER III

THE ARTICLES

As we have seen, nouns in German have:

(*a*) Three Genders:

masculine (= **männlich**, from **der Mann**, man).
feminine (= **weiblich**, from **das Weib**, woman, our "wife").
neuter (= **sächlich**, from **die Sache**, thing).

Gender is generally shown not by the noun itself, but by the noun qualifiers: the articles, adjectival pronouns, adjectives.

(*b*) Four cases:

Nominative (= **der Werfall**, who-case).
Accusative (= **der Wenfall**, whom-case).
Genitive (= **der Wessenfall**, whose-case).
Dative (= **der Wemfall**, to-whom-case).

In German Grammars for Germans the order is: Nominative, Genitive, Dative, Accusative, but English German grammars usually follow the Latin order, as I have done. The cases are also named: Nom. **der erste Fall** (= 1st case); Gen. **der zweite Fall** (= 2nd case); Dat. **der dritte Fall** (= 3rd case); Acc. **der vierte Fall** (= 4th case).

The cases are shown partly by the nouns themselves, but mainly by the noun qualifiers.

(*c*) Two numbers:

Singular (= **die Einzahl**, one-number).
Plural (= **die Mehrzahl**, more-number).

Most nouns add an inflection to show the number, which is also shown by the noun-qualifiers. Gender is not shown in the plural by either the noun or its qualifiers.

Let us now tackle the most important noun-qualifiers, the Definite Article, " the ", and the Indefinite Article, " a, an ". Until you have mastered them thoroughly you will not be able to handle the noun correctly.

THE DEFINITE ARTICLE

In German it is called **das bestimmte Geschlechtswort** (= the definite sex- or gender-word). Here is its declension :

	Singular.			Plural.
	Masc.	Fem.	Neut.	All genders.
Nom.	**der**	**die**	**das**	**die**
Acc.	**den**	**die**	**das**	**die**
Gen.	**des**	**der**	**des**	**der**
Dat.	**dem**	**der**	**dem**	**den**

Note that the masculine and neuter differ only in the Nominative and Accusative singular. Further note particularly that the genders and cases are not all clearly shown by the form of the article : there are four **der** forms, four **die** forms, two **den** forms and two **das** forms.

Thus in the sentence :

Der Wagen der Bäcker steht in der Mitte der Strasse,

which means " The cart of the bakers (the bakers' cart) stands in the middle of the street ", the first **der** is the Nominative, masculine, singular ; the second **der** is the Genitive plural ; the third **der** is the Dative, feminine, singular ; the fourth **der** is the Genitive, feminine, singular. Nevertheless the meaning is perfectly clear, and no confusion is caused by the four **der's**. Why ? Because their function is shown both by their word-order and by the gender of the nouns. You will have to watch this point, and not jump to the conclusion that every **der** you see qualifies a masculine noun in the Nominative singular.

You must learn the declension of **der, die, das,** so that you have it perfectly by heart; it will be good discipline for you. But as you never meet with the Definite Article alone, but always in combination with nouns, the mere learning of the declension is not enough: you must learn it in the proper setting. I give you below three sentences in the singular and plural, the first being masculine throughout, the second feminine and the third neuter, and they show the order: Nominative; Accusative; Genitive; Dative. The English is:

The man sees the son of the king (the king's son) in the garden.

The woman sees the daughter of the queen in the church.

The child sees the lamb of the sheep on the field.

These are repeated in the plural. Here they are in German:

Singular.

	Nominative.	Verb.	Accusative.	Genitive.	Dative.
M.	**Der Mann**	**sieht**	**den Sohn**	**des Königs**	**in dem Garten**
F.	**Die Frau**	**sieht**	**die Tochter**	**der Königin**	**in der Kirche**
N.	**Das Kind**	**sieht**	**das Lamm**	**des Schafs**	**auf dem Feld**

Plural.

M.	**Die Männer**	**sehen**	**die Söhne**	**der Könige**	**in den Gärten**
F.	**Die Frauen**	**sehen**	**die Töchter**	**der Königin-nen**	**in den Kirchen**
N.	**Die Kinder**	**sehen**	**die Lämmer**	**der Schafe**	**auf den Feldern**

Note that **König,** king, makes the feminine **Königin,** by adding **-in**; this is like the English -ess, but is much more widely used. If you will learn those six little sentences by heart so that you can write any one of them out without a mistake, you will be well on your way to the conquest of the Definite Article. Do not worry about the various plurals for the moment; just learn them by heart.

The Definite Article is unstressed in speech in German as it is in English: we do not say THEE book, but th' book.

Owing to this slurring the German Article often fuses with the preceding preposition as follows :

an dem becomes **am**, as in **am Montag**, on Monday ; **am Himmel**, in the sky ;

in dem ,, **im**, as in **im Zimmer ist es warm**, it is warm in the room ;

bei dem ,, **beim**, as in **er fasste den Mann beim Kragen**, he seized the man by the collar ;

von dem ,, **vom**, as in **der Herr vom Hause**, the master of the house ;

zu dem ,, **zum**, as in **ich gehe zum Bruder**, I am going to my brother's ;

an das ,, **ans**, as in **ich gehe ans Haus**, I am going towards the house ;

in das ,, **ins**, as in **er geht ins Zimmer**, he goes into the room ;

auf das ,, **aufs**, as in **sie singt aufs schönste**, she sings most (very) beautifully ;

zu der ,, **zur**, as in **zur Not**, at a pinch, on the off-chance ; this is the only feminine contraction.

You will be well advised to learn all the above examples by heart.

Qualifiers declined like **der, die, das**, are ; **dieser**, this ; **jener**, that, yon ; **welcher ?**, which? ; **mancher**, many a ; **solcher**, such, together with **wer ?**, who ?, and other words which we shall meet with later on. Here is the declension of **dieser**, which you already know if you have learnt the Definite Article properly.

	Singular.			Plural.
	Masc.	Fem.	Neut.	All genders.
Nom.	**dieser**	**diese**	**dieses**	**diese**
Acc.	**diesen**	**diese**	**dieses**	**diese**
Gen.	**dieses**	**dieser**	**dieses**	**dieser**
Dat.	**diesem**	**dieser**	**diesem**	**diesen**

THE INDEFINITE ARTICLE

The Indefinite Article—**das unbestimmte Geschlechtswort**—has the same case-endings as the Definite Article, except that the Nominative masculine and the Nominative and Accusative neuter in the singular are not inflected. If you know your **der, die, das,** you know your **ein, eine, ein.** The Indefinite Article has of course no plural—the plural of **ein Mann** is **Männer,** just as " a man " becomes " men " in the plural in English. In the negative we use **kein,** not any, no, as in " I have no ink, I haven't any ink "—**ich habe keine Tinte.**

	The Indefinite Article Singular only.			Kein Singular			Plural
	Masc.	Fem.	Neut.	Masc.	Fem.	Neut.	(all genders)
Nom.	**ein**	**eine**	**ein**	**kein**	**keine**	**kein**	**keine**
Acc.	**einen**	**eine**	**ein**	**keinen**	**keine**	**kein**	**keine**
Gen.	**eines**	**einer**	**eines**	**keines**	**keiner**	**keines**	**keiner**
Dat.	**einem**	**einer**	**einem**	**keinem**	**keiner**	**keinem**	**keinen**

Concentrate on : **DER Mann,** but **EIN Mann,** and **DAS Kind,** but **EIN Kind,** and you will not be tempted to add the **-er** of **der** to **ein,** or the **-s** of **das** to **ein.** This temptation is especially strong with the possessive adjectives, which are all declined like **ein, eine, ein : mein,** my ; **dein,** thy ; **sein,** his (or its) ; **ihr,** her (or its) ; **unser,** our ; **euer,** your (familiar plural) ; **ihr,** their ; **Ihr,** your (polite form in singular and plural).

Ein, eine, ein, the Indefinite Article, does not contract with a preceding preposition, but it is slurred in speech by the **ei** being dropped : **ein Mann = 'n Mann ; einen Mann = 'nen Mann ; eine Frau = 'ne Frau.** This occurs in all cases, whether there is a preposition or not.

In order to distinguish **ein, eine, ein,** the Indefinite Article, from **ein, eine, ein,** the numeral " one ", the latter is sometimes printed by spacing out the letters : **ein Mann,** a man ; **e i n Mann,** one man.

HOW THE ARTICLES ARE USED

On the whole the use of the Articles is much the same in German as in English : " A man once loved a woman. The man was young, the woman was beautiful." " A " picks out one from amongst a number ; " the " indicates a person or thing already referred to and is equivalent to " this " or " that ". And so in German : **Ein Mann liebte einmal eine Frau. Der Mann war jung, die Frau war schön.** But there are some differences in usage which I now detail below.

The Definite Article is used before a noun which represents a whole class : **der Mensch is sterblich,** man is mortal. Hence names of metals require the Definite Article, as in **das Eisen ist nützlich,** iron is useful. Of course if the name of a material is used to mean only a certain quantity, then there is no Definite Article : **ich trinke gern Tee,** I like (drinking) tea ; but **der Tee ist eine Tropenpflanze,** tea is a tropical plant.

Names of countries—which are mostly neuter in German—do not take the Definite Article unless they are qualified : **Deutschland is ein schönes Land ;** Germany is a beautiful country ; but **das besetzte Deutschland,** occupied Germany. Those that are feminine do take the Definite Article : **die Schweiz ist gebirgig,** Switzerland is mountainous ; **die Türkei ist ein Staat in Kleinasien,** Turkey is a state in Asia Minor.

Names of rivers, mountains, lakes, take the Article : **der Rhein,** the Rhine ; **die Themse,** the Thames ; **der Bodensee,** Lake Constance ; **der Brocken,** the Brocken ; **der Rigi,** Mount Rigi.

Names of streets and squares, etc., take the Article : **die Friedrichstrasse ist sehr lang,** Frederick Street is very long ; **der Königsplatz ist in Berlin,** King's Square is in Berlin. It is omitted when giving one's address : **ich wohne Königstrasse, 15,** I live at 15 King Street.

The names of the days, seasons, months, meals, require the Definite Article : **im Winter ist es kalt,** it is cold in winter; **am Montag,** on Monday; **der Juli ist ein schöner Monat,** July is a lovely month; **das Frühstück ist um 8 Uhr,** breakfast is at eight.

Personal names take the Definite Article if qualified: **der junge Werther,** young Werther. In familiar speech the Article is used even if the name is not qualified: **der Hans geht in die Schule,** Johnny is going to school.

The Definite Article is used instead of the possessive adjective with parts of the body and clothing if the sense is clear: **er öffnete den Mund,** he opened his mouth; **er hielt den Hut in der Hand,** he held his hat in his hand.

The Indefinite Article is omitted when referring to a quality or a profession: **er ist Arzt,** he is a doctor; **er kam als Freund,** he came as a friend.

German uses the Definite Article where English uses the Indefinite when dealing with quantities: **es kostet zehn Mark das Pfund,** it costs ten marks a pound; **zweimal in der Woche,** twice a week.

Nothing very difficult about those few rules, is there? Read them over carefully, think them over, and learn the examples by heart.

CHAPTER IV

THE NOUN

The noun, **das Hauptwort** (= headword), must next be examined. It is usual to deal first with the declension of the noun in the singular and plural, but, as the declension depends largely on gender, I will put in a short section on gender first.

GENDER OF NOUNS

Natural gender is often indicated by different pairs of words, as in English : **Mann, Frau** ; **Vater, Mutter** ; **Hengst,** stallion, **Stute,** mare. The young of animals are generally neuter : **das Kind,** child ; **das Kalb,** calf ; **das Lamm,** lamb ; **das Fohlen,** foal.

The feminine is often formed from the masculine by adding **-in** (and modifying the vowel) : **der Freund,** friend ; **die Freundin,** lady friend ; **der Schwager,** brother-in-law ; **die Schwägerin,** sister-in-law ; **der Löwe,** lion ; **die Löwin,** lioness. German insists on the gender (or sex) being made clear whenever possible ; we do not in English. Thus we speak of " a friend " without worrying whether it is a he or a she, and in the same way " a teacher " is genderless ; in German you must use **Freund** and **Lehrer** for the males and **Freundin** and **Lehrerin** for the females. You may find yourself embarrassed if you forget to do this. A very few masculines are formed from the feminines : **die Witwe,** widow, **der Witwer,** widower ; **die Gans,** goose, **der Gänserich,** gander.

Grammatical gender can to a certain extent be brought under a few useful rules, but has mainly to be learnt by practice. Here are some of the rules that will help you :

Masculines

The days of the week, the months, the seasons, compass points and mountains are masculine: **der Dienstag,** Tuesday; **der Mai,** May; **der Winter,** winter, **der Herbst,** autumn, der **Frühling,** spring; **der Norden,** the North; **der Osten,** the East; **der Brocken,** the Brocken.

Most monosyllabic nouns derived from verbs are masculine: **der Fall,** case, from **fallen; der Biss,** bite, from **beissen; der Tanz,** dance, from **tanzen; der Guss,** gush, from **giessen.**

Nouns with the suffix **-er,** meaning the doer of an action: **der Bäcker,** baker; **der Fischer,** fisherman; **der Weber,** weaver; and those with the suffix **-el,** meaning an instrument to do something: **der Sattel,** saddle; **der Gürtel,** girdle, belt; **der Stachel,** sting. Add to these the nouns in **-ig: der König,** king; **der Honig,** honey; and those in **-ling: der Eindringling,** intruder (= in-throng-ling); **der Jüngling,** youth; **der Findling,** foundling; **der Frühling,** spring (= early-ling).

Finally a number of nouns ending in **-e** which indicate a living creature: **der Rabe,** raven; **der Löwe,** lion; **der Preusse,** Prussian.

Feminines

Nouns ending in **-e** derived from verbs: **die Bitte,** the request, from **bitten,** to ask; **die Frage,** question, from **fragen;** and also those derived from adjectives: **die Härte,** hardness, from **hart; die Güte,** goodness, kindness, from **gut; die Röte,** redness, from **rot.**

Nouns having the following suffixes: **-e** as above and those denoting lifeless objects: **die Stube,** room; all those ending in **-ung, -heit, -keit, -schaft: die Zeitung,** newspaper; **die Lösung,** solution; **die Kindheit,** childhood; **die Ähnlichkeit,** similarity; **die Freundschaft,** friendship; **die Wissenschaft,** science.

A few nouns ending in **-nis** and **-sal: die Finsternis,** darkness; **die Betrübnis,** sadness; **die Trübsal,** affliction.

Most nouns with these endings are, however, neuter: **das Schicksal**, fate; **das** (or **die**) **Drangsal**, hardship (see below under Neuter).

Neuters

All diminutives in **-chen** (our -kin) and **-lein** are neuter: **das Männchen**, little man, male of animals; **das Büchlein**, little book; **das Bächlein**, brooklet. Note that the addition of **-chen** and **-lein** causes modification of the root vowel.

All nouns ending in **-tum** (our -dom as in kingdom) are neuter except **der Reichtum**, riches, and **der Irrtum**, error; **das Bistum**, bishopric, see; **das Kaisertum**, empire; **das Altertum**, antiquity; **das Christentum**, christianity.

Most nouns formed with the prefix **Ge-**: **das Gespräch**, conversation; **das Geräusch**, noise; **das Gehör**, hearing; **das Gefecht**, fight, battle; **das Getue**, fuss, goings-on. A few common ones are (*a*) masculine: **der Gebrauch**, use; **der Gedanke**, thought; **der Gefallen**, favour, kindness; **der Genuss**, enjoyment; **der Geschmack**, taste; and (*b*) feminine: **die Gefahr**, danger; **die Geburt**, birth; **die Geduld**, patience; **die Geschichte**, history; **die Gewalt**, power.

Most nouns in **-nis**, **-sal** and **-sel** are neuter: **das Hindernis**, obstacle; **das Begebnis**, event; **das Begräbnis**, funeral, burial; **das Labsal**, refreshment, comfort; **das Rätsel**, riddle.

All Infinitives of verbs used as nouns are neuter: **lesen**, to read, **das Lesen**, reading. All other parts of speech used as nouns: **das Für und das Wider**, the for and against, the pros and cons; and adjectives used as abstract nouns: **das Schöne**, the beautiful.

Foreign Words

Nouns derived from foreign words generally keep the gender they have in the foreign language, but there are exceptions, e.g. words in **-age** from the French are feminine: **die Sabotage**, sabotage; **die Courage**, courage.

The following foreign endings are feminine: **-ion**, **die**

Nation, nation; **-tät, die Universität**, university; **-ie, die Harmonie**, harmony; **die Familie**, family; **-ik, die Fabrik**, factory; **-ei, die Bücherei**, library.

Masculine foreign endings are: **-or, der Humor**; **-us, der Autobus**; **-ismus, der Realismus**, realism.

Neuters are: **-ett, das Duett**; **-um, das Verbum**, verb, **das Museum**, museum.

Read the above over when you have a spare moment in the train or bus, so that you become familiar with the words and their genders. Note that all the nouns are preceded by the Definite Article, so that you learn the gender as you read.

THE DECLENSION OF THE NOUN

Before discussing the various declensions let us set down five general rules:

1. Feminine nouns are not declined in the singular: Nom. **die Frau**, Acc. **die Frau**, Gen. **der Frau**, Dat. **der Frau**.
2. The Nominative, Accusative and Genitive of the plural all have the same form: Nom. **die Tische**, Acc. **die Tische**, Gen. **der Tische**.
3. The Dative plural always ends in **-n**, but this **-n** is not added to a noun which already ends in **-n**: Nom. **Die Tische**, Dat. **den Tischen**; but Nom. **Die Mädchen**, Dat. **den Mädchen**.
4. Most masculines and neuters add **-s** or **-es** to form the Genitive singular.

   If they end in a sibilant (**s, sz, z, sch, x**) they must add **-es**: Nom. **der Tisch**, Gen. **des Tisches**.

   If they end in **-er, -el, -en** they must add **-s**: Nom. **der Vater**, Gen. **des Vaters**; **der Mantel, des Mantels**; **das Mädchen, des Mädchens**.

   All other masculine and neuter nouns may add either **-s** or **-es**. In modern German, however, the

-es is being replaced more and more by **-s**, especially in the spoken language. You should therefore write and say **des Königs** rather than **des Königes.**

5. Certain masculines and neuters may add **-e** to form the Dative singular; but this is not added to those ending in **-er, -el, -en.**

   This **-e** is, however, almost dead in modern German, and very seldom heard in the spoken language, except in some set expressions. You will be well advised not to use it, as it sounds old-fashioned and very formal.

   In the model declensions below we will put a bracket round the **e** in **-es** (thus: **(e)s**) and round the **-e** (**(e)**) to show that they may be omitted: **des Tag(e)s ; dem Tag(e).**

CLASSIFICATION OF THE DECLENSIONS

The great German grammarian Jacob Grimm (1785–1863) was the first to classify nouns into Weak, Strong and Mixed, and as this classification still holds good, we shall adopt it.

The Weak Declension

This comprises all nouns which add **-n** or **-en** to the Nominative singular to form all the other cases of both the singular and the plural.

As no feminine nouns change in the singular they should not, strictly speaking, be classified as Weak, but we shall, following the example of all German grammars, put them in that class.

The Strong Declension

This comprises all nouns which add **-s** or **-es** to form the Genitive singular, excepting the few feminine nouns in this declension, which, of course, do not change in the singular.

The Mixed Declension

This comprises all nouns which are Strong in the singular but Weak in the plural, i.e. they add **-s** or **-es** to make the Genitive singular but add **-n** or **-en** to form the plural.

Let us now examine the Declensions in detail.

THE WEAK DECLENSION

Characteristic: Plural in **-n** or **-en**.

This includes:

A. Practically all the feminines in the language.
If they end in **-e** or **-er** or **-el**, they add **-n**; otherwise they add **-en**: **die Frau, die Frauen**; **die Fahne, die Fahnen**, flag; **die Schachtel, die Schachteln**, box; **die Feder, die Federn**, feather, pen.

Here are examples fully declined:

Singular.

Nom.	**die Frau**	**die Fahne**	**die Schachtel**	**die Feder**
Acc.	**die Frau**	**die Fahne**	**die Schachtel**	**die Feder**
Gen.	**der Frau**	**der Fahne**	**der Schachtel**	**der Feder**
Dat.	**der Frau**	**der Fahne**	**der Schachtel**	**der Feder**

Plural.

Nom.	**die Frauen**	**die Fahnen**	**die Schachteln**	**die Federn**
Acc.	**die Frauen**	**die Fahnen**	**die Schachteln**	**die Federn**
Gen.	**der Frauen**	**der Fahnen**	**der Schachteln**	**der Federn**
Dat.	**den Frauen**	**den Fahnen**	**den Schachteln**	**den Federn**

B. Masculine nouns ending in **-e** and denoting living creatures, together with a few which formerly had the **-e** but have lost it.
Here are some common ones to note: **der Affe die Affen**, ape; **der Bote, die Boten**, messenger; **der Junge, die Jungen**, lad, boy; **der Knabe, die Knaben**, boy; **der Löwe, die Löwen**, lion; **der Neffe, die Neffen**, nephew; **der Ochse, die Ochsen,**

ox; **der Rabe, die Raben,** raven; **der Riese, die Riesen,** giant; **der Zeuge, die Zeugen,** witness.
der Bär, die Bären, bear; **der Christ, die Christen,** Christian; **der Fürst, die Fürsten,** prince; **der Herr, die Herren,** master, Mr.; **der Mensch, die Menschen,** human being; **der Narr, die Narren,** fool.

C. Masculine nouns of foreign origin referring to living beings and accented on the last syllable: **der Monarch, die Monarchen,** monarch; **der Philosoph, die Philosophen,** philosopher; **der Student, die Studenten,** student; **der Advokat, die Advokaten,** advocate, lawyer; **der Poet, die Poeten,** poet; **der Tyrann, die Tyrannen,** tyrant.

Here are examples of the above masculines fully declined:

Singular.

N.	**der Junge**	**der Mensch**	**der Herr**	**der Student**
A.	**den Jungen**	**den Menschen**	**den Herrn**	**den Studenten**
G.	**des Jungen**	**des Menschen**	**des Herrn**	**des Studenten**
D.	**dem Jungen**	**dem Menschen**	**dem Herrn**	**dem Studenten**

Plural.

N.	**die Jungen**	**die Menschen**	**die Herren**	**die Studenten**
A.	**die Jungen**	**die Menschen**	**die Herren**	**die Studenten**
G.	**der Jungen**	**der Menschen**	**der Herren**	**der Studenten**
D.	**den Jungen**	**den Menschen**	**den Herren**	**den Studenten**

Note particularly that **Herr** adds **-n** in the singular and **-en** in the plural.

THE STRONG DECLENSIONS

These are classified into three groups, according to the way they form their plurals:

Class I.

Characteristic: Nothing is added to make the plural.

Nouns in this Class add nothing to form the plural, but some of them modify the vowel.

They make the Genitive singular by adding **-s**
The Dative singular never adds **-e.**
Nouns in this Class are:

A. Masculines and neuters ending in **-er, -el, -en,** and Neuters in **-chen** and **-lein**: **der Spaten, die Spaten,** spade; **der Maler, die Maler,** painter; **der Deckel, die Deckel,** lid; **das Mädchen, die Mädchen,** girl; **das Büchlein, die Büchlein,** little book.

The majority of the masculines ending in **-er, -el, -en** do NOT modify; only one neuter modifies: **das Kloster, die Klöster,** cloister.

The neuters in **-chen** and **-lein** are already modified, and hence cannot modify again in the plural.

There are only two feminines in this Class, and both modify: **die Mutter, die Mütter; die Tochter, die Töchter.**

Here are the most useful words to know which modify in the plural, but remember that the majority in **-er, -el, -en** do NOT modify:

Der Apfel, die Äpfel, apple; **der Bruder, die Brüder,** brother; **der Vater, die Väter,** father; **der Schwager, die Schwäger,** brother-in-law; **der Garten, die Gärten,** garden; **der Laden, die Läden,** shop; **der Ofen, die Öfen,** stove; **der Sattel, die Sättel,** saddle; **der Vogel, die Vögel,** bird.

B. Neuter nouns commencing with **Ge-** and ending with **-e,** such as **das Gebäude, die Gebäude,** building; **das Gerippe, die Gerippe,** skeleton; **das Gerede,** no plural, talk, gossip. These nouns do not modify.

Here are examples of the above Class fully declined:

Singular.

N.	**der Maler**	**der Vater**	**das Mädchen**	**das Gebäude**	**die Mutter**
A.	**den Maler**	**den Vater**	**das Mädchen**	**das Gebäude**	**die Mutter**
G.	**des Malers**	**des Vaters**	**des Mädchens**	**des Gebäudes**	**der Mutter**
D.	**dem Maler**	**dem Vater**	**dem Mädchen**	**dem Gebäude**	**der Mutter**

Plural.

N. **die Maler**	**die Väter**	**die Mädchen**	**die Gebäude**	**die Mütter**
A. **die Maler**	**die Väter**	**die Mädchen**	**die Gebäude**	**die Mütter**
G. **der Maler**	**der Väter**	**der Mädchen**	**der Gebäude**	**der Mütter**
D. **den Malern**	**den Vätern**	**den Mädchen**	**den Gebäuden**	**den Müttern**

Class II.

Characteristic: Add **-e** to form the plural.

The nouns in this Class add **-e** to form the plural.
They add **-s** or **-es** to form the Genitive singular.
They may add **-e** to form the Dative singular.
Nouns in this Class are:

A. Most masculine monosyllables. The majority of those that are modifiable (i.e. containing the vowels **a, o, u, au**) DO modify, such as:
der Bach, die Bäche, brook; **der Ball, die Bälle**, ball; **der Bart, die Bärte**, beard; **der Fall, die Fälle**, case, fall; **der Fuss, die Füsse**, foot; **der Hut, die Hüte**, hat; **der Knopf, die Knöpfe**, button; **der Korb, die Körbe**, basket; **der Schlag, die Schläge**, blow; **der Sohn, die Söhne**, son; **der Strom, die Ströme**, river; **der Stuhl, die Stühle**, chair; **der Traum, die Träume**, dream; **der Wunsch, die Wünsche**, wish.

Examples of those which do NOT modify are:

der Arm, die Arme, arm; **der Hund, die Hunde**, dog; **der Laut, die Laute**, sound; **der Schuh, die Schuhe**, boot; **der Tag, die Tage**, day.

B. Most neuter nouns of one syllable. They do NOT modify in the plural, except **das Floss, die Flösse**, raft. Here are some examples:
das Bein, die Beine, leg; **das Boot, die Boote**, boat; **das Haar, die Haare**, hair; **das Heft, die Hefte**, exercise-book; **das Jahr, die Jahre**, year; **das Mal, die Male**, time; **das Meer, die Meere**, sea; **das Paar,**

die Paare, pair; **das Pfund, die Pfunde,** pound; **das Reich, die Reiche,** empire; **das Schaf, die Schafe,** sheep; **das Schiff, die Schiffe,** ship; **das Stück, die Stücke,** piece; **das Tuch, die Tuche,** cloth (also **Tücher**); **das Tier, die Tiere,** animal.

C. All neuters and feminines in **-nis** and **-sal.** Those in **-nis** double the **-s** in the plural: **die Finsternis, die Finsternisse,** darkness; **das Ereignis, die Ereignisse,** event; **die Trübsal, die Trübsale,** sadness; **das Schicksal, die Schicksale,** fate. They do NOT modify.

D. About thirty common feminine nouns. They all modify. Here are the most frequently used ones: **die Angst, die Ängste,** anguish, fear; **die Bank, die Bänke,** bench; **die Braut, die Bräute,** fiancée; **die Faust, die Fäuste,** fist; **die Frucht, die Früchte,** fruit; **die Gans, die Gänse,** goose; **die Hand, die Hände,** hand; **die Kraft, die Kräfte,** power; **die Kuh, die Kühe,** cow; **die Kunst, die Künste,** art, trick; **die Macht, die Mächte,** might, power; **die Magd, die Mägde,** maid; **die Maus, die Mäuse,** mouse; **die Nacht, die Nächte,** night; **die Nuss, die Nüsse,** nut; **die Stadt, die Städte,** town; **die Wand, die Wände,** wall; **die Wurst, die Würste,** sausage.

Here are examples of nouns of this Class fully declined: The **e** in brackets—(e)—means that it can be omitted.

Singular.

Nom.	**der Bach**	**der Arm**	**das Jahr**	**die Hand**
Acc.	**den Bach**	**den Arm**	**das Jahr**	**die Hand**
Gen.	**des Bach(e)s**	**des Arm(e)s**	**des Jahr(e)s**	**der Hand**
Dat.	**dem Bach(e)**	**dem Arm(e)**	**dem Jahr(e)**	**der Hand**

Plural.

Nom.	**die Bäche**	**die Arme**	**die Jahre**	**die Hände**
Acc.	**die Bäche**	**die Arme**	**die Jahre**	**die Hände**
Gen.	**der Bäche**	**der Arme**	**der Jahre**	**der Hände**
Dat.	**den Bächen**	**den Armen**	**den Jahren**	**den Händen**

Singular.

Nom.	**die Finsternis**	**das Schicksal**	**das Gefängnis**
Acc.	**die Finsternis**	**das Schicksal**	**das Gefängnis**
Gen.	**der Finsternis**	**des Schicksals**	**des Gefängnisses**
Dat.	**der Finsternis**	**dem Schicksal(e)**	**dem Gefängnis** (or **Gefängnisse**)

Plural.

Nom.	**die Finsternisse**	**die Schicksale**	**die Gefängnisse**
Acc.	**die Finsternisse**	**die Schicksale**	**die Gefängnisse**
Gen.	**der Finsternisse**	**der Schicksale**	**der Gefängnisse**
Dat.	**den Finsternissen**	**den Schicksalen**	**den Gefängnissen**

Class III.

Characteristic : add **-er** and modify to make the plural.

Nouns in this Class are :

A. All neuter monosyllables not included in Class II, such as :
das Amt, die Ämter, office ; **das Bad, die Bäder,** bath ; **das Bild, die Bilder,** picture ; **das Buch, die Bücher,** book ; **das Dach, die Dächer,** roof ; **das Dorf, die Dörfer,** village ; **das Ei, die Eier,** egg ; **das Feld, die Felder,** field ; **das Gras, die Gräser,** grass ; **das Glas, die Gläser,** glass ; **das Haupt, die Häupter,** head ; **das Haus, die Häuser,** house ; **das Holz, die Hölzer,** wood ; **das Horn, die Hörner,** horn ; **das Kind, die Kinder,** child ; **das Kalb, die Kälber,** calf ; **das Kleid, die Kleider,** dress, clothes ; **das Lamm, die Lämmer,** lamb ; **das Land, die Länder,** land ; **das Lied, die Lieder,** song ; **das Loch, die Löcher,** hole ; **das Nest, die Nester,** nest ; **das Rad, die Räder,** wheel, cycle ; **das Schloss, die Schlösser,** lock, castle ; **das Tal, die Täler,** valley, dale ; **das Tuch, die Tücher,** cloth.

B. All nouns in **-tum**, including the two masculine nouns **der Irrtum, die Irrtümer,** error, and **der Reichtum, die Reichtümer,** riches, all the others being neuter : **das Bistum, die Bistümer,** bishoprick ; **das Fürstentum, die Fürstentümer,** principality.

C. A few masculine nouns, of which the following are the most frequently used : **der Geist, die Geister,** spirit ; **der Gott, die Götter,** God, god ; **der Leib, die Leiber,** body ; **der Mann, die Männer,** man ; **der Rand, die Ränder,** edge ; **der Wald, die Wälder,** wood ; **der Wurm, die Würmer,** worm.

Here are some examples of this Class fully declined :

		Singular.	
Nom.	**das Buch**	**das Bistum**	**der Mann**
Acc.	**das Buch**	**das Bistum**	**den Mann**
Gen.	**des Buch(e)s**	**des Bistums**	**des Mann(e)s**
Dat.	**dem Buch(e)**	**dem Bistum**	**dem Mann(e)**
		Plural.	
Nom.	**die Bücher**	**die Bistümer**	**die Männer**
Acc.	**die Bücher**	**die Bistümer**	**die Männer**
Gen.	**der Bücher**	**der Bistümer**	**der Männer**
Dat.	**den Büchern**	**den Bistümern**	**den Männern**

THE MIXED DECLENSION

There are only a few masculine and neuter nouns in this Class, which we can sum up as follows :

A. A small group of masculines : **der Dorn, des Dorn(e)s, die Dornen,** thorn ; **der Schmerz, des Schmerzes, die Schmerzen,** pain ; **der See, des Sees, die Seen,** lake ; **der Sporn, des Sporn(e)s, die Sporen,** spur ; **der Staat, des Staat(e)s, die Staaten,** state ; **der Strahl, des Strahl(e)s, die Strahlen,** ray, beam ; **der Vetter, des Vetters, die Vettern,** cousin ; **der Bauer, des Bauers, die Bauern,** farmer ; **der Nachbar, des Nachbars, die Nachbarn,** neighbour (also Weak).

B. Most foreign nouns in **-or: der Direktor, des Direk-**

tors, die Direktoren, manager; der Doktor, des Doktors, die Doktoren.

C. A small group of nouns which used to end in **-en** but have dropped the final **-n** in the Nominative singular, though they may be sometimes still found with this **-n**. They make **-ens** in the Genitive singular and -en in all the other cases: **der Funke, des Funkens, die Funken**, spark; **der Glaube, des Glaubens, die Glauben**, belief; **der Haufe, des Haufens, die Haufen**, heap; **der Name, des Namens, die Namen**, name; **der Same, des Samens, die Samen**, seed; **der Schade, des Schadens, die Schäden**, damage, but nowadays this is more frequently declined as **der Schaden, des Schadens, die Schäden**; **der Wille, des Willens, die Willen**, will (= willpower); **der Friede, des Friedens**, no plural, peace; **der Gedanke, des Gedankens, die Gedanken**, thought.

D. A small group of neuters: **das Auge, des Auges, die Augen**, eye; **das Bett, des Bett(e)s, die Betten**, bed; **das Ende, des Endes, die Enden**, end; **das Hemd, des Hemdes, die Hemden**, shirt; **das Ohr, des Ohr(e)s, die Ohren**, ear. Also all foreign words in **-um**: **das Museum, des Museums, die Museen, das Adverbium, des Adverbiums, die Adverbien**, adverb.

Here are examples of this Class fully declined:

Singular.

Nom.	der Staat	der Doktor	der Name	das Ohr
Acc.	den Staat	den Doktor	den Namen	das Ohr
Gen.	des Staat(e)s	des Doktors	des Namens	des Ohr(e)s
Dat.	dem Staat(e)	dem Doktor	dem Namen	dem Ohr(e)

Plural.

Nom.	die Staaten	die Doktoren	die Namen	die Ohren
Acc.	die Staaten	die Doktoren	die Namen	die Ohren
Gen.	der Staaten	der Doktoren	der Namen	der Ohren
Dat.	den Staaten	den Doktoren	den Namen	den Ohren

That, I am glad to say, concludes the chapter on the Declension of the Noun—except, of course, for the exceptions! There are just a few odd words that have no plural or no singular or double gender and such-like freaks which are so annoying to the tidy mind. It will not, however, take long to set them out, even if we include the Proper Nouns.

ODDMENTS

1. The following words are usually found only in the singular: **das Blut,** blood; **das Fleisch,** meat; **das Gold,** gold; **das Heu,** hay; **das Mehl,** flour; **das Obst,** fruit (in general); **das Vieh,** cattle; **das Wild,** game.
2. The following are used only in the plural: **die Leute,** people; **die Ferien,** holidays; **die Kosten,** cost; **die Geschwister,** brothers and sisters.
3. Nouns compounded with **-mann** usually make the plural in **-leute**: **der Kaufmann, die Kaufleute,** merchant; **der Hauptmann, die Hauptleute,** captain (army); but **der Staatsmann, die Staatsmänner,** statesman.
4. Many foreign nouns have the plural in **-s**: **der Lord, des Lords, die Lords,** lord; **das Restaurant, des Restaurants, die Restaurants,** restaurant. In familiar speech and in dialect German words also add -s for the plural: **der Junge, die Jungens,** lad; **das Mädel, die Mädels,** girl.
5. Some nouns have two forms which vary in gender, plural and meaning. Here are the most frequently used of this class: **der Band, die Bände,** volume; **das Band, die Bänder,** ribbon; **das Band, die Bande,** tie, fetter.
   der Bauer, peasant, farmer; **das Bauer,** bird-cage.
   der Bund, alliance; **das Bund,** bundle.
   der Erbe, heir; **das Erbe,** inheritance.

das Gesicht, die Gesichter, face; **das Gesicht, die Gesichte,** vision.
der Heide, heathen; **die Heide,** heath.
der Hut, hat; **die Hut,** guard.
der Kunde, customer; **die Kunde,** information.
das Licht, die Lichter, light; **das Licht, die Lichte,** candle.
der Laden, die Läden, shop; **der Laden, die Laden,** shutter.
das Land, die Länder, land, country; **das Land, die Lande,** districts, provinces.
der See, die Seen, lake; **die See, die Seen,** sea.
der Stock, die Stöcke, stick; **der Stock, die Stockwerke,** storey of a house.
der Teil, part; **das Teil,** share.
das Tuch, die Tücher, piece of cloth; **das Tuch, die Tuche,** kind of cloth.
der Verdienst, wages; **das Verdienst,** merit.
das Wort, die Worte, connected words in speech; **das Wort, die Wörter,** words not connected with speech or meaning.

6. Proper nouns are declined as follows:

   1. They take an -s in the Genitive: **Peters Hund,** Peter's dog; **Annas Katze,** Ann's cat; **die Universitäten Frankreichs,** the universities of France; **Sudermanns Werke,** the works of Sudermann. If however the noun has a qualifier they drop the inflection: **die Katze der Anna; die Siege des mächtigen Frankreich,** the victories of powerful France; **die Werke des jungen Sudermann.** Christian names ending in a sibilant and feminine ones in **-e** may add (e)ns: **Hans, Hansens Mutter,** Johnny's mother; **Maries** or **Mariens Garten,** Mary's garden.

2. If a title without the article precedes the name, then the name alone is inflected: **Kaiser Wilhelms Geburtstag,** the Emperor William's birthday: **Professor Ostwalds Entdeckungen,** Professor Ostwald's discoveries. HERR is however always inflected: **Herrn Stadens Haus,** Mr. Staden's house; **das Haus des Herrn Staden.**
3. The plural of surnames is generally formed by adding **-s**: **Ich wohne bei Schmidts,** I am living at the Smiths (house); **Brauns sind nicht zu Haus,** the Browns are not at home.
4. The feminine names of countries do not add **-s** in the Genitive: **die Berge der Schweiz,** the mountains of Switzerland. (See page 26: The Declension of the Noun. I.)

7. Compound nouns have the gender of the last element: **der Schularzt,** school doctor; **die Schulprüfung,** school examination; **das Schulbuch,** school book. The compounds of **der Mut,** courage, are an exception to this rule, those with a feminine characteristic being feminine: **die Demut,** humility; **die Anmut,** grace; **die Sanftmut,** gentleness; **die Langmut,** patience, long-suffering. Those with masculine characteristics are masculine: **der Hochmut,** haughtiness; **der Freimut,** frankness; **der Übermut,** arrogance.

8. A noun placed alongside another to qualify it is said to be in apposition and in German it agrees with the noun it qualifies: **mein Onkel, der bekannte Arzt, wohnt hier,** my uncle, the well-known doctor, lives here, but: **ich helfe meinem Onkel, dem bekannten Arzt,** I am helping my uncle, the well-known doctor. In dates usage is: **am Montag, dem ersten Mai,** or **Montag, den ersten Mai** (for dates on letters). In expressions of quantity such as **eine**

Tasse Kaffee, a cup of coffee, **ein Paar Schuhe,** a pair of boots, **ein Pfund Obst,** a pound of fruit, we are dealing with apposition; but with the Genitive singular of the noun of quantity the qualifying noun remains in the Nominative: **der Preis des Pfundes Obst,** not **Obstes.**

FORMATION OF NOUNS

Suffixes

The following suffixes are much used in forming nouns:

-chen and **-lein** form diminutives, the root vowel being modified except in the case of christian names (**Karl, Karlchen**); the endings **-e** and **-en** are dropped: **die Blume,** flower, **das Blümchen,** flowerlet; **der Garten,** garden, **das Gärtchen,** little garden. The suffix **-chen** is more used than **-lein,** this latter being mainly added to words ending in **-ch** and **-g**: **der Bach,** stream, **das Bächlein,** streamlet. The diminutive suffix is sometimes added to a plural: **die Kinder,** children, **die Kinderchen** or **Kinderlein,** little children. Such words are used only as plurals.

-in, generally with modification of the root vowel, forms the feminines of masculine persons and animals: **der Lehrer,** teacher, **die Lehrerin**; **der Franzose,** Frenchman, **die Französin,** Frenchwoman; **der Hund,** dog, **die Hündin,** bitch; **der Fuchs,** fox, **die Füchsin,** vixen. Those formed from masculines in **-er** do not modify: **der Maler,** painter, **die Malerin,** and there are a few others which do not modify: **der Gatte,** husband, **die Gattin,** wife, consort; **der Herzog,** duke, **die Herzogin,** duchess.

-er added to a verbal stem is widely used for the doer or instrument of an action: **backen,** to bake, **der Bäcker,** baker; **heizen,** to heat, **der Heizer,** stoker; **-ler** is used to form agents from nouns: **Tisch,** table, **der Tischler,** joiner; **der Sommerfrischler,** the (Summer) holiday-maker; **die Kunst,** art, **der Künstler,** artist; **-ner** is also thus used: **das Bild**, picture, image, **der Bildner**, sculptor, modeller.

-e added to an adjective with modification forms feminines: **warm**, warm, **die Wärme**, heat, warmth; **kalt**, cold, **die Kälte**, cold, coldness; **hoch**, high, **die Höhe**, height. It is also added to the verbal stem: **geben**, to give, **die Gabe**, gift; **bitten**, to beg, **die Bitte**, request.

-ei, originally French, forms feminines often meaning an activity or the place where it is carried on: **die Bäckerei**, bakery; **die Fischerei**, fishing; **die Pfarrei**, vicarage; **die Bücherei**, library. It is also used pejoratively: **die Kinderei**, childishness; **die Schurkerei**, rascality; **die Ausländerei**, aping foreign ways.

-heit forms abstract nouns when added to adjectives and nouns: **die Kindheit**, childhood; **die Mannheit**, manliness; **die Sicherheit**, safety; **-keit** is added to adjectives ending in **-el**, **-er**, **-ig**, **-sam**, **-bar**: **die Fruchtbarkeit**, fertility, fruitfulness; **die Ewigkeit**, eternity; **-ig** is often inserted before the **-keit**: **süss**, sweet, **die Süssigkeit**, sweetness.

-ling forms masculines: **der Findling** foundling; **der Sträfling**, convict; **der Jüngling**, youth, young man.

-nis forms mainly neuters from verbs, nouns and adjectives: **bedürfen**, to need, **das Bedürfnis**, necessity; **der Zeuge**, witness, **das Zeugnis**, evidence, certificate. A few of those in **-nis** are feminine: **die Erlaubnis**, permission, **die Finsternis**, darkness.

-sal and **-sel** are added to verbs and form mostly neuters: **das Schicksal**, fate; **das Rätsel**, puzzle; **das Drangsal**, oppression. A few are feminine: **die Mühsal**, trouble.

-schaft forms feminines from nouns and adjectives: **der Bote**, messenger, **die Botschaft**, message; **der Vater**, father, **die Vaterschaft**, fatherhood, paternity; **eigen**, own, **die Eigenschaft**, quality; **bereit**, ready, **die Bereitschaft**, readiness.

-st and **-t** form feminines when added to a verbal stem:

tragen, to wear, **die Tracht**, costume; **schreiben**, to write, **die Schrift**, writing.

-ung is used for forming feminine verbal nouns: **die Festung**, fortress; **die Kleidung**, clothing; **die Schöpfung**, creation.

Prefixes

Ge- (often equivalent to our con- or com-) makes collectives: **der Stern**, star, **das Gestirn**, constellation; **der Berg**, mountain, **das Gebirge**, mountain chain; it frequently indicates the result of an action: **das Gebäude**, building; or the action itself: **das Gebrüll**, roaring; or a repeated action: **das Getue**, doings, goings-on; **das Gerede**, talk, gossip, rumour.

Un- is generally equivalent to our un- or in- or im- with a negative meaning: **das Unrecht**, injustice; **die Unmöglichkeit**, impossibility; **die Unsicherheit**, insecurity. It is also a pejorative as in: **der Unmensch**, monster; **das Unwetter**, stormy weather; **das Unwesen**, disorder; or it is intensive: **die Unmenge**, enormous crowd; **die Unzahl**, enormous number.

Ur- has the meaning of " original ", " very old ", " primitive ": **der Urwald**, primeval forest; **der Ursprung**, origin; **die Ursache**, cause; **das Urbild**, prototype, archetype; **der Urgrossvater**, great-grandfather.

CHAPTER V

THE ADJECTIVE

Qu'ils s'accordent entre eux ou se gourment, qu'importe?
Whether they agree amongst themselves or have a fight, what does it matter?

(Molière, " Les Femmes savantes ".)

Molière pokes fun at the pedant Bélise, who, shocked at the maid's bad grammar, tells her that grammar teaches the laws that regulate the agreement of the noun with its verb and the adjective with its noun. Martine, the maid, unable to make head or tail of his rigmarole, asks, very sensibly, what does it matter whether they agree or fight?

The foreigner who learns English, lucky man, has no need to worry about the agreement of the noun and adjective, but we British who learn German (or most other foreign languages) have to toil and moil over this agreement business, though many of us, like Martine, think it does not matter.

The German adjective (**das Eigenschaftswort** = quality word) agrees with its noun in number, gender and case, except when it forms part of the predicate: **er ist krank,** he is ill; **sie ist krank,** she is ill; **wir bleiben treu,** we remain faithful; **ich werde alt,** I am getting old. When the adjective follows its noun—mostly in poetic style—it also does not agree, as in Goethe's: **Röslein rot,** rosebud red; **Haar weiss wie Schnee,** hair as white as snow.

The adjective has three declensions: Strong, Weak, Mixed, but if you have really learnt your **der, die, das,** you have not so very much more to learn.

STRONG DECLENSION

When the noun is preceded by an adjective without any other noun-qualifier (such as **der, dieser, mein,** etc.), then the adjective has itself to take on the case endings of **dieser** so as to show the gender, number and case clearly. If therefore you know your **dieser, diese, dieses,** you know the Strong Declension of the adjective. There is just one point: in modern German the Genitive singular masculine and neuter is in **-en** and not in **-es,** except in a few set expressions. Here is a skeleton of the endings:

	Masc.	Fem.	Neut.	Plural.
Nom.	**-er**	**-e**	**-es**	**-e**
Acc.	**-en**	**-e**	**-es**	**-e**
Gen.	**-en** *	**-er**	**-en** *	**-er**
Dat.	**-em**	**-er**	**-em**	**-en**

This declension is mainly met with in the singular in the case of nouns denoting substances: sweet wine, fresh milk, cold beer, black ink. In the plural it is more common: old people; interesting books; tall trees. Here is the full declension of **süsser Wein, frische Milch, kaltes Bier, gute Getränke** (good beverages):

Nom.	**süsser Wein**	**frische Milch**	**kaltes Bier**	**gute Getränke**
Acc.	**süssen Wein**	**frische Milch**	**kaltes Bier**	**gute Getränke**
Gen.	**süssen Weins**	**frischer Milch**	**kalten Biers**	**guter Getränke**
Dat.	**süssem Wein**	**frischer Milch**	**kaltem Bier**	**guten Getränken**

Not much to worry about there.

WEAK DECLENSION

When **der, die, das** or any qualifier declined like it—**dieser, jener,** etc.—precedes the adjective, the gender, number and case are already shown and the adjective can take things easy. It does so by ending in **-e** in the Nominative masculine, feminine and neuter and in the Accusative

* May be **-es** in set expressions, e.g. **reines Herzens,** of pure heart.

feminine and neuter; everywhere else in the singular and plural it ends in -en. Here is the skeleton declension:

	Singular.			Plural.
	Masc.	Fem.	Neuter.	All genders.
Nom.	-e	-e	-e	-en
Acc.	-en	-e	-e	-en
Gen.	-en	-en	-en	-en
Dat.	-en	-en	-en	-en

Here is the declension in full of **der süsse Wein, die frische Milch, das kalte Bier, die guten Getränke**:

	Singular.		
Nom.	**der süsse Wein**	**die frische Milch**	**das kalte Bier**
Acc.	**den süssen Wein**	**die frische Milch**	**das kalte Bier**
Gen.	**des süssen Weins**	**der frischen Milch**	**des kalten Biers**
Dat.	**dem süssen Wein**	**der frischen Milch**	**dem kalten Bier**

	Plural.
Nom.	**die guten Getränke**
Acc.	**die guten Getränke**
Gen.	**der guten Getränke**
Dat.	**den guten Getränken**

MIXED DECLENSION

When the adjective is preceded by **ein, eine, ein**, or any qualifier declined like it, then the Nominative masculine singular and the Nominative and Accusative neuter singular all have **ein**, thus:

Nom.	**ein Wein**	**ein Bier**
Acc.		**ein Bier**

The adjective must therefore bear the burden of showing that **Wein** is masculine Nominative and that **Bier** is Nominative and Accusative neuter. It does so by taking on the appropriate endings. The feminine already shows its gender by the **-e** of **eine**, and hence remains the same as in the Weak declension ; all the other cases, singular and plural, end in **-en**, as was the case with the Weak declension. Our skeleton now is thus :

	Singular.			Plural.
	Masc.	Fem.	Neut.	All genders.
Nom.	-er	-e	-es	-en
Acc.	-en	-e	-es	-en
Gen.	-en	-en	-en	-en
Dat.	-en	-en	-en	-en

Here is the full declension of : **Ihr kleiner Sohn,** your little son ; **meine hübsche Tochter,** my pretty daughter ; **unser liebes Kind,** our dear child ; **seine strengen Eltern,** his strict parents. I have used the possessive adjectives in preference to **ein, eine, ein,** as they require more care :

Singular.

N. **Ihr kleiner Sohn**	**meine hübsche Tochter**	**unser liebes Kind**
A. **Ihren kleinen Sohn**	**meine hübsche Tochter**	**unser liebes Kind**
G. **Ihres kleinen Sohns**	**meiner hübschen Tochter**	**unsres lieben Kinds**
D. **Ihrem kleinen Sohn**	**meiner hübschen Tochter**	**unsrem lieben Kind**

Plural.

Nom.	**seine strengen Eltern**
Acc.	**seine strengen Eltern**
Gen.	**seiner strengen Eltern**
Dat.	**seinen strengen Eltern**

To sum up :

A. Adjective alone : endings of **dieser, diese, dieses**
B. Adjective preceded by **der, die, das,** etc. :

	Masc.	Fem.	Neut.	
Nom.	-e	-e	-e	(in the singular)
Acc.		-e	-e	

and **-en** everywhere else.

C. Adjective preceded by **ein, eine, ein,** etc. :

	Masc.	Fem.	Neut.	
Nom.	**-er**	**-e**	**-es**	(in the singular)
Acc.		**-e**	**-es**	

and **-en** everywhere else.

Not so frightfully difficult, after all !

THE ADJECTIVE AS A NOUN

In English we speak of " the blind ", " the rich ", " the poor ", meaning " blind people ", " rich people ", " poor people ". We also speak of " the beautiful ", " the good ", " the unexpected ", meaning " that which is beautiful, beauty ", " that which is good " and so on. The former are all plural, the latter singular.

In German we can make an adjective into a noun by writing it with a capital letter, but though it is a noun it is still declined exactly like an adjective. Thus we have it declined strong in **ich Armer,** I poor (wretch) ; weak in **der Arme,** the poor man ; **die Arme,** the poor woman ; **die Armen,** the poor (people). We have it declined mixed in **ein Armer,** a poor man ; **eine Arme,** a poor woman ; **meine Armen,** my poor (people). Words from adjectives of this type are widely used and are neat ; here are a few common ones : **der Reisende,** traveller ; **der Vorsitzende,** chairman ; **der Geschworene,** juryman ; **der Bediente,** servant ; **der Gesandte,** ambassador ; **der Bekannte,** acquaintance. Of course they can all be feminine and plural as well as masculine singular. Here is the full declension of **der Arme,** etc. :

Singular.

	Masc.		Fem.	
Nom.	**der Arme**	**ein Armer**	**die Arme**	**eine Arme**
Acc.	**den Armen**	**einen Armen**	**die Arme**	**eine Arme**
Gen.	**des Armen**	**eines Armen**	**der Armen**	**einer Armen**
Dat.	**dem Armen**	**einem Armen**	**der Armen**	**einer Armen**

Plural.

Nom.	**die Armen**	**meine Armen**
Acc.	**die Armen**	**meine Armen**
Gen.	**der Armen**	**meiner Armen**
Dat.	**den Armen**	**meinen Armen**

You will have noticed that there were no neuters in the above noun-adjectives, which all referred to persons. The neuters are, however, important. **Das Schöne** means "the beautiful, beauty"; **das Gute,** "the good, that which is good"; **das Unerwartete,** "the unexpected". This kind of noun is very common in German and is really neat and useful, especially in prose which has a philosophical bent. Here are a few examples I have just culled from a book I have been reading recently: **das Gold, dieses Symbol des Feststehenden und Bleibenden,** gold, this symbol of what is established and enduring (literally "fast-standing and remaining"); **der Drang ins Unendliche,** the urge into the infinite; **kaum hat die Menschheit das Nötigste bereitgestellt, so geht sie an das Unnötige,** scarcely has mankind made the most necessary things, when it starts on the unnecessary. These neuter noun-adjectives can, of course, be strong, weak or mixed in declension.

We find the strong form in such cases as: **ich habe Schönes gesehen,** I have seen lovely things—often used ironically. This form is frequently found with **etwas,** something, and **nichts,** nothing: **ich habe nichts Neues gefunden,** I have found nothing new; **ich weiss von etwas Neuem,** I know of something new—note the Dative in **-em.** The **etwas** is often abbreviated to **was**: **gibt es was Neues?** is there anything new? Also with **was?** we have the same form: **was Interessantes haben Sie gehört?**, what have you heard that is of interest?

ODDMENTS

Below I discuss one or two points of agreement on which German grammarians are themselves not in agreement.

Do not blame them, gentle reader; they are as human as you are!

1. After the indefinite numeral adjectives in the plural **alle**, all; **einige**, some, a few; **etliche**, some, several, a few; **keine**, no, not any; **manche**, many; **mehrere**, several; **sämtliche**, all, all included; **verschiedene**, various, different; **viele**, many; **wenige**, few; and also after **solche**, such; **welche**, which; **folgende**, the following, present-day usage varies. Most of the above prefer the strong form in the Nominative and Accusative plural, i.e. the form in **-e**: **einige gute Bücher**, a few good books; **manche kluge Kinder**, many clever children; **mehrere alte Häuser**, several old houses; **verschiedene gute Freunde**, various good friends; **solche hohe Bäume**, such lofty trees. But with **alle** and **keine** the weak declension is preferred: **alle kleinen Kinder**; **keine alten Leute**. That means you GENERALLY find, let us say, **einige gute Bücher** and **alle kleinen Kinder**, but you may very well find **einige guten Bücher** and **alle kleine Kinder**. I am sorry about this but you must just blame the German language and not me.

2. With personal pronouns accompanied by an adjective we also have a spot of bother: the adjective is weak, except in the Nominative singular, viz. with **ich, du, er**: **ich elender armer Sünder**, I miserable poor sinner; **du lieber Freund**, you, dear friend; **er armer Mann**, he poor man. But **wir armen Leute**, we poor people; **ihr tapfern Brüder**, ye bold brothers; **mir armen Frau**, to me poor woman. The same rule applies in cases like: **ich Armer**, I poor (wretch); **du Deutscher**, you German; but **ihr Deutschen**, you Germans; **wir Armen**, we poor (wretches).

The adjective-noun is indeclinable when in set expressions in pairs and is then written with a small letter: **alt und jung**, old and young; **gross und klein**, big and little, great and small; **arm und reich**, rich and poor; **durch dick und dünn**, through thick and thin; **über kurz oder lang**, sooner or later; **schwarz auf weiss**, black on white, in black and white; **von klein auf**, from childhood on.

The adjectives formed from the names of towns by adding **-er**, such as **Londoner, Berliner, Pariser**, are indeclinable: **die Berliner Zeitung**, the Berlin Times; **die Pariser Mode**, the Paris fashion.

The names of languages are not declined unless referring to a particular national language as contrasted with another national language: **wie sagt man das auf Deutsch?** What's that in German?; **er spricht gebrochenes Deutsch**, he speaks broken German; **auf gut Deutsch**, in plain German, frankly, in plain English; **im heutigen Deutsch**, in present-day German. But: **er übersetzte das Buch aus dem Englischen ins Deutsche**, he translated the book from English into German.

THE COMPARISON OF ADJECTIVES

In English we have two ways of comparing adjectives: cheap, cheaper, cheapest, but wonderful, more wonderful, most wonderful. German comparison (**die Steigerung**, from **steigern**, to raise, increase) has only one method: **billig, billiger, billigst; wunderbar, wunderbarer, wunderbarst.** You add **-er** for the comparative and **-st** or **-est** for the superlative. The **-est** may be added if the positive ends in a sibilant: **frisch, frischer, frischest**, but **frischst** is also found. After **-d** or **-t**, **-est** is used: **hart, härter, härtest.**

Adjectives ending in **-el, -er, -en** often drop the **e** of the ending in the comparative but keep it in the superlative: **edel**, noble, **edler, edelst; bitter, bittrer, bitterst; trocken, trockner, trockenst**, dry.

A number of monosyllables containing the vowels **a, o, u** modify in the comparative and superlative: **lang, länger, längst**, long, but some do not modify and others vary according to the dialectal origin of the speaker. The following are always modified: **arm**, poor, **ärmer, ärmst; gross**, big, **grösser, grösst; hart**, hard, **härter, härtest; hoch,** high, **höher, höchst**; **jung,** young, **jünger, jüngst**; **kalt,** cold, **kälter, kältest**; **krank,** sick, **kränker, kränkest**; **kurz,** short, **kürzer, kürzest**; **lang,** long, **länger, längst**; **nah,** near, **näher, nächst**; **scharf,** sharp, **schärfer, schärfst**; **stark,** strong, **stärker, stärkst**; **warm,** warm, **wärmer, wärmst.**

The following are found both with and without modification: **bang,** anxious, **banger** or **bänger,** etc.; **dumm,** stupid, **dummer** or **dümmer,** etc.; **fromm,** pious, **frommer** or **frömmer,** etc.; **gesund,** healthy, **gesünder** or **gesunder,** etc.; **glatt,** smooth, **glatter** or **glätter,** etc.; **nass,** wet, **nasser** or **nässer,** etc.; **rot,** red, **roter** or **röter,** etc.; **schmal,** narrow, **schmaler** or **schmäler,** etc.; **zart,** tender, **zarter** or **zärter,** etc.

Lastly we have those which do not modify: **voll,** full, **voller**; **matt,** faint, dim, **matter**; **starr,** stiff, **starrer**; **klar,** clear, **klarer**; **sanft,** gentle, **sanfter**; **stolz,** proud, **stolzer**; **schlank,** slender, **schlanker.**

The best way to learn the above is to memorize them by saying them aloud with the comparative and superlative. It is little use to memorize something like this: "The following adjectives **lang,** etc. . . . modify", as your memory will play you tricks. If you learn **lang, länger** aloud you will have something that the memory can grip and hold on to.

The comparative and the superlative are, of course, adjectives, and are declined as such. Thus, just as we have **der arme Mann,** so we have **der ärmere Mann,** the poorer man, and **der ärmste Mann,** the poorest man, and in the same way we get: **mein junges Kind,** my young child; **mein jüngeres Kind,** my younger child; **mein jüngstes Kind,** my youngest child.

In English we use the conjunction "than" with the comparative: Henry is older than his brother. German uses **als**: **Heinrich ist älter als sein Bruder.** You will however often find **wie,** especially in North Germany, but this is frowned on by German grammarians, and you should avoid it. German uses **weniger**, less, in descending comparison: **sie ist weniger schön als ihre Mutter**, she is less beautiful than her mother or she is not so beautiful as her mother. Note the idiom **nichts weniger als**, anything but, nothing less than, as in **er ist nichts weniger als intelligent**, he is anything but intelligent.

Wie is the conjunction used with the positive: **sie ist eben so schön wie ihre Mutter**, she is just as beautiful as her mother. It is found in all sorts of useful phrases: **schwarz wie die Nacht**, as black as night; **leicht wie die Luft**, light as air; **sanft wie ein Lamm**, gentle as a lamb; **rein wie frisch gefallener Schnee**, pure as freshly fallen snow, as driven snow.

German also uses the comparative, not to compare one thing with another, but rather to indicate a higher degree of the quality expressed by the adjective. Thus **eine ältere Dame** means not "an older lady" but "an elderly lady"; **ich bin seit längerer Zeit hier**, I have been here some time.

The superlative of the adjective, e.g. **längst**, is never found in that form, being always accompanied by a qualifier and inflected. Thus "This is the longest street" is: **dies ist die längste Strasse**, and "This street is (the) longest" is: **diese Strasse ist die längste.**

German has another form of the superlative which is adverbial: **am längsten, am besten, am schönsten.** The ordinary superlative is used when comparing one thing with others; the adverbial superlative is used when comparing a thing with itself. Thus "This street is the widest" is: **diese Strasse ist die breiteste**, for we compare "this street" with other streets. In "This street is widest here" we compare "this street" at this spot with the same street at another spot, and the German is: **diese Strasse ist hier am breitesten.** This form of the superlative is, of course, not further declinable.

The positive may be emphasized by means of: **ganz,**

quite; **sehr,** very; **höchst,** extremely (highest), as in: **ich bin ganz müde,** I am quite tired; **ein sehr glückliches Kind,** a very fortunate child; **es war höchst unangenehm,** it was extremely (highly) unpleasant.

The comparative is reinforced by means of **noch,** still, yet; **viel,** much; **bei weitem,** by far: **er ist viel stärker als ich,** he is much stronger than I; **das ist noch teurer, als ich bezahlen wollte,** that is still dearer than I wanted to pay; **sie ist bei weitem älter als Marie,** she is older by far than Mary.

The superlative is reinforced by combining it with **aller-**: **er war der allerletzte,** he was last of all. Women are rather partial to this exaggerated form: **ein allerliebstes Kind,** a perfectly sweet child.

Let us set out a few comparisons for memorizing:

Positive.	Comparative.	Superlative.	Adverbial Super.
arm wie	**ärmer als**	**der, die, das ärmste**	**am ärmsten**
kurz wie	**kürzer als**	**der, die, das kürzeste**	**am kürzesten**
edel wie	**edler als**	**der, die, das edelste**	**am edelsten**
hart wie	**härter als**	**der, die, das härteste**	**am härtesten**

If you learn it that way you automatically get the conjunctions fixed in your mind: poor as; poorer than.

The following comparisons are irregular:

gut wie	**besser als**	**der, die, das beste**	**am besten** (good)
gross wie	**grösser als**	**der, die, das grösste**	**am grössten** (big)
***hoch wie**	**höher als**	**der, die, das höchste**	**am höchsten** (high)
nah wie	**näher als**	**der, die, das nächste**	**am nächsten** (near)
wenig wie	**weniger als**	**der, die, das wenigste**	**am wenigsten** (little)
	minder als	**der, die, das mindeste**	**am mindesten** (little)

Of course there are cases where the above rules do not apply, but they are not very important. I will just mention one: in English we say "It is more pretty than strong", not: "It is prettier than stronger". That is just common sense; and so in German too: **es ist mehr hübsch als stark.**

* **hoch** changes the **ch** to **h** when followed by a vowel; **der hohe Baum,** the high tree.

FORMATION OF ADJECTIVES

The following suffixes are useful:

-bar, equivalent frequently to our -able, is added to verbs and occasionally to nouns and adjectives: **essbar**, edible; **furchtbar**, terrible, frightful; **brauchbar**, serviceable, usable; **wunderbar**, wonderful; **offenbar**, evident, public.

-en and **-ern** are added to names of substances: **golden**, golden; **hölzern**, wooden; **eisern**, iron; **ledern**, leathern.

-haft is added to nouns and some adjectives and verbs: **heldenhaft**, heroic; **mannhaft**, manly, virile; **riesenhaft**, gigantic; **krankhaft**, diseased, morbid; **zaghaft**, timorous, from **zagen**, to be afraid.

-ig forms many adjectives from adverbs of place and time: **dort**, there, **dortig, die dortigen Verhältnisse**, the conditions at that place; **hier**, here, **hiesig**, local, **das hiesige Bier**, the local beer; **gestern**, yesterday, **gestrig**, **unser gestriger Brief**, our letter of yesterday; **heute**, today, **heutig, die heutigen Schwierigkeiten**, the present-day difficulties. It is also added to nouns, often with modification: **die Macht**, power, **mächtig**, powerful; **die Gunst**, favour, **günstig**, favourable, but **der Durst**, thirst, **durstig**, thirsty; **das Blut**, blood, **blutig**, bloody; **die Gewalt**, power, **gewaltig**, powerful.

-isch is added to nouns: **der Teufel**, devil, **teuflisch**, devilish; **die Erde**, earth, **irdisch**, earthly; **Berlin**, **berlinisch**; and many form nationalities: **spanisch**, Spanish; **französisch**, French; **russisch**, Russian; **holländisch**, Dutch. From nouns in **-er**: **malerisch**, picturesque; **künstlerisch**, artistic; it is also used pejoratively: **kindisch**, childish.

-lich (our " like " and -ly) is added to nouns, adjectives and verbal stems: **möglich**, possible; **fröhlich**, joyful; **begreiflich**, comprehensible; **käuflich**, saleable, venal; **bläulich**, bluish; **rötlich**, reddish; **sterblich**, mortal; **wöchentlich**, weekly; **unsäglich**, unutterable.

-los, less, is added to nouns: **sinnlos,** thoughtless, mad, foolish; **kindlos,** childless; **arbeitslos,** unemployed; **heimatlos,** homeless, stateless.

-sam (our -some) is added to adjectives and verbs: **einsam,** lonely, lonesome; **ratsam,** advisable, prudent; **biegsam,** supple, lissom; **langsam,** slow; **schweigsam,** silent.

CASES GOVERNED BY ADJECTIVES

The Dative

A large number of adjectives govern the Dative. They generally correspond to English adjectives with " to " and imply such ideas as likeness to; service to, kindness to, advantage to; obedience to; nearness to, faithfulness to, harm to, and their opposites. Here are some examples:

ähnlich, like: **er ist seinem Bruder ähnlich,** he is like his brother; **treu,** faithful, **er blieb seinem Eide treu,** he remained faithful to his oath; **böse,** angry, cross: **ich war ihm böse** (or **auf ihn**), I was angry with him; **bekannt,** known: **das ist mir bekannt,** I know that, that is known to me; **dienlich,** serviceable: **es ist der Gesundheit dienlich,** it is wholesome: **nötig,** necessary: **ein neuer Hut ist mir nötig,** I need a new hat; **nützlich,** useful: **das Buch ist mir sehr nützlich,** the book is very useful to me; **nahe,** near: **das Lachen war ihr sehr nahe,** she was very near to laughing; **unentbehrlich,** indispensable: **seine Hilfe war mir unentbehrlich,** his help was indispensable to me.

Following the example of Classical languages, German also uses the dative sometimes to give the idea of "*from*": **abhold,** averse from: **der Gewalt abhold,** averse from violence (even here we often say " to "); **abgeneigt,** averse, disinclined: **dem Weine abgeneigt,** averse from (to) wine.

Many of these adjectives (such as " **abgeneigt** ") are really past participles of verbs which take this " dative of deprivation " e.g. **sie raubten ihm Geld und Ehre,** they took his money and his honour *away from* him.

The Genitive

Many adjectives require the Genitive in literary German but the present-day tendency is to replace this case by a preposition or by an accusative. Here are some of the more usual:

ansichtig (werden), to catch sight of: **ich bin seiner ansichtig geworden**, I caught sight of him; **bedürftig**, in need of: **sie ist eines neuen Kleides bedürftig**, she needs a new dress; **bewusst**, aware of: **er war sich dessen wohl bewusst, dass . . .**, he was well aware that . . .; **fähig**, capable of: **er ist jeder Anstrengung fähig** (or **zu jeder Anstrengung**) he is capable of any effort; **mächtig**, master of, (have) a command of: **ich bin der deutschen Sprache mächtig**, I have a command of the German language; **verdächtig**, suspected of: **eines Mordes verdächtig sein**, to be under suspicion of murder; **wert**, worthy of: **es ist nicht der Mühe wert**, it is not worth the trouble; **aller Achtung wert**, worthy of all respect (but **es ist diesen Preis wert**, it is worth this price); **würdig**, worthy: **einer besseren Sache würdig**, worthy of a better cause. Note that practically all of the above have "of" in the English translation.

CHAPTER VI

THE NUMERALS

1. The Cardinals (**die Grundzahlen**) are:

1 **ein, eins**
2 **zwei** *
3 **drei**
4 **vier**
5 **fünf**
6 **sechs**
7 **sieben**
8 **acht**
9 **neun**
10 **zehn**
11 **elf**
12 **zwölf**
13 **dreizehn**

14 **vierzehn**
15 **fünfzehn**
16 **SECHZEHN**
17 **SIEBZEHN**
18 **achtzehn**
19 **neunzehn**
20 **zwanzig**
21 **einundzwanzig**
22 **zweiundzwanzig**
30 **DREISSIG**
40 **vierzig**
50 **fünfzig**

60 **SECHZIG**
70 **SIEBZIG**
80 **achtzig**
90 **neunzig**
100 **hundert**
101 **hunderteins** †
200 **zweihundert**
1000 **tausend**
10000 **zehntausend**
1000000 **eine Million**
2000000 **zwei Millionen**
0 **Null (die)**

Here are some numbers to give you practice: 199, **hundert(und)neunundneunzig**; 1101, **tausendeinhundert(und)eins**; 1949, **neunzehnhundertneunundvierzig** or **tausendneunhundertneunundvierzig**; 999 999 (in English we write it: 999,999; the comma in German figures is the decimal point; see below) **neunhundertneunundneunzigtausendneunhundertneunundneunzig**; 2 345 678, **zwei Millionen dreihundertfünfundvierzigtausendsechshundertachtundsiebzig.**

Eins is used when no substantive follows: **einmal eins ist eins**; **die Uhr schlug eins**, the clock struck one; **es ist mir alles eins**, it's all one (the same) to me; **eins nach dem**

* **zwo** over the telephone. † Also **hundertundeins.**

andern, one after the other. **Ein** is declined like the indefinite article when there is no other qualifier in front of it: **e i n Tisch,** one table; **e i n e Frau,** one woman; **sie sind von e i n e r Farbe,** they are of one colour. If there is a qualifier preceding **ein,** then it is declined like an ordinary adjective: **das e i n e Kind,** the one child; **sein e i n e s Kind,** his one child. When used as a pronoun it is declined like **dieser**: **einer meiner Freunde,** one of my friends; note the idiom **in einem fort,** continually: **sie arbeiteten in einem fort,** they went on working.

Zwei and **drei** are declined in the Genitive when it is necessary to show the case: **durch zweier Zeugen Mund wird die Wahrheit kund,** through the mouths of two witnesses the truth is made known; **das Haus dreier verwandter Familien,** the house of three related families, but: **das Haus dieser drei verwandten Familien,** the house of these three related families. The Dative in **-en** is also found: **niemand kann zwei** (or **zweien**) **Herren dienen,** a man cannot serve two masters; **zu zweien,** by twos. The numbers from **zwei** to **zwölf** may be inflected when they do not stand before a substantive: **er streckt alle viere von sich,** he lies at full length (as if dead); **er fuhr mit sechsen,** he drove a team of six horses; **auf allen vieren gehen,** to walk on all fours; **ich bin in den Sechzigern,** I am in my sixties; **wir spielten zu dreien,** we made up a party of three, three of us played the game.

Useful words are formed by adding **-er**: **ein Vierziger,** a man in his forties; **in den vierziger Jahren dieses Jahrhunderts,** in the forties of this century, i.e. 1940 to 1949.

Die Million is a substantive; **Hundert** and **Tausend** are also used substantively and are neuter: **das Hundert,** plural **die Hunderte**; **das Tausend, die Tausende**: **das geht in die Tausende,** it runs into the thousands; **man verkauft es zu Hunderten,** they sell it by hundreds.

The figures 1, 2, 3, etc., are feminine: **die Eins, die Einsen**; **die Sechs, die Sechsen,** etc. **Die Sieben** does not change in the plural : **es ist eine böse Sieben**, she is a shrew —seven being an unlucky number, like thirteen.

2. The Ordinals (**Ordnungszahlen**) are all except three regularly formed from the cardinals by adding **-te** to the first nineteen : **der zweite, der fünfte** ; and **-ste** to all the rest : **der zwanzigste, der zweiunddreissigste, der hundertste,** etc. The three exceptions are : **der erste**, the first ; **der dritte**, the third ; **der achte**, the eighth. They are declined like ordinary adjectives : **die Ersten werden die Letzten und die Letzen die Ersten sein**, the first shall be last and the last first ; **der erste beste**, the first comer, anyone ; **die erste Hilfe ist die beste**, the first help is the best. Note **der** (**die, das**) **letzte**, the last ; **vorletzte**, last but one ; **drittletzte**, last but two ; **viertletzte**, last but three, etc.

3. From the ordinals we get the adverbs : **erstens**, firstly, in the first place ; **zweitens**, secondly, etc., and also the fractional numbers (**die Bruchzahlen**) which are all neuter nouns : **dritte**, third, **das Drittel**, the third part ; **vierte**, fourth, **ein Viertel**, a quarter ; **ein Hunderstel**, a hundredth ; **ein Tausendstel**, a thousandth. As you see, you add **-l** to the ordinal number. This **-l** was originally the noun **Teil**, a part, and thus **das dritte Teil** was fused into **das Drittel**. The plural of these fractions is the same as the singular : **drei Viertel**, three fourths, three quarters. **Ein Halb** is used instead of **ein Zweitel**, but it is mainly used as an adjective : **ein halbes Pfund**, half a pound ; **ein halber Tag**, half a day. **Die Hälfte** is used as the substantive : **geben Sie mir nur die Hälfte der Summe**, give me only half of the amount. Note : **anderthalb**, $1\frac{1}{2}$; **dritthalb**, $2\frac{1}{2}$, etc.

4. Multiplicatives (**Vervielfachungszahlen**) are made by adding **-fach** or **-fältig** to the cardinals: **einfach**, single (or simple in character), **einfältig**, onefold (or silly); **zweifach**, two-fold or double (also **doppelt**), **zweifältig**, twofold, etc. They are adjectives.

5. Iteratives (**Wiederholungszahlen**) are made by adding **-mal** (= time) to the cardinals: **einmal**, once, **zweimal**,

twice, **dreimal,** three times, etc. Note the adverbs: **manchmal,** sometimes, **allemal,** always.

6. Variatives (**Gattungszahlen**) are formed from the cardinals by adding **-erlei**; they are indeclinable: **einerlei,** of one sort; **zweierlei,** of two sorts; **vielerlei,** of many kinds; **allerlei,** of all sorts. **Es ist mir einerlei,** it's all the same to me; **allerlei Menschen,** all sorts and conditions of people.

The decimal point, as already mentioned, is represented by a comma in German: 12,25 (= 12·25) is read as **zwölf Komma zwei fünf. Der Dezimalbruch** is the German for decimal fraction.

THE TIME AND THE DATE

The Germans have three ways of telling the time: A, as in English by counting " past " the hour: **es ist zehn Minuten nach zehn (Uhr),** it is ten minutes past ten (o'clock); and by counting " to " the hour: **es ist zehn Minuten vor elf,** it is ten minutes to eleven. Half past the hour is, however, always counted as half into the following hour: **es is halb zehn** means " it is half past nine "; **halb elf** is half past ten, etc. B and C both count into the following hour, not only for the half hours but also for the quarters, system B using **auf**: **es ist (ein) Viertel auf fünf,** it is a quarter past four; system C using no preposition: **es ist (ein) Viertel fünf,** it is a quarter past four. And of course there is the quick " railway " time method: **es ist zehn Uhr zehn,** it is ten ten. Germany uses the twenty-four clock.

To get this matter straight I will give the various systems in the following order: A, the easiest one for you to learn, as it uses **nach** and **vor** like the English " past " and " to ", the only snag being the half hours; B and C, counting both the half hours and the quarters into the following hour; D, the snappy " railway " time, e.g. 8.15, i.e. eight fifteen (the train you so often miss in the morning !).

Wieviel Uhr ist es?

o'clock.	A.	B. & C.	D.
	Es ist . . .		
5	**fünf Uhr**	**fünf Uhr**	**fünf Uhr**
5.10	**zehn Minuten nach fünf (Uhr)**	**zehn Minuten nach fünf (Uhr)**	**fünf Uhr zehn**
5.15	**fünfzehn Minuten nach fünf (Uhr)**	**(ein) Viertel auf sechs (Uhr)**	**fünf Uhr fünfzehn**
	(ein) Viertel nach fünf (Uhr)	**(ein) Viertel sechs (Uhr)**	
5.20	**zwanzig Minuten nach fünf (Uhr)**	**zwanzig Minuten nach fünf (Uhr)**	**fünf Uhr zwanzig**
5.30	**halb sechs (Uhr)**	**halb sechs (Uhr)**	**fünf Uhr dreissig**
5.40	**zwanzig Minuten vor sechs (Uhr)**	**zwanzig Minuten vor sechs (Uhr)**	**fünf Uhr vierzig**
5.45	**(ein) Viertel vor sechs (Uhr)**	**dreiviertel auf sechs (Uhr)**	**fünf Uhr fünfundvierzig**
		dreiviertel sechs (Uhr)	
5.55	**fünf Minuten vor sechs (Uhr)**	**fünf Minuten vor sechs (Uhr)**	**fünf Uhr fünfundfünfzig**

Exactly five o'clock, five " on the dot ", is **Punkt fünf** or **Schlag fünf.** At what time ? is **um wieviel Uhr ?**; at five o'clock is **um fünf Uhr.** My watch is right is **meine Taschenuhr geht richtig** ; it is slow is **sie geht nach** ; it is fast is **sie geht vor.**

The date is fairly simple. In answer to the question : **Der wievielte ist heute?**, what is the date today?, or **den wievielten haben wir heute?**, we get the answers : **es ist der 5. (fünfte) November** or **wir haben den 5. (fünften) November.** Note the usual way of marking the ordinal number by means of a full stop : 5. = **fünfte.** On the fifth of November is **am fünften November** ; on Monday is **am Montag** : he comes on Mondays is **er kommt Montags.** On Monday the fifth November is **am Montag, dem fünften November.** I am coming on Monday is **ich komme Montag,** without any preposition.

At the head of a letter the date is written : **den 5. Novem-**

ber 1949, and frequently the **den** is printed on the letter-heading: **den. . . .**

Care is needed with the year: he was born in 1876 is either **er wurde 1876 geboren** or **er wurde im Jahre 1876 geboren**, but never, as in English, with **in** alone before the figure.

Here are some useful time words: **heute**, today; **heute abend**, this evening; **heute über acht Tage**, a week today; **morgen**, tomorrow; **übermorgen**, the day after tomorrow; **gestern**, yesterday; **vorgestern**, the day before yesterday; a.m., **vormittags**; p.m., **nachmittags**; midday, noon, **der Mittag**; midnight, **die Mitternacht**: **der Schlaf vor Mitternacht ist der beste**, the sleep before midnight is the best, the beauty sleep.

CHAPTER VII

THE PRONOUNS

PERSONAL PRONOUNS

Singular.

	1st Person.	2nd Person.	3rd Person.		
Nom.	**ich**	**du**	**er**	**sie**	**es**
Acc.	**mich**	**dich**	**ihn**	**sie**	**es**
Gen.	**meiner** *	**deiner** *	**seiner** *	**ihrer**	**seiner** *
Dat.	**mir**	**dir**	**ihm**	**ihr**	**ihm**

Plural.

Nom.	**wir**	**ihr**		**sie**	
Acc.	**uns**	**euch**		**sie**	
Gen.	**unser**	**euer**		**ihrer**	
Dat.	**uns**	**euch**		**ihnen**	

The polite form of the 2nd person is, of course, the same as the 3rd person plural, written with a capital letter: Nom. **Sie**, Acc. **Sie**, Gen. **Ihrer**, Dat. **Ihnen**.

The reflexive pronouns are the same as the above except in the Accusative and Dative of the 3rd persons (and the polite form), where they are replaced by **sich**, himself, herself, itself, themselves, yourself, yourselves.

The prepositions **halben**, **wegen**, on account of, and **willen**, for the sake of, which govern the Genitive, combine with the Genitive of the personal pronouns as follows: **meinethalben**, **um meinetwillen**, for my sake; **unsertwegen**, on account of us. The Genitive is also found in **unsereiner**, literally " one of us ", which is used for both the masculine

* The older forms, **mein**, **dein**, **sein**, are still found in poetry and some set expressions: **Gedenke mein**, remember me; **vergiss mein nicht**, forget me not.

and feminine and can be translated as " people like us " : **unsereiner ist nicht gut genug dazu**, people like us are not good enough for that ; **mit unsereinem macht man nicht viel Umstände**, they don't put themselves out for folk like us, they make short work of people like us.

Du is used between husband and wife and close relations ; between bosom friends (= **Duzfreunde**) ; to small children ; to animals ; when addressing oneself in a soliloquy ; in prayers ; by an author to his " gentle reader " ; in poetry. The plural of **du, ihr,** is of course used when addressing two or more familiars. In all other cases the polite form **Sie** is used. In older German, **Er** and **Sie**, he and she, written with a capital, were used by a superior to an inferior. **Du** is written with a capital letter if the writing is to be seen by the person thus addressed, e.g. in a letter : **Lieber Hans ! Warum hast Du meinen letzten Brief nicht beantwortet ?**, Dear Johnny, Why haven't you replied to my last letter ?

When the antecedent of the Nominative of the relative pronoun **der** or **die** is a pronoun of the 1st or 2nd person, the latter is usually repeated : **ich, der ich ihn so liebe,** I who love him so ; **du, der du hier wohnst,** you who live here ; **unser Vater, der Du bist im Himmel,** our Father which art in Heaven ; but **er, der es weiss,** he who knows it.

The Genitive and Dative of the 3rd persons and the Accusative governed by a preposition are not generally used for inanimate objects. Thus in English we say : we possess a large garden but only plant a part of it ; German cannot use **seiner** to translate " of it ", but uses the Genitive of **derselbe,** the same : **wir besitzen einen grossen Garten, bepflanzen aber nur einen Teil desselben.** Again, we can say in English : My pen is out of order, I cannot write with it ; German will not use **mit ihr** to translate " with it ", but the pronominal adverb : **Meine Feder ist kaputt, ich kann damit nicht schreiben ; man zeigte uns ein grosses Zimmer und wir traten hinein,** we were shown a large room and went into it.

For the uses of es see " Impersonal Verbs ", p. 125.

Note that the reflexive pronoun **sich** may be used reciprocally : **sie lieben sich** may mean " they love themselves " or " they love each other ". In order to make clear what is meant, **selbst** is used to strengthen the reflexive : **sie lieben sich selbst,** they love themselves ; and **einander,** each other, is used reciprocally : **sie lieben einander,** they love each other.

Selbst and **selber,** which are indeclinable, are used for emphasis with nouns and pronouns : **wir haben das selbst bezahlt,** we paid it ourselves ; **der Kaiser selbst kann es nicht tun,** the Emperor himself cannot do it : **selbst der Kaiser kann es nicht tun,** even the Emperor cannot do it.

Sich refers back generally to the subject of the sentence, but when the 3rd person stands after a preposition and refers back to the subject, German, unlike English, uses the reflexive **sich** : **er hat Geld bei sich,** he has money on him ; **er zog das Buch an sich,** he drew the book to him.

POSSESSIVE PRONOUNS

These are the English mine, thine, his, hers, its, ours, yours, theirs, as in : My book and yours ; I have his book and mine ; his father and hers are friends but not mine.

German has four forms :

1. **meiner, meine, meines** ; **deiner,** etc. ; **seiner,** etc., **ihrer,** etc., **unsrer,** etc., **eurer,** etc., **ihrer,** etc.
   These are declined like **dieser, diese, dieses.**
2. **der meine, die meine, das meine** ; **der deine,** etc.
   These are declined like the Weak adjective.
3. **der meinige, die meinige, das meinige,** etc.
   These are also declined like the Weak adjective.

These all have exactly the same meaning. Here are some examples : **Mein Buch und Ihres (das Ihre, das Ihrige),** my book and yours ; **ich habe sein Buch und meines (das meine, das meinige),** I have his book and mine ; **ich habe**

keine Federn, geben Sie mir ihre (die ihren, die ihrigen), I have no pens, give me hers (or theirs).

The first form, **meiner, meine** etc. of the above seems to be the most used in modern German.

4. This is the uninflected form: **mein, dein, sein, ihr, unser, euer, ihr,** and of course **Ihr,** the polite form.

This is used as part of the predicate, especially with **sein, werden, bleiben, scheinen,** to indicate ownership: **dieses Haus ist mein,** this house is mine; **die Bücher sind sein,** the books are his; **das Geld ist unser,** the money is ours. One very rarely finds **ihr,** hers or theirs, and **Ihr,** yours, used in this way; they are replaced by the inflected forms: **der Hut ist ihrer,** the hat is hers (theirs). Note that these forms indicate possession and so could not be used in a case like " your wishes are mine ", **Ihre Wünsche sind meine.** And here is a cynical example: **was dein ist, ist mein, und was mein ist, geht dich nichts an,** what is thine is mine, and what is mine is none of your business.

When forms 1, 2 and 3 are pure substantives they are written with a capital: **die Meinigen,** my family, my folks; **er has das Seinige getan,** he has done his best. The short forms, 4, are neuters, used as we do meum and tuum: **kommt's aufs Mein und Dein, wird's mit der Freundschaft zu Ende sein,** when it comes to a question of mine and thine (property), there's an end to friendship; **er verwechselt Mein und Dein,** he mistakes mine for thine (meum for tuum), a kindly way of calling somebody a thief.

To avoid ambiguity the Genitive of the demonstrative pronoun, **der, die, das,** is used instead of the possessive: **die Mutter kam mit ihrer Tochter hierher, um deren Angelegenheiten in Ordnung zu bringen,** the mother came with her daughter in order to put the latter's affairs in order; **ihre** could refer either to the mother or the daughter and would be ambiguous, **deren** can refer only to the daughter.

Note the polite form used when referring to a person's

relatives: **Ihr Herr Vater,** your father; **Ihre Frau Mutter,** your mother; **Ihre Fräulein Schwester;** note further that the possessive adjective agrees in these examples with **Vater, Mutter, Schwester,** but it could also agree with the title, **Ihr Fräulein Schwester.**

DEMONSTRATIVE PRONOUNS AND ADJECTIVES

The adjectives are: **dieser,** this; **jener,** that; **solcher,** such; **derjenige,** that; **derselbe,** the same; **der,** that.

Der is declined like the Definite Article; **dieser** and the others are declined as follows:

	Masc.	Fem.	Neut.	Plural.
Nom.	**dieser**	**diese**	**dieses**	**diese**
Acc.	**diesen**	**diese**	**dieses**	**diese**
Gen.	**dieses**	**dieser**	**dieses**	**dieser**
Dat.	**diesem**	**dieser**	**diesem**	**diesen**

When used substantively **dieser, jener,** etc., are declined as above, but **der, die, das** adds **-en** to all the Genitives and to the Dative plural.

Nom.	**der**	**die**	**das**	**die**
Acc.	**den**	**die**	**das**	**die**
Gen.	**dessen**	**deren**	**dessen**	**deren** *
Dat.	**dem**	**der**	**dem**	**denen**

Dieser. When this is used substantively in the neuter **dies** is generally used instead of **dieses**: **dies ist mein Bruder,** this is my brother; **dies sind meine Kinder,** these are my children. Note that **dies** is invariable in such cases, i.e. with **sein** followed by a noun. Before a neuter noun the shorter form is frequent: **dies Buch,** this book, for **dieses Buch.**

Dieser means something at hand, present, near by, whereas **jener** refers to something distant, and is indeed generally used only as a contrast with **dieser**: **ich kenne nicht diesen Herrn, sondern jenen,** I don't know this gentleman, but that

* In place of **deren** in the plural **derer** is used when a relative clause follows: **die Kinder derer, die im Krieg starben,** the children of those who died in the war (see also below).

one. The two are used to mean "the former" and "the latter": **Karl und Wilhelm sind beide intelligent; dieser ist aber fleissiger als jener,** Charles and William are both intelligent; the latter is however more diligent than the former.

Jener has no shortened form, like **dies.** It is used when referring to a person or thing already mentioned or known to the reader or listener, where English would use "the": **man kennt jenes alte Sprichwort: Du sollst den Tag nicht vor dem Abend loben,** one knows the old proverb: Don't praise the day before the evening (i.e. we are not yet out of the wood).

Dieser and **jener** may be used to express something indefinite: **ich habe dieses und jenes gesehen,** I have seen this and that, one thing and another. **Dieser oder jener mag es getan haben, ich weiss es nicht,** somebody or other may have done it, I don't know.

Der is the most used demonstrative; it has no reference to nearness or distance, as is the case of **dieser** and **jener.** As an adjective it is always emphatic and strongly stressed, whereas the Definite Article **der, die, das** is not. Hence the stem vowel **e** is long in **der, den, dem,** etc.—but short in **dessen**—and is thus different in pronunciation from the Definite Article. It is often printed spaced out to show the emphasis: **d e r Mann ist ganz dumm,** *that* man is quite stupid; **d e n Kerl kann ich nicht leiden,** I can't bear *that* fellow; **er ist schlau, vor d e m muss ich Sie warnen,** he is cunning, I must caution you against *him*; **d i e sind zu beneiden, deren Glück ist ohne Grenzen,** *those* people are to be envied whose happiness is without limits. Note the use of the Genitive **deren** in the last example. Here are some more examples of the use of the Genitive: **er nahm Abschied von seinem Freund und dessen Schwester,** he took leave of his friend and his (the latter's) sister; **der Brief muss von dem Direktor oder dessen Stellvertreter unterschrieben werden,** the letter must be signed by the manager or his deputy. As said above, instead of the Genitive plural **deren**, the form **derer** is used when followed by a relative clause: **die Nachkommen derer, die hier gewohnt haben**, the descendants of those who have lived here, but **ich grüsse meine alten Freunde und deren Kinder**, I greet my old friends and their children.

The neuter Dative **dem** is used as an indefinite neuter: **ich bin mit dem, was Sie sagen, nicht einverstanden**, I do not agree with that which (what) you say; **dem sei, wie es wolle**, be that as it may.

Instead of a preposition plus **dem** German prefers to use a pronominal adverb such as: **daran, dafür, darauf, damit**, etc. when referring to inanimate objects: **ich erkenne ihn daran**, I recognize him by that; **dagegen habe ich nichts**, I have nothing against that; **hiermit kann ich nichts anfangen**, I can't do anything with this.

Derjenige, diejenige, dasjenige, that, is both adjective and substantive; it is emphatic. It is declined as a weak adjective. Examples are: **derjenige Schüler, der zu spät ankommt, wird bestraft**, that (the) pupil who arrives (too) late is punished; **diejenigen, die fleissig arbeiten, werden belohnt**, those who work hard are rewarded.

He who, she who, those who are translated by **derjenige, der (welcher), diejenige, die (welche), diejenigen, die (welche)**: **derjenige, der hier wohnt, heisst Schmidt**, he who lives here is named Schmidt. **Wer** can be used in this way: **wer ein bös Weib hat, der bedarf keines Teufels**, he who has a bad wife needs no devil.

Derselbe, dieselbe, dasselbe, the same, is both adjectival and substantival: **du sagst immer dasselbe**, you always say the same; **du sagst immer dieselben Dummheiten**, you always say the same foolish things.

Dergleichen, derlei, solcherlei, such, are all indeclinable; they can be used adjectivally or substantively: **dergleichen habe ich nie gegessen**, I have never eaten anything like this;

dergleichen Bücher sind spannend, books of that kind are thrilling; **derlei Dinge,** suchlike things.

Solcher, solche, solches, such, is declined like **dieser.** The shortened uninflected form **solch** may be used before adjectives: **solch bravem Manne können Sie trauen,** you can trust such an honest man; it must be used before **ein, eine, ein**: **solch ein Mann, solch eine Frau, solch ein Kind,** instead of **ein solcher Mann, eine solche Frau, ein solches Kind,** such a man, such a woman, such a child. As a pronoun it is used in cases like: **er verkauft deutsche Waren und auch solche aus der Fremde,** he sells German goods and also goods from abroad. In spoken German **so ein** is used instead of the more formal **solcher**: **so ein Mann würde es zustande bringen,** such a man would accomplish it; this is abbreviated to **so'n.**

RELATIVE PRONOUNS

In English we have two sets of relative pronouns: A, who and that for persons; B, which and that for things. We use " who " and " which " when we do not define or pick out the antecedent but merely describe it: the man, who was very old, suddenly sat down; the house, which was to let, stood in its own garden. Note that we separate the relative clauses by commas from the principal, and in speaking we drop the voice on " who " and " which ". When we define the antecedent we tend to use " that " (though " who " and " which " are correct), we do not use a comma or drop the voice: the man that was very old suddenly sat down; the house that was to let stood in its own garden. You could not say: Gladstone that was the G.O.M. of England . . . because there was only one Gladstone, so he does not need defining. You could say: the Gladstone that our forefathers knew. . . . In English we can omit the relative pronoun if it is not the subject: the man I know; the house we bought.

In German there are only two relative pronouns: **der** and **welcher**; they have no difference in meaning, they can never be omitted, and they are always preceded by commas; moreover, they apply to either persons or things indifferently. **Der** is more used than **welcher**, especially in the spoken language. **Der** is preferred after a proper name: **Wilhelm II, der Deutscher Kaiser war,** William II who was German Emperor; after a personal or interrogative pronoun: **ich, der ich das wünsche,** I who wish that; **wer, der dies gesehen hat, könnte es vergessen?,** who that has seen this could forget it?

Der is declined like the demonstrative pronoun **der**; **welcher** like **dieser**, except in the Genitives. Here they are:

Singular.

	Masc.	Fem.	Neut.	Masc.	Fem.	Neut.
Nom.	**der**	**die**	**das**	**welcher**	**welche**	**welches**
Acc.	**den**	**die**	**das**	**welchen**	**welche**	**welches**
Gen.	**dessen**	**deren**	**dessen**	**dessen**	**deren**	**dessen**
Dat.	**dem**	**der**	**dem**	**welchem**	**welcher**	**welchem**

Plural.

	All genders.	All genders.
Nom.	**die**	**welche**
Acc.	**die**	**welche**
Gen.	**deren**	**deren**
Dat.	**denen**	**welchen**

Here are some examples of the relative pronouns: **unter den Offizieren erhob sich ein schallendes Gelächter, in das der General einstimmte,** there arose amongst the officers a resounding peal of laughter, in which the General joined; **in welches** could, of course, be used instead of **in das. Ein Herr, der nach Raritäten suchte, kam an einem Bauernhofe vorüber, dessen Besitzer an der Tür stand,** a gentleman who was looking for curiosities passed a farm whose owner was standing at the door; we could use **welcher** instead of **der,** but the Genitive **dessen,** whose, must be used. Note the use of the pronominal adverb instead of the relative in: **die Schüssel, woraus der Hund frass,** the dish out of which the dog was eating, although **aus der der Hund frass** would be correct. **Für den Nachrichtendienst genügten früher ein paar verwegene Burschen, auf deren Verschmitztheit man sich verlassen konnte,** Formerly for the Intelligence Service a few bold fellows sufficed whose cunning could be relied on. **Japan brauchte keinen andern Nachrichtendienst als den, welchen Deutschland ihm selbst aufbaute,** Japan needed no other Intelligence Service than the one which Germany itself built up for her; note that: **als den, den Deutschland,** though correct, is not as elegant as **den, welchen. Die Leute, mit denen (welchen) er umging, waren reich,** the people with whom he associated were rich. I think you have now enough examples to guide you; learn them by heart.

Wer is used as a " condensed relative " equal to the English " who " or " he who ": **wer das sagte, hat gelogen,** (he) who said that, lied; **wes(sen) Brot ich esse, des(sen) Lied ich singe,** whose bread I eat, his song I sing, i.e. who pays the piper calls the tune; **wem es hier nicht gefällt, der kann gehen,** literally: to whom it is not pleasing here, he can go, or: if you don't like it here you can go.

Was is similarly used for " that which, what ": **sie kauften, was sie nötig hatten,** they bought what they needed. **Was** is also used when the antecedent is of indefinite meaning or implies an indefinite quantity, such as: **das, etwas, nichts, alles : alles, was er sagte, war falsch,** all that he said was untrue; **ich habe etwas, was interessant ist,** I have something that is interesting. It is also used when the antecedent is a neuter adjective used as a substantive: **das Gute, was er tat,** the good that he did; and when the antecedent is the whole sentence: **er bezahlte**

pünktlich, was mich sehr erstaunte, he paid punctually, which greatly astonished me. The Genitive is generally supplied by **dessen : dieser Laden bietet alles, dessen man bedarf,** this shop offers everything that one needs, the verb **bedürfen** taking the Genitive.

The pronominal adverbs are also used as relatives : **die Schüssel, woraus der Hund frass,** the dish out of which the dog was eating ; **die Städte, wovon wir sprechen,** the towns of which we are speaking ; but **die Leute, von denen wir sprechen,** the people of whom we are speaking.

INTERROGATIVE PRONOUNS AND ADJECTIVES

In English the interrogative pronouns are "who ?" and "what ?" "Who ?" may be plural in English : who are coming tonight ? The German pronouns are **wer** and **was ;** they are always singular : **wer kommt heute abend ?,** who is (or are) coming this evening ? The plural idea can be expressed by **alles : wer alles kommt heute abend ?** who are coming this evening ?

Wer and **was** are declined as follows :

Nom.	**wer**	**was**
Acc.	**wen**	**was**
Gen.	**wessen**	**(wessen)**
Dat.	**wem**	

Examples are : **wer hat das getan ?** who has done (did) that ? ; **wen sehe ich dort ?,** whom do I see there ? ; **wessen Fahrrad ist das ?,** whose bicycle is that ? ; **wem schickte er den Brief ?,** to whom did he send the letter ?

Examples of the use of **was** are : **was liegt auf dem Tisch ?** what is (lying) on the table ? ; **was sagen Sie ?,** what do you say ? ; **wessen rühmen Sie sich ?,** of what are you boasting ?

There is no Dative form. Instead of **was ?** with a preposition we use our old friends the pronominal adverbs, **womit,** with what ?, etc. : **womit schreiben Sie ?,** what are you writing with? ; **wozu soll das dienen?**, what is that to serve for? what's the use of it? If emphasis is desired, then **was** can be used with a preposition: **zu w a s soll das dienen?**, *what* is that to serve for? In everyday German such constructions of **was** plus preposition are common, even when no emphasis is intended.

The interrogative adjective is **welcher, welche, welches,** declined like **dieser.** It corresponds to the English "which?" or "what?", as in: **welches Buch lesen Sie?**, which (or what) book are you reading? The neuter **welches** is used like **das, es** and **dies** (e.g. **das ist mein Freund, dies sind meine Freunde,** that is my friend, these are my friends) without regard to gender or number: **welches sind Ihre Freunde?**, which are your friends? ; **welches ist Ihre Absicht?**, what is your intention?

Was für ein is equivalent to the English "what sort of", as in: **was für ein Bleistift ist das?**, what sort of a pencil is that? The **ein** is NOT governed by the preposition **für,** but takes its case from its function in the sentence: **was für einen Bleistift haben Sie?**, what sort of a pencil have you? **Was für ein** may be used substantively, and then, of course, takes the endings of **der, die, das**: **wir haben ein Haus gekauft. Was für eines?**, we have bought a house. What sort of (a) one? When used before a plural or an abstract noun or the name of a substance the **ein** is dropped: **was für Leute sind das?**, what sort of people are those? **was für Bier trinken Sie?**, what sort of beer do you drink? In the plural when used substantively **welche** is used: **ich habe ja Bücher, aber was für welche!**, I have books all right, but what sort! The **was** may be separated from **für ein,** as in: **was ist das für Unsinn?**, what nonsense is that?

The old Genitive of **was,** namely **wes,** is found in proverbs and in Biblical language: **wes das Herz voll ist, des geht der Mund über,** out of the abundance of the heart the mouth speaketh (Matthew xii. 34).

INDEFINITE PRONOUNS AND ADJECTIVES OF QUANTITY

Jemand, somebody, and **niemand,** nobody, make the Genitive by adding **-s**; they are generally uninflected in the Accusative and Dative but may add **-en** for the former and **-em** for the latter. Here are some examples: **es ist jemand im Garten,** there is somebody in the garden; **ich sehe niemand,** I see nobody. Note the following: **jemand anders,** somebody else; **ich habe niemand Fremdes getroffen,** I met nobody who was a stranger.

Jedermann, everybody, takes an **-s** in the Genitive, but is not otherwise declined: **jedermanns Freund ist niemands Freund,** the friend of everybody is the friend of nobody; **Herr Jedermann regiert die Welt,** the man-in-the-street rules the world.

Jeder, jede, jedes, each, every, any, is declined like **dieser**; when used substantively it is often equivalent to "everybody": **jeder muss sich nach der Decke strecken,** everybody must stretch himself according to the coverlet, i.e. one must cut one's coat according to one's cloth; **jeder kehre vor seiner Tür !,** let everybody sweep before his own door, i.e. let everybody mind his own business; **man kann es nicht jedem recht machen,** one cannot please everybody. Here are examples of its adjectival use: **jeder Zoll ein König,** every inch a king; **jeder Tag hat seine Plagen,** every day has its worries, i.e. sufficient for the day is the evil thereof; **er kommt jeden Tag,** he comes every day. It often has the meaning of "any": **er kann jeden Augenblick hier sein,** he may be here at any moment; **ohne jede Gefahr,** without any danger; **ohne jeden Zweifel,** without any doubt.

Einer, one, and **keiner,** none, are both declined like **der, die, das**; they are often used in everyday language for **jemand** and **niemand**: **gestern fragte mich einer, ob ich hier geboren sei,** somebody asked me yesterday if I was born here; **ich werde es keinem sagen,** I will tell nobody. The adjective **kein, keine, kein,** "no" or "not any", presents no difficulties: **ich trinke keinen Wein,** I do not drink any wine or I do not drink wine; **ich habe keine Zeit für solche Dummheiten,** I have no time for such nonsense. **Kein Mensch** is equivalent to "not a soul": **kein Mensch weiss, dass ich hier bin,** not a soul knows I am here.

Man is our "one", the French "on"; it is the noun **Mann** spelt with one **n** and a small letter; it is found only in the Nominative: **überstandner Leiden gedenkt man gern,** one likes to remember sorrows (sufferings) overcome —note that the verb **gedenken** takes the Genitive; **durch Lehren lernt man,** one learns by teaching. The other cases of **man** are taken by **einer**: **wenn's einem am besten schmeckt, soll man aufhören zu essen,** one should stop eating when it tastes best (to one), i.e. one should leave off with an appetite; **er kann einen nicht treffen, ohne etwas Unangenehmes zu sagen,** he cannot meet one without saying something disagreeable. **Man,** as we see under "Passive Voice", is much more used in German than "one" in English.

Etwas, something, is used as in: **ich wünsche etwas zu essen,** I want something to eat; **geben Sie mir etwas Butter,** give me some butter; **haben Sie irgend etwas für mich?,** have you anything at all for me? In everyday German **was** frequently replaces **etwas**: **haben Sie was (etwas) anderes?,** have you something else? In a shop the customer is asked: **sonst noch was?,** anything else? **Was** is also used with the meaning of "how": **was ist das Kind klug!,** how clever the child is!

Nichts, nothing, is indeclinable: **es gab nichts zu essen,** there was nothing to eat; **was sagten Sie? Nichts!,** what did you say? Nothing! Remember the idioms with **etwas** and **nichts**: **er hat etwas Dummes gesagt,** he has said something silly; **wissen Sie nichts Neues?** do you know nothing new?, i.e. have you no news? Here are a few proverbs with **nichts**: **er weiss aus nichts etwas zu machen,** he knows how to make something out of nothing; **mit nichts kann man kein Haus bauen,** you can't build a house out of nothing; **mir nichts, dir nichts,** without more ado, unceremoniously; **wo nichts ist, hat der Kaiser das Recht verloren,** where there is nothing the Emperor has lost his rights. **Nichts weniger als** means "anything but": **sie ist nichts weniger als schön,** she is anything but beautiful.

All, all, generally remains uninflected when it stands in front of a noun qualified by a possessive adjective or the definite article: **all das Geld,** all the money; **all meine Kinder,** all my children; **mit all seiner Kraft,** with all his might. It is also found inflected: **alles dieses Glück,** all this happiness; **alle diese Waren,** all these goods. It is declined like a strong adjective when used alone before a noun: **aller Anfang ist schwer,** the first step is the difficulty (*c'est le premier pas qui coûte*); **aller Leute Freund,** the friend of everybody, **aller** being Genitive plural; **allen Leuten recht getan, ist eine Kunst, die niemand kann,** to do justice to everybody is an art that nobody understands.

As a pronoun it is declined like a strong adjective: **wir sind alle arme Sünder,** we are all miserable sinners; **alles zu seiner Zeit,** everything in its own good time; **alles besiegt die Liebe,** love conquers all; **aller Dinge Anfang ist gering,** the beginning of all things is small; **alles** is used with the meaning of everybody: **alles rannte dahin,** everybody rushed to it. Note the idiomatic meaning of **alle** in: **mein Geld ist alle,** my money has all gone.

"All" is to be translated by **ganz,** whole, in cases like all day, all the year: **den ganzen Tag, das ganze Jahr**; **ganz Deutschland,** all Germany.

Sämtlich, all, all together, entire, is a useful adjective: **sein sämtliches Hab und Gut,** his entire goods and chattels.

Manch, many a, **solch,** such, and **welch,** which, what, are uninflected before the indefinite article: **manch ein Mann,** many a man; **solch eine Freude,** such a pleasure; **welch**

ein schönes Buch, what a lovely book! They are frequently not declined before an adjective: **manch edler Mann**, many a noble man; **solch traurige Nachrichten**, such sad news; **welch süsses Kind**, what a sweet child.

Otherwise **manch** and **solch** are declined like strong adjectives: **mancher gute Mann**, many a good man; **mancher Mann**, many a man; **eine solche Freude**, such a pleasure; **solche traurigen Nachrichten**, such sad news.

Examples of their use as pronouns are: **mancher kehrte nicht nach Haus**, many a one did not return home; **ich habe noch manches zu tun**, I have still a great many things to do, much to do; **solche, die hier wohnen**, such as live here, those who live here.

Solch is often replaced by **so ein**, especially in speech: **so ein kleiner Kerl**, such a little fellow. (For **solch** see also p. 69.)

Beide, both, is declined like an adjective: **er hat zwei Töchter, aber beide sind in der Fremde**, he has two daughters, but both are abroad; **seine beiden Söhne sind zu Hause**, his two sons (both his sons) are at home; **sie sind alle beide froh, mich zu sehen**, they are both glad to see me; the neuter **beides** is used when two objects are considered as a whole: **beides, Geld und Ehre, habe ich verloren**, I have lost both money and honour.

Ein paar, a few, is indeclinable: **geben Sie mir ein paar Kirschen**, give me a few cherries; **nach ein paar Jahren**, after a few years. But **ein Paar**, a pair, is regular: **mit einem Paar Strümpfe**, with a pair of stockings. This **Paar** is neuter: **das Paar**.

Viel, much, many, and **wenig**, little, few, may be inflected or uninflected. They are always inflected when they follow the definite article or an adjectival pronoun: **es ist schade um das viele Geld**, it is a pity about all that money; **mein weniges Geld war bald ausgegeben**, my little money was soon spent; **die wenigen Bücher**, the few books. When used substantively in the plural to designate persons they are generally inflected: **viele haben viel, niemand genug,** many (people) have much, nobody has enough; **nach der Meinung vieler (weniger),** in the opinion of many (few).

If they are not preceded by a pronominal adjective they may be inflected or not: **viel** or **viele Bücher,** many books; **mit viel** or **vieler Mühe,** with much trouble.

The uninflected forms **viel** and **wenig** used to express an indefinite quantity are indeclinable adverbs. They may then stand alone or be followed by the Genitive or the Dative with **von: lerne viel, sage wenig, höre alles,** learn much, say little, hear all things; **lerne viel, dass du viel vergessen kannst,** learn much so that you may forget much; **mit wenig von diesem Wein,** with (a) little of this wine; **viel des besten Stoffes,** much of the best material.

The neuter pronouns, **vieles** and **weniges,** are collectives and mean "many things", "few things", as in: **manches soll man hören und vieles verschweigen,** you should hear many things and keep silent about many; **lerne nicht auf einmal vieles, sondern viel,** do not learn many things at once but much (of one subject).

Mehrere, several, derived from the comparative of **viel,** viz. **mehr,** is used only in the plural: **er hat mehrere Geschwister,** he has several brothers and sisters; **vor mehreren Jahren,** several years ago.

CHAPTER VIII

THE VERB

" Verb " means THE word, and is, indeed, the most important element of the sentence—the fulcrum on which it turns. Let us run over the verbal machinery before setting out the conjugations; it is common to most European languages, and our survey will help us to understand much that would otherwise be obscure.

THE VERB AS A NOUN

A verb is defined as a " part of speech which predicates, e.g. the italicized words in: Time *flies*; Salt *is* good; you *surprise* me " (Concise Oxford Dictionary). And " to predicate " is " to assert something about a subject ". Now, in: to fly is an exciting experience; to be good is a moral duty; to surprise the enemy is an advantage, " to fly ", " to be " and " to surprise " do not assert anything about a subject, since they are all subjects themselves. They are in fact verbal nouns.

In: I can fly; you must be good; that will surprise him, " fly ", " be ", " surprise " are not verbs as defined above, since they have no subject and do not predicate, " can ", " must " and " will " being the predicating verbs. What are they, then? They, too, are verbal nouns. " Fly " differs from " to fly " in that it cannot be used as a subject: we can say " to fly is pleasant ", but not " fly is pleasant ".

Again in: flying is pleasant; being good is a moral duty; surprising the enemy is an advantage, we are evidently dealing with a noun, a verbal noun. There is a slight difference in meaning between " seeing is believing " and " to see is to believe ", but from the point of view of grammar " seeing " and " to see " are both verbal nouns.

What names shall we give these three verbal nouns? Some grammarians call " to fly " the Supine and " fly " the Infinitive—also called, wrongly, the Infinitive Mood—but most grammarians lump them together under the term Infinitive, with or without " to ", and we shall do the same. " Flying " is called the Gerund, and is evidently much more of a noun than the Infinitive, since we can qualify it with an adjective : " high flying is pleasant ", or use it with a preposition : " by flying we can travel quickly ". Note that the Gerund is the only one of the forms which has an inflection, viz. -ing.

German has only one form for the above three : the Infinitive, **die Nennform** (= name-form, i.e. the form that names the action), which ends in **-en** or **-n** : **loben,** to praise ; **singen,** to sing ; **springen,** to jump. If the verbal stem ends in **-er** or **-el** it adds **-n** to form the Infinitive : **klettern,** to climb ; **vereiteln,** to thwart. Other verbs in **-n** are **sein,** to be ; **tun,** to do ; and **sehen,** to see, **gehen,** to go, are often written **sehn, gehn.**

The German Infinitive is so much of a noun that it has only to be written with a capital letter to become a pure noun : **ich kann das Singen der Vögel nicht hören,** I cannot hear the singing of the birds. Here are some examples :

Borgen macht Sorgen, borrowing makes sorrowing, he who goes a-borrowing, goes a-sorrowing.

Bieten und Widerbieten macht den Kauf, bidding and counter-bidding make the bargain.

Ich tat es mit Zittern und Beben, I did it in fear (= dithering) and trembling (= quaking).

Sehen ist Glauben, seeing is believing.

The Infinitive with " to " after certain verbs corresponds to the German **zu** in most cases : **ich wünsche, nach Hause**

zu gehen, I wish to go home ; **ich will nach Hause gehen,** I will go home ; **ich befehle Ihnen, hier zu bleiben,** I order you to remain here ; **Sie dürfen hier bleiben,** you may remain here ; good to eat, **gut zu essen** (or **zum Essen**) ; easy to understand, **leicht zu verstehen** ; **ein Zimmer zu vermieten,** a room to let.

In German the Infinitive is used as an Imperative, especially in official orders : **Nicht rauchen !,** no smoking ; **rechts halten !,** keep to the right ; **hier öffnen !,** open here.

There is a curious use of the Infinitive in both English and German (and in French, too) as an exclamation : What ! he say that ? ! **Wie ! er das sagen ? !** (*Quoi ! lui dire ça? !*).

The English Gerund in -ing must be translated into German in various ways, often by the Infinitive, e.g. seeing is believing, **Sehen ist Glauben.** He took it without paying is : **er nahm es, ohne zu bezahlen** ; I like drinking tea, **ich trinke gern Tee** ; he obtained the book by paying a high price, **er bekam das Buch dadurch, dass er einen hohen Preis bezahlte.** You will have to be on the look-out in your reading for these Gerund equivalents.

You must not confuse our Gerund in -ing with the German pure nouns in **-ung** derived from verbs : **die Begegnung,** meeting ; **die Kleidung,** clothing ; **die Wohnung,** dwelling ; **die Zeichnung,** drawing. ALL English verbs can make a Gerund in -ing ; the German nouns in **-ung** are restricted in number.

THE VERB AS AN ADJECTIVE

The Present Participle

In : the flying Dutchman ; a surprising assertion ; running to the door, he opened it ; he is always singing, the form in -ing is not a noun, but an adjective. It is the Present Participle, a most useful and neat part of speech.

The German Participle, **das Partizip** (or **Partizipium**) **Präsens,** is made by adding **-end** to the verbal stem ; **lobend,** praising; **singend**, singing; but **seiend**, being; **tuend**, doing. Its use as a pure adjective is common in German: **der fliegende Holländer**, the flying Dutchman; **eine überraschende Behauptung**, a surprising assertion; **das laufende Jahr**, the current (running) year; **eine reizende Frau**, a charming woman. Of course verbs in **-er** and **-el** make the Present Participle in **-nd**: **kletternd**; **vereitelnd**.

If these participial adjectives are modified as in: the Dutchman flying through the storm; an assertion surprising on account of its violence, in German the modifying phrase precedes the adjective: **der durch den Sturm fliegende Holländer**; **eine wegen ihrer Heftigkeit überraschende Behauptung**.

In cases like: running to the window, he opened it, German uses the same construction: **ans Fenster laufend, öffnete er es**, but it is much less common in German and has a much more literary flavour. Here are some examples: **sie stand zitternd da**, she stood there trembling; **da trat die Heilige zu mir, ein Schwert und Fahne tragend**, then the Saint (St. Joan) stepped up to me, bearing a sword and banner.

In cases like: I saw him coming; I heard him calling, German uses the Infinitive: **ich sah ihn kommen**; **ich hörte ihn rufen**. Note that in: I hear the orator speak and I hear the word spoken, German has the Infinitive: **ich höre den Redner sprechen** and **ich höre das Wort sprechen**.

When an action is further particularized by a Present Participle in English, as in: a bird came flying into the room, German uses the Past Participle: **ein Vogel kam ins Zimmer geflogen**; **eine Kugel kam geflogen**, a bullet came flying; this construction is used only with "kommen".

German has no form corresponding to our: I am singing, which presents an action as proceeding at a given moment, and it must in most cases be translated by the simple Present Tense **ich singe**, I sing. German can, however, express this idea by means of **am** with the Infinitive: **ich bin am Singen.**

The Past Participle

The Past Participle is also an adjective, as in: the closed door; a badly written letter; the fallen leaves. It is also used with the auxiliary verb "to have" to form tenses: I have closed the door. The English Past Participle is formed by adding -ed or -d to the Infinitive of the Weak (or Regular) verbs: jump, jumped; praise, praised. With the Strong (or Irregular) verbs the Past Participle is made by vowel change and often by adding -en: speak, spoken; sing, sung; break, broken.

In German **das Partizip Perfekt** is formed by prefixing **ge-** to the stem of the verb and adding **-t** in the case of Weak verbs; **loben,** to praise, **gelobt,** praised; if the stem ends in **-t** or **-d,** then **-et** must be added: **beten,** to pray, **gebetet; zünden,** to ignite, **gezündet.** With strong Verbs **-en** is added: **singen, gesungen; kommen, gekommen; brechen, gebrochen;** but **sein,** to be, **gewesen; tun,** to do, **getan.**

Verbs which are compounded with an inseparable prefix such as **be-, er-, zer-, ent-, ver-,** etc. (see p. 128) drop the **ge-: erlauben,** to allow, **erlaubt; zerbrechen,** to smash to pieces, **zerbrochen; versprechen,** to promise, **versprochen.**

Verbs derived from foreign words and accented on the last syllable, the majority of which end in **-ieren,** also omit the **ge-: spazieren,** to go for a walk, **spaziert; boykottieren,** to boycott, **boykottiert.**

See p. 141 for **können, mögen, dürfen, müssen, sollen, wollen** and for **lassen, sehen, hören, helfen, heissen, lernen, machen, fühlen, wissen,** which use the Infinitive instead of the Past Participle when connected with an Infinitive, e.g. **ich habe es nicht tun wollen,** I have not wanted to do it, i.e. **wollen** and not **gewollt; wir haben ihn sprechen hören,** we have heard him speak, i.e. **hören** and not **gehört.** And see p. 138 under Passive for the Past Participle of **werden.**

Here are typical examples of the use of the Past Participle in German: **das gelobte Buch,** the praised book; **das von jedermann gelobte Buch,** the book praised by everybody; **die gefallenen Blätter,** the fallen leaves; **die von den Bäumen gefallenen Blätter,** the leaves fallen from the trees; **da lag er ermüdet und verwundet,** there he lay tired and wounded; **in seinem Mantel gehüllt, schlief er ruhig,** wrapped in his cloak he slept calmly.

The Past Participle can, of course, be used as a noun: **der Verwundete,** the wounded man; **die Verwundeten,** the wounded; we pray for the fallen, **wir beten für die Gefallenen**; **das Erwartete,** the expected.

It is used as a noun in the following examples, but is not inflected: **aufgeschoben ist nicht aufgehoben** (Luther), postponed is not abandoned, forbearance does not mean acquittance; **gesagt, getan,** no sooner said than done; **jung gewohnt, alt getan** (= young accustomed, old done), what is learnt in youth is remembered in old age.

The Past Participle is used to form compound tenses with the auxiliaries **haben** and **sein**: **ich habe gelobt,** I have praised, but **ich bin gekommen,** I have come; **ich bin gewesen,** I have been. (See p. 96 for verbs which take **sein** as the auxiliary.)

The Past Participle is used in German to give an urgent command: **Bücher zugemacht!,** books closed!; **stillgestanden!,** attention!

THE FINITE VERB

We now come to the verb proper—that is to say, the verb which predicates something of a subject, which presents the action as being done by somebody or something at a certain time: he praises; they praised; I have praised; lest he praise, etc.

Tense and Time

The verb shows the time of the action by means of the Tense mechanism (**das Tempus,** tense) which indicates present, **die Gegenwart,** past, **die Vergangenheit,** and future, **die Zunkunft,** Only the Present and Past are simple tenses, the others being created by means of the auxiliary verbs, **haben, sein,** and **werden.**

Concord of the Finite Verb with the Subject

Of course the finite verb agrees with the subject in person and number : **du bist, ihr seid, Sie sind.** A singular noun takes a singular verb : **das Kind lacht** ; a plural noun takes a plural verb : **die Kinder lachen.** In English collective nouns generally take a plural verb : the Government have decided . . .; the L.C.C. are going to . . .; the police think that . . .; England are playing well ; the Bank of England have agreed that . . ., etc. In German these collective nouns take a singular verb : **die Regierung hat entschieden . . .** ; **die Polizei glaubt, dass . . .,** etc. They may, however, especially when followed by a dependent word in the plural, take a plural verb : **Eine Menge Wagen standen vor der Tür,** a crowd of carriages stood in front of the door ; **eine Anzahl Bücher lagen vor ihr,** a number of books lay before her ; **Hundert Soldaten sind gefallen,** a hundred soldiers have fallen ; **ein Paar Handschuhe lagen auf dem Tisch,** a pair of gloves lay on the table.

When two substantives closely related or contrasted in meaning form the subject the verb is frequently found in the singular : **Salz und Brot macht Wangen rot,** salt and bread make cheeks red ; **gleich und gleich gesellt sich gern,** birds of a feather flock together ; **frischer Sinn und froher Mut ist besser, als viel Geld und Gut,** quick wit and merry humour are better than much money and land ; **da ist alle Mühe und Arbeit verloren,** it is not worth while (all trouble and work is lost) ; **Morgenregen und Weibertränen ist nicht zu trauen,** morning rain and women's tears are not to be trusted.

With titles such as **Eure (Euer) Majestät,** your Majesty, **Ew. (= Euer) Exzellenz,** your Excellency, **Eure Hoheit,** your Highness, the verb is usually in the plural: **Eure Majestät scheinen erregt,** Your Majesty seems excited. This is also the case when speaking of the titled person: **Sind Seine Exzellenz zu Hause?**, is his Excellence at home? It is also used by servants when speaking of their master or mistress, though I doubt whether in the Germany of today it will be much used: **die gnädige Frau ist (sind) nicht zu sprechen,** my mistress is not to be seen.

Mood

The verb shows whether the action is reported as a factual happening—the Indicative Mood, **die Wirklichkeitsform** (= reality-form)—as an order to be obeyed—the Imperative, **die Befehlsform** (= order-form)—or as an action which is desired or possible or purely imaginary—the Subjunctive Mood, **die Wunsch-** or **Möglichkeitsform** (= wish or possibility-form).

That sounds difficult, but it is not nearly as difficult as it sounds. Remember that language is the creation of the average human mind, not of philosophers and grammarians, and that the human beings who have built up language over the centuries were, and are, on the whole pretty simple-minded. The peasant, the charwoman, the cobbler, the man-in-the-street have all co-operated in creating our language, and they use the Subjunctive Mood without blenching at the idea. When a little French child says: *il faut bien que je le fasse,* I'll have to do it, it is using the Subjunctive; the child may be quite ignorant, unable to read or write, but it will use the Subjunctive correctly. Why? Because that is "how you say it". The English child will say: I wish I *were* at home now; or a countryman: I'll be sixty *come* Christmas, and both of them will be using the Subjunctive, without being aware of the fact. The German child looking into a shop window will say without the least effort: **wenn ich nur etwas Geld hätte!**, if only I had some money! The poor little wretch does not suspect that he is using this dreadfully difficult Subjunctive. There is nothing more democratic than language which has been created by the common effort of all who speak it or have spoken it. Behind all grammar lies the simple human mind struggling to interpret the universe. These Moods were created by the human mind in its effort to communicate the impressions thronging on it through the senses, and roughly sorting out those impressions into facts which occur in the world outside us and non-facts which exist only in our inner world; into the objective and the subjective, or, in other words, into the Indicative and the Subjunctive.

As I sit here at my desk typing this chapter I look out over the garden and see the leafless trees. A dog runs on to the lawn and barks. I report those seen facts by saying "The trees are leafless. The neighbour's dog runs on to the lawn. It barks." Tomorrow I will report those events as being past: "The trees were leafless. The neighbour's dog ran on to the lawn. It barked."

Then I turn my mind inwards and create a scene which exists only in my imagination; I say: "Were the trees in leaf, it would be summer. If that dog were lame and dumb, it could not run on the lawn or bark." In order to show that the trees are *not* in leaf, that it is *not* summer, that the dog is *not* lame and dumb, I use a special form of the verb, the Subjunctive, and thus make clear to my hearer that this scene is purely in the realm of the imagination.

Another example: the baby next door suddenly cries out; I exclaim: "God bless the child, I hope it isn't hurt!" Why do I use "bless" and not "blesses"? Because "bless" indicates that it is merely a wish on my part, something that I hope will happen but which is not actually happening; the "blessing" is only in my mind. "Bless" is here Subjunctive.

The Imperative Mood is very like the Subjunctive, since

when you order a person to do something, you do not know that the order will be carried out: open the door! The "opening" is not a fact, though it may become a fact.

Now English has almost lost the Subjunctive as a special form of the verb, and has invented all sorts of tricks to indicate the non-factuality of a happening, and this is what makes it rather difficult for us to get used to a language, like German or French, which has pretty full Subjunctive forms. We do not say: if he praise me, but: if he praises me; or: if he should praise me, using either the Indicative (praises) or an auxiliary (should) to express the idea.

Voice

There are two ways of reporting an action: by looking at it from the point of its origin, or from the point towards which it is directed. When I say: "The man fells the tree," I am presenting the action of felling as originating in "the man". When I say: "The tree is felled by the man," I am presenting the action as directed towards the tree; the first is the Active Voice, the second the Passive, **die Tätigkeitsform** (= activity-form) and **die Leideform** (= suffering-form).

In English we use the verb "to be" as the auxiliary to form the Passive, making no difference between: the door is closed, I can't get out, and: the door is closed by the porter at ten o'clock. As we shall see on p. 134, the first is not Passive at all. You can feel this if I replace "close" by the verb "open": the door is open; the door is opened by the porter at ten o'clock. In German you have to distinguish between the mere description (the door is closed; the door is open) and the action (is closed by the porter; is opened by the porter), which latter are Passive. German uses **sein** for the description, **werden** for the Passive: **die Tür ist geschlossen; die Tür wird von dem Portier geschlossen.** We will discuss these more in detail on p. 134.

REFLEXIVE VERBS

The origin of the action may lie in the subject and return to the subject, in which case we have a Reflexive Verb, **das rückbezügliche Zeitwort** (= back-referring verb) : he washes himself : **er wäscht sich,** the action originates in " he " and is directed towards " himself ", the same person. There are no serious difficulties with the German Reflexive Verb, which you will find fully treated on p. 123.

We have now cleared the ground for the conjugation of the verb and a more detailed discussion of some of the above phenomena. I think they deserve a fresh chapter.

CHAPTER IX

CONJUGATION OF THE VERB

German grammarians divide verbs into: (*a*) Regular Verbs, subdivided into Weak and Strong; (*b*) Irregular Verbs.

Weak verbs, like **loben**, to praise, make their Past Tense 1st person by adding **-te** to the verbal stem: **lobte**, and their Past Participle by prefixing **ge-** and adding **-t**: **gelobt**.

Strong verbs, like **singen**, to sing, make their Past Tense by vowel change (**der Ablaut**) in the verbal stem: **ich sang**, and their Past Participle by prefixing **ge-** and adding **-(e)n**: **gesungen**.

Irregular verbs do not conform to either of the above rules: **können**, to be able, **konnte, gekonnt** or **können**; **brennen**, to burn, **brannte, gebrannt**.

The Personal Pronoun subjects are in English: I, you, he, she, it, singular, and we you, they, plural. I omit "thou" as being quite obsolete in English. The German pronouns are: **ich, du, er, sie, es**, singular; **wir, ihr, sie**, plural. **Du**, thou, and **ihr**, you, ye, are very much alive in German, being used when addressing close relatives and intimate friends, small children, and animals. The polite form of **du** and **ihr** is **Sie**, you, which is probably the only form you will ever use. Historically it is merely the 3rd person plural **sie**, they, with a capital letter: **sie loben**, they praise; **Sie loben**, you praise. I shall omit it in the conjugation of the verbs, as it is always the same as the 3rd person plural.

WEAK VERBS

Let us first examine the simple tenses of the Weak verbs and then look at the Strong verbs. Here are the endings of the Weak verbs for: the Present Indicative, the Present Subjunctive; the Imperfect Indicative and the Imperfect Subjunctive, which are exactly alike:

	Present.		Imperfect.
	Indic.	Subj.	Indic. and Subj.
ich	**-e**	**-e**	**-(e)te**
du	**-(e)st**	**-est**	**-(e)test**
er	**-(e)t**	**-e**	**-(e)te**
wir	**-en**	**-en**	**-(e)ten**
ihr	**-(e)t**	**-et**	**-(e)tet**
sie	**-en**	**-en**	**-(e)ten**

Note that you can form the Imperfect by inserting a **-t** before the endings of the Present, except for the 3rd person singular, when you add an **e**, thus making the 1st person and 3rd person singular alike: **ich lobte, er lobte.**

The rules for the omission or inclusion of the (**e**) in the Present are:

A. The great majority of Weak verbs always omit the (**e**) in the 2nd person singular: **du lobst,** and in the 3rd person singular: **er lobt**; but it may be included in the 2nd person plural: **ihr lobt** or **ihr lobet,** the latter being much more formal and literary.

B. Verbs whose stem ends in **-t** or **-d** always insert the (**e**) before the **-t** of the ending: **er redet,** he speaks; **er betet,** he prays; **ihr redet,** ye speak; **ihr betet,** ye pray; they generally insert it also in the 2nd person singular but may drop it: **du redest** or **du redst.**

C. Verbs whose stem ends in **-m** or **-n** preceded by a different consonant insert the (**e**): **atmen,** to breathe, **du atmest**; **er atmet**; **ihr atmet**; **trocknen,** to dry, **du trocknest**; **er trocknet**; **ihr trocknet.**

D. Verbs whose stem ends in a sibilant generally insert the (**e**) before **-st**: **reisen,** to travel, **du reisest,** or contract the **-est** to **-t**: **du reist.** They do not insert the (**e**) before the **-t** of the ending.

E. Verbs whose Infinitive ends in **-ern** or **-eln** generally drop the **e** of the stem in the first 1st person singular of the Present Indicative: **klettern**, to climb: **ich klettre**, but **du kletterst**, **wir klettern**, etc.; **wandeln**, to walk, travel: **ich wandle**.

In the Imperfect the **(e)** is inserted by all verbs whose stem ends in **-t**, **-d**, **-m**, **-n**, as above: **reden, ich redete**; **beten, ich betete**; **atmen, ich atmete**; **trocknen, ich trocknete**.

Here are examples of all these classes in the Present Indicative, neither the Present Subjunctive nor the Imperfect Indicative requiring any further help.

Infinitive:	lob-en	bet-en	atm-en	reis-en	wandeln
ich	lobe	bete	atme	reise	wandle
du	lobst	betest	atmest	reisest (reist)	wandelst
er	lobt	betet	atmet	reist	wandelt
wir	loben	beten	atmen	reisen	wandeln
ihr	lob(e)t	betet	atmet	reis(e)t	wandelt
sie	loben	beten	atmen	reisen	wandeln

THE IMPERATIVE

This is also a simple form. You can only give a direct order to a person to whom you are speaking, and not to a third person. Thus in English the Imperative of "to praise" is: praise! To give an order to a person not present we use a subterfuge: let him praise; let them praise. If we include ourselves in the order we say: let us praise.

In German we have three forms for the direct order, corresponding to **du**, **ihr** and **Sie**:

lobe! praise (thou) **loben Sie!** praise (you)
lob(e)t! praise (ye)

The 2nd person singular is also found without the **-e**: **lob!**

For the 3rd person singular we can use the Subjunctive:

er lobe !, let him praise; or **er soll loben,** he is to praise; for the 3rd person plural: **sie sollen loben,** they are to praise; for the 1st person plural: **loben wir,** let us praise, or **lass uns loben, lasst uns loben !**

Note that in German the Imperative is always followed by a note of exclamation (**das Ausrufszeichen**): **lobe !; lobt !; loben Sie !**

THE STRONG VERBS

The Strong verbs make the Present Indicative and Subjunctive in the same way as the Weak verbs, but the majority modify the vowel in the verbal stem of the Infinitive in the 2nd and 3rd persons singular of the Present Indicative, **a** changing into **ä**, **e** into **i** or **ie**: **ich falle, du fällst, er fällt; ich lese, du liesest** or **liest, er liest; ich gebe, du gibst, er gibt.** Verbs whose stem ends in **-t** or **-d**, of course, like Weak verbs, insert an **e** before the **-t** of the ending: **finden, er findet.** Verbs whose stem ends in a sibilant may insert the **e** before **-st** or contract as with Weak verbs: **ich esse, du issest** or **isst; lesen, du liesest** or **liest.**

The verbs **gelten,** to be worth, be valid; **treten,** to step, walk; **fechten,** to fight, fence; **halten,** to hold; **raten,** to advise, guess, all of which modify in the 2nd and 3rd persons singular, contract the **-t** of the stem and the **-t** of the 3rd person singular ending into a single **t**: **er gilt; er ficht; er hält; er rät; er tritt.**

Here are examples of the Present Indicative of typical strong verbs:

Infinitive:	sing-en	find-en	fall-en	rat-en	les-en
ich	singe	finde	falle	rate	lese
du	singst	findest	fällst	rätst	liesest (liest)
er	singt	findet	fällt	rät	liest
wir	singen	finden	fallen	raten	lesen
ihr	sing(e)t	findet	fallt	ratet	lest
sie	singen	finden	fallen	raten	lesen

The Present Subjunctive has the same endings as the

Present Subjunctive of the Weak verbs and there is no vowel change in the 2nd and 3rd persons singular :

ich	**singe**	**finde**	**falle**	**rate**	**lese**
du	**singest**	**findest**	**fallest**	**ratest**	**lesest**
er	**singe**	**finde**	**falle**	**rate**	**lese**
wir	**singen**	**finden**	**fallen**	**raten**	**lesen**
ihr	**singet**	**findet**	**fallet**	**ratet**	**leset**
sie	**singen**	**finden**	**fallen**	**raten**	**lesen**

The Imperfect Indicative is formed by vowel change in the 1st person and 3rd person singular : **singen, ich sang, er sang**; **fallen, ich fiel, er fiel,** etc. In the other persons there is the same vowel change plus the endings **-st** for **du, -en** for **wir, -t** for **ihr** and **-en** for sie as follows :

ich	**sang**	**fand**	**fiel**	**riet**	**las**
du	**sangst**	**fandst**	**fielst**	**rietst**	**lasest**
er	**sang**	**fand**	**fiel**	**riet**	**las**
wir	**sangen**	**fanden**	**fielen**	**rieten**	**lasen**
ihr	**sangt**	**fandet**	**fielt**	**rietet**	**last**
sie	**sangen**	**fanden**	**fielen**	**rieten**	**lasen**

The Imperfect Subjunctive is formed by modifying the vowel of the Imperfect Indicative and adding the endings of the Present Subjunctive, i.e. **-e, -est, -e, -en, -et, -en.** In verbs which have a modifiable vowel, like **sang, sänge,** the 2nd person singular may drop the **e** : **du sängest** or **du sängst,** and also it may drop the **e** in the 2nd person plural : **ihr sänget** or **ihr sängt.** In verbs in which the vowel in the Imperfect is unmodifiable, e.g. **fiel,** this **e** must be used in order to distinguish the Subjunctive from the Indicative ; thus the Indicative is **du fielst** and **ihr fielt** and the Subjunctive **du fielest** and **ihr fielet.**

ich	**sänge**	**fände**	**fiele**	**riete**	**läse**
du	**säng(e)st**	**fändest**	**fielest**	**rietest**	**läsest**
er	**sänge**	**fände**	**fiele**	**riete**	**läse**
wir	**sängen**	**fänden**	**fielen**	**rieten**	**läsen**
ihr	**säng(e)t**	**fändet**	**fielet**	**rietet**	**läs(e)t**
sie	**sängen**	**fänden**	**fielen**	**rieten**	**läsen**

Perhaps the best translation of this Imperfect Subjunctive is: (if) I were to sing; if I were to find, etc. We shall discuss this further when we deal with the use of the Subjunctive.

The Imperative is like the Weak verbs except that the **-e** of the **du** form is generally dropped: **sing!** rather than **singe!** We thus get:

sing(e)!	**find (e)!**	**fall(e)!**	**rat(e)!**
sing(e)t!	**findet!**	**fall(e)t!**	**ratet!**
singen Sie!	**finden Sie!**	**fallen Sie!**	**raten Sie!**

The verbs which modify **e** into **i** or **ie** in the 2nd and 3rd persons of the Indicative keep this modification in the Imperative singular and never use the ending **-e**, e.g.:

Lesen makes its Imperative thus:

lies!
les(e)t!
lesen Sie!

The Strong verbs are divided into classes corresponding to the vowel changes in the stem of which the following are examples:

Class I. **bleiben, blieb, geblieben,** to remain
beissen, biss, gebissen, to bite

Class II. **fliegen, flog, geflogen,** to fly
bieten, bot, geboten, to offer

Class III. **werfen (er wirft), warf, geworfen,** to throw
binden, band, gebunden, to bind, tie
schwimmen, schwamm, geschwommen, to swim float
sprechen (er spricht), sprach, gesprochen, to speak
nehmen (er nimmt), nahm, genommen, to take
stehlen (er stiehlt), stahl, gestohlen, to steal

Class IV. **geben (er gibt), gab, gegeben,** to give
essen (er isst), ass, gegessen, to eat
sehen (er sieht), sah, gesehen, to see

Class V. **graben (er gräbt), grub, gegraben,** to dig
waschen (er wäscht), wusch, gewaschen, to wash
fahren (er fährt), fuhr, gefahren, to go, travel, drive

Class VI. **fallen (er fällt), fiel, gefallen,** to fall
fangen (er fängt), fing, gefangen, to catch
schlafen (er schläft), schlief, geschlafen, to sleep

Irregulars. These Weak Irregulars have the vowel in the Imperfect and Past Participle different from that in the Infinitive: **brennen,** burn, **brannte, gebrannt; kennen,** know, **kannte, gekannt; rennen,** run, **rannte, gerannt; senden, sandte** (or **sendete**), **gesandt** (or **gesendet**); **wenden,** turn, **wandte** (or **wendete**), **gewandt** (or **gewendet**). Also: **bringen,** bring, **brachte, gebracht; denken,** think, **dachte, gedacht; dünken,** seem, **dünkte** (or **deuchte**), **gedünkt** (or **gedeucht**).

You will find a full list of Strong and Irregular verbs in Appendix A, and I advise you to consult it frequently and to learn the parts of the verbs by heart in batches of ten.

THE COMPOUND TENSES

These are tenses which are formed by means of auxiliary verbs (**das Hilfszeitwort** = help-time-word)—namely: **haben,** to have, **sein,** to be, and **werden,** to become.

Haben and **sein** are used to form Past Tenses; **werden** is used to form the Future and Conditional Tenses. We shall find **werden** again when we come to the Passive Voice.

Haben or Sein?

Haben meant originally " to hold ": " I have an arrow ", meant " I hold an arrow ". Hence when a man had made an arrow he said: " I have an arrow (which is) made," meaning " I hold an arrow made " or, since we now put the adjective before the noun: "I have a made arrow." When the meaning of "to hold" gradually weakened, "have" came to be used as a Tense former, and "I have made an arrow" resulted.

If, however, the verb had no object (which could be "held"), e.g. to come, "to have" could not be used: "I have come" is ridiculous, since "I hold come" is nonsense! Our far-off forbears had to say: "I am (the man who is) come; I am (the) come (man)."

English and Spanish have in modern times ousted out "to be" and used "to have" for both types of verb: I have made an arrow; I have come. German and French have been more conservative, and still keep up the old usage: **ich habe einen Pfeil gemacht,** *j'ai fait une flèche*; **ich bin gekommen,** *je suis venu(e)*.

English has not quite shed the old construction: "I have an arrow made," as is proved by the following quotation from a novel I have just been reading. The hero goes to a guest-house, and when he is received at the door he says: "My name is Warren. I have a room booked." Not: "I have booked a room," because that insists too much on the action, and he wants to insist on the "having" of the room. You often find the construction in Irish, where they will say of a man who has taken too much: "He has the drink taken." Here again it insists on his possessing NOW the taken drink!

Here are a few useful rules as to the use of **haben** and **sein**, but German still fluctuates from one to the other in a number of cases, the North preferring **haben**, the South **sein**.

All Transitive verbs—i.e. verbs that take an object—use **haben: ich habe ihn gelobt; wir hatten ihn gesehen.** Note that the Past Participle falls to the end of the sentence.

All Reflexive verbs and nearly all Impersonal verbs use **haben: er hat sich gewaschen,** he has washed himself; **es hat geregnet,** it has rained.

Intransitive verbs which express a state of rest at a place take **haben** in the North of Germany, but **sein** in the South: **liegen**, to lie; **sitzen**, to sit; **stehen**, to stand; **hangen**, to hang; **schweben**, to hover: **das Buch ist** (or **hat**) **lange auf dem Tisch gelegen; ich habe** (or **bin**) **den ganzen Tag gestanden**, I have been standing the whole day. **Sein** and **bleiben**, to remain, are always conjugated with **sein: ich bin krank gewesen**, I have been ill; **er ist zwei Tage hier geblieben**, he has remained here two days.

Intransitives which express the starting of an action (**erwachen**, to awake) or the completion of an action (**kommen**, to come; **ankommen**, to arrive) take **sein**, especially if they have one of the following prefixes: **ge-**, **ver-**, **ent-**, **er-**, **zer-**, as in **gelingen**, to succeed, **es ist mir gelungen**, I have succeeded; **genesen**, to recover, get well, **er ist genesen**, he has got better; **geschehen**, to happen, **was ist ihm geschehen?**, what has happened to him?; **verschwinden**, to disappear, **sie ist in jenem Haus verschwunden**, she has disappeared in that house; **verhungern**, to die of starvation, **viele Leute sind verhungert**, many people have starved to death; **entgehen**, to escape, **er ist dem Feind entgangen**, he has escaped from the enemy; **entstehen**, to arise, **was ist daraus entstanden**, what has come of it?; **erkalten**, to grow cold, **die Suppe ist erkaltet**, the soup has grown cold; **zerfliessen**, to dissolve, melt away, **sie ist in Tränen zerflossen**, she has dissolved in tears; **zerspringen**, to crack, fly in pieces, **das Glas ist plötzlich zersprungen**, the glass has suddenly cracked.

Werden, to become; **fallen**, to fall; **kommen**, to come; **gehen**, to go, like **sein** and **bleiben**, always take **sein: ich bin krank geworden**, I have fallen sick, etc.

The following verbs of motion (in a very wide sense) take **sein: bersten**, to burst; **wachsen**, to grow (to wax), **er ist in die Höhe gewachsen**, he has shot up, grown tall; **reifen**, to ripen, mature, **diese Äpfel sind früh gereift**, these apples have ripened early; **schwellen**, to swell; **fahren**, to go, drive, travel, **ich bin nach der Stadt gefahren,** I have driven (gone) to town; **folgen,** to follow, **ich bin dem Mann gefolgt,** I have followed the man; **treten,** to step; **reisen,** to travel, **er ist nach Berlin gereist,** he has gone on a journey to Berlin; **schwimmen,** to swim, float, **ich bin über den Fluss geschwommen; springen,** to jump; **reiten,** to ride; **fliegen,** to fly; **rennen,** to run; **wandern,** to wander, walk; **altern,** to grow old. But again the North often uses **haben,** whereas the South prefers **sein.**

In the case of verbs of real motion, like **reiten, laufen, schwimmen, fliegen, fahren,** etc., if the idea is one of motion towards a destination, **sein** is used: **ich bin nach Köln geritten,** I have ridden to Cologne; **ich bin über den Fluss geschwommen,** I have swum over the river. If, however, the underlying idea is merely to describe the manner of the motion, **haben** is used: **ich habe den ganzen Morgen geritten,** I have ridden the whole morning; **wir haben am Montag schön geschwommen,** we had a lovely swim on Monday. Again I warn you that North Germans prefer **haben,** even in cases where the destination is mentioned.

You will find that the verbs which require **sein** are marked with an asterisk in the Verb List on p. 199, and that will help you to remember them. Perhaps the best way to get hold of the verbs requiring **sein** is to note them down whenever you come across them in your reading, jotting down the sentence, and then learning it by heart. After all, when you boil down the above " rules " it comes down mainly to this: use **sein** ALWAYS with, **sein, werden, bleiben, gehen, kommen, fallen,** but be cautious with other intransitive verbs.

Let us now run over the conjugation of the auxiliary verbs **haben, sein, werden.**

THE AUXILIARY VERBS

Infinitive	**haben**, to have	**sein**, to be	**werden**, to become
Pres. Part.	**habend**, having	**seiend**, being	**werdend**, becoming
Past. Part.	**gehabt**, had	**gewesen**, been	**geworden**, become (or **worden**, see p. 138)

Present Tense

	Indic.	Subj.	Indic.	Subj.	Indic.	Subj.
ich	**habe**	**habe**	**bin**	**sei**	**werde**	**werde**
du	**hast**	**habest**	**bist**	**sei(e)st**	**wirst**	**werdest**
er	**hat**	**habe**	**ist**	**sei**	**wird**	**werde**
wir	**haben**	**haben**	**sind**	**seien**	**werden**	**werden**
ihr	**habt**	**habet**	**seid**	**seiet**	**werdet**	**werdet**
sie	**haben**	**haben**	**sind**	**seien**	**werden**	**werden**

Imperfect Tense

	Indic.	Subj.	Indic.	Subj.	Indic.	Subj.
ich	**hatte**	**hätte**	**war**	**wäre**	**wurde** *	**würde**
du	**hattest**	**hättest**	**warst**	**wär(e)st**	**wurdest** *	**würdest**
er	**hatte**	**hätte**	**war**	**wäre**	**wurde** *	**würde**
wir	**hatten**	**hätten**	**waren**	**wären**	**wurden**	**würden**
ihr	**hattet**	**hättet**	**wart**	**wär(e)t**	**wurdet**	**würdet**
sie	**hatten**	**hätten**	**waren**	**wären**	**wurden**	**würden**

Imperative

habe!	**sei!**	**werde!**
habt!	**seid!**	**werdet!**
haben Sie!	**seien Sie!**	**werden Sie!**

We can now conjugate the verb in the compound Tenses: the Perfect and Pluperfect: I have praised, and I had praised; and the Future and Conditional: I shall praise, and I should praise. To these we can add the Future Perfect: I shall have praised, and the Past Conditional: I should have praised. Strictly speaking, I ought not to have called the Conditional a Tense; it is a Mood—a Subjunctive, in fact. You will see the point of this when we discuss the use of the Tenses and Moods later on.

* An older form: **ich ward, du wardst, er ward** is still used in poetry.

The Perfect Tense

I have praised; I have come.

	Indic.	Subj.	Indic.	Subj.
ich	habe gelobt	habe gelobt	bin gekommen	sei gekommen
du	hast „	habest „	bist „	seist „
er	hat „	habe „	ist „	sei „
wir	haben „	haben „	sind „	seien „
ihr	habt „	habet „	seid „	seiet „
sie	haben „	haben „	sind „	seien „

The Pluperfect Tense

I had praised; I had come.

	Indic.	Subj.	Indic.	Subj.
ich	hatte gelobt	hätte gelobt	war gekommen	wäre gekommen
du	hattest „	hättest „	warst „	wär(e)st „
er	hatte „	hätte „	war „	wäre „
wir	hatten „	hätten „	waren „	wären „
ihr	hattet „	hättet „	wart „	wäret „
sie	hatten „	hätten „	waren „	wären „

The Future Tense

I shall praise; I shall come.

	Indic.	Subj.	Indic.	Subj.
ich	werde loben	werde loben	werde kommen	werde kommen
du	wirst „	werdest „	wirst „	werdest „
er	wird „	werde „	wird „	werde „
wir	werden „	werden „	werden „	werden „
ihr	werdet „	werdet „	werdet „	werdet „
sie	werden „	werden „	werden „	werden „

The Conditional

I should praise; I should come.

ich	würde	loben	ich	würde	kommen
du	würdest	„	du	würdest	„
er	würde	„	er	würde	„
wir	würden	„	wir	würden	„
ihr	würdet	„	ihr	würdet	„
sie	würden	„	sie	würden	„

Note.—As the Conditional is formed by the Past Subjunctive of **werden**, there is, of course, no Indicative form, as in the Tenses proper.

The Future Perfect: I shall have praised, and the Past Conditional: I should have praised, are not much used, but I will give the singular to show how they run:

Future Perfect

I shall have praised;	I shall have come
ich werde gelobt haben	**ich werde gekommen sein**
du wirst gelobt haben	**du wirst gekommen sein**
er wird gelobt haben	**er wird gekommen sein**

Past Conditional

I should have praised;	I should have come
ich würde gelobt haben	**ich würde gekommen sein**
du würdest gelobt haben	**du würdest gekommen sein**
er würde gelobt haben	**er würde gekommen sein**

Note that the Infinitives, **haben** and **sein**, come after the Past Participles **gelobt** and **gekommen.**

THE NEGATIVE AND INTERROGATIVE

We noted in the first chapters that English has a curious trick with the Negative and Interrogative, using the verb "to do": I praise; I do not praise; do I praise? German is much simpler: **ich lobe nicht; ich habe nicht gelobt; ich werde nicht loben; ich werde nicht gelobt haben; lobe ich?; habe ich gelobt?; werde ich loben?; werde ich gelobt haben?** Perhaps I had better set out the Present of **loben** in the Affirmative, the Negative, the Interrogative and the Negative Interrogative:

Affirmative.	Negative.	Interrogative.	Neg.-Interr.
I praise.	I do not praise.	Do I praise?	Do I not praise?
ich lobe	**ich lobe nicht**	**lobe ich?**	**lobe ich nicht?**
du lobst	**du lobst nicht**	**lobst du?**	**lobst du nicht?**
er lobt	**er lobt nicht**	**lobt er?**	**lobt er nicht?**
wir loben	**wir loben nicht**	**loben wir?**	**loben wir nicht?**
ihr lobt	**ihr lobt nicht**	**lobt ihr?**	**lobt ihr nicht?**
sie loben	**sie loben nicht**	**loben sie?**	**loben sie nicht?**

Do not be dismayed by the large number of forms that the verbs assume in German and the multiplicity of the personal pronouns. In real life you will not need **du** and **ihr**, and we could have replaced them both by **Sie**. Thus the Present of **loben**, so far as you are concerned when you speak German, is as follows:

ich lobe	**wir loben**
Sie loben	**Sie loben**
er lobt	**sie loben**
sie lobt	
es lobt	

The Tenses themselves are not as numerous as they appear, for, as I shall tell you when I discuss them, the Future, **ich werde loben**, is replaced in the spoken language by the Present, **ich lobe**. The Future Perfect, I shall have praised, occurs rarely in practice in English, and still more rarely in German. All languages look dreadfully complicated when the grammatical machinery is analysed and set down methodically, but all languages, in so far as the needs of daily life are concerned, are fairly simple.

We had better close this chapter now, and start another to discuss the uses of the various tenses and moods.

CHAPTER X

THE TENSES

Tense in language is not the same thing as mathematical time, which neatly parcels it out into seconds, minutes, hours, and so on, measuring it with inexorable precision. We feel time as a flow of events, starting in our Present, then gliding back to the Past and at the same time slipping into the Future. A Past event is definitely over and done with as an event, though it may leave a Present result; a Present event is fugitive, containing a parcel of the Past and merging into the Future; a Future event is uncertain, nebulous, prophetic. This flow of time causes Past, Present and Future to merge into each other, so that the distinction between the Tenses becomes blurred, and this is especially the case with the Present, which, Janus-like, faces both ways.

When I say "Mary sang 'Home Sweet Home' at the concert last Friday," I describe a definite, dated event in the Past. When, however, I say "Mary sings beautifully, she has a good voice," I do not refer to a definite event at a definite time in the Present; I assert that she sings beautifully at this moment, she sang beautifully in the Past and will sing beautifully in the Future; the time element is indefinite. It is still more indefinite in: "Water solidifies at 0° Centigrade" or in "Water is a liquid," "Water boils when you heat it." A real Present is expressed in "Mother, the water's boiling," but, as we have already seen, German has no comparable Tense.

When I say "Arsenal play Everton next Saturday," I use the Present Tense, although the event is distinctly Future; so also in "When George arrives he'll be hungry," his arrival is in the Future. In "Is George coming tomorrow?" his "coming" is a Future event, but the Tense is Present. Language tends always to use a Present Tense for a Future event, and especially the German language, as we shall see shortly.

The Present contains a parcel of the Past, and language uses the Present Tense to make the Past come vividly to life again. "Ah!" says he, "I can't do that", is more lively than "said he"; "I saw Fred yesterday; he says he is working hard", is more vivid, more dramatic, than "he said he was working hard". In literary style this Historic Present, as it is called, is common: "The men were exhausted; they were discouraged. Suddenly a bugle rings out, they spring up and charge the enemy"; the bugle-call in the Present Tense makes us see the action of the men. This dramatic Historic Present is greatly used in conversation, especially amongst those who are not inhibited by too much academic schooling: "Well, I'm just going down the street when up she comes to me and starts laughing", is very much more exciting than the educated: "Well, I was just going down the street when she came up to me and started laughing". German and French use this Tense much more than English does, being less poker-faced, more inclined to show emotion.

The Future is essentially doubtful, and hence language will use the Future Tense to express doubt about an event: "Where's Jack? Oh, he'll be at the office, I expect," and a doubtful event in the Past can be expressed by the Conditional: "There was a ring at ten o'clock. Was there? That would be the milkman, no doubt."

The Past Tense can be used to express Present Time. When I say, "I've got your book", I mean simply, "I have your book", but the Past "getting" has so faded away that it no longer exists in my mind, which is wholly occupied with the presence of the book here and now. If I am uneducated I will say, "I got your book", and the Simple

Past Tense becomes a Present. This is what happened many centuries ago with can, may, must, which were once Past in Tense, but are now Present, and are called by grammarians Past–Present verbs. They still bear traces of their past existence, for we cannot say "he cans", as the -s is an ending of the Present Tense. The same is true of the German verbs **können, er kann; müssen, er muss; mögen, er mag.** Languages are continually changing, and the vulgarism of one generation may become the classically correct form of a later one.

In English the Perfect Tense is linked with Present Time, as in: "I have come to see you", my Past "coming" resulting in my being here now; "I have written many letters today, this week, this year" is contrasted with "I wrote many letters yesterday, last week, a year ago"; "I have written" extends the action into the Present (today, etc.), whereas "I wrote" cuts the action off from the Present (yesterday, etc.). We shall see that German has a different time-value for these two Tenses. We use the Perfect for single events which have some connection with the Present: "I have lived in Holland" means "I have lived there (but am not living there now)"; "I lived in Holland" makes us expect some addition, like: "in 1910", "before the war", "when I was a youth", etc., cutting us off from the Present.

The Simple Past is the Tense for narrating a series of past events: "Harry materialized without a sound. He stood watching Gibson. He noted the sharp features, the blue eyes and the fair hair. He waited a moment and then announced . . ." We could not substitute the Perfect "Harry has materialized, etc."; German could and does, especially in the spoken language.

I think you will now be ready for a discussion of the German Tenses, as you have had a chance of thinking over our own Tense mechanism, which, after all, very much resembles the German.

THE PRESENT TENSE

The German Present is used, like the English, to present an event as being universally true: **der Mensch ist sterblich,** man is mortal; **das Wasser erstarrt bei o°,** water solidifies at o°.

It is used to report an action which extends to some extent into the Past and into the Future: **Marie singt ganz schön,** Mary sings quite nicely; or to report an action as taking place at the moment of speaking: **Horch !, man klopft !,** Listen, somebody is knocking!

In spoken German the Present is used instead of the formal Future with **werden,** which is a "paper" Tense: **kommt er?,** is he coming?; **warten Sie einen Augenblick, ich bringe es sofort,** wait a moment, I'll bring it at once; **ich reise morgen nach Berlin,** I'm off to Berlin tomorrow; **wenn er die Tür öffnet, so gehe ich auf ihn zu,** when he opens the door I will go up to him; in which both the "opening" and the "going" are future actions, but both are Present Tenses in German. In **wenn du morgen kommst, habe ich die Arbeit schon fertig,** when (or if) you come tomorrow, I shall have the work ready, both actions are again Future, but the Tenses are Present. If we change the text slightly we can get a Perfect instead of a Future Perfect: **wenn du morgen kommst, habe ich die Arbeit gemacht,** when you come tomorrow I shall have the work done (I shall have done the work).

German, like English, uses the Present to report a Past event in order to make it more dramatic, especially in conversation: **Georg hat mir gestern alles erzählt, aber ich lache ihn aus,** George told me everything yesterday, but I laughed at him. **Was !, sagt er, du lachst?,** what, says he, you laugh? In literary style it is frequently used: **Als Hans diese Worte sprach, rief eine Stimme aus der Menge: "Warte noch ein paar Wochen, Hans!" Da springt der Minister, bleich wie eine Leiche, vom Sessel auf und wirft**

die Karten auf den Tisch, when John spoke these words a voice called from the crowd: " Wait a couple of weeks longer, John." Thereupon the minister, white as a corpse, jumps up from his arm-chair and throws the cards on the table.

The Present is also used as an Imperative: **" Du bleibst hier ! " rief ihm der Alte,** " You (will) remain here," the old man cried out to him. In English we have a similar usage: " You do that immediately, I tell you ! "

THE PERFECT TENSE

The German Perfect is used to present a Past action with a Present result: **ich habe in Holland gewohnt,** I have lived in Holland; **ich habe meinen Schlüssel verloren,** I have lost my key; **ich bin glücklich gewesen,** I have been happy; **ich habe ihn einmal besucht,** I have called on him once. But German will say: **Goethe hat *Hermann und Dorothea* geschrieben,** Goethe wrote *Hermann and Dorothea*; German thinks of the poem as being a result of the past action of writing; English thinks of Goethe's writing as being a Past action cut off from the Present.

This leads me to an important difference between English and German: English says, " I have seen him today " but " I saw him yesterday ", whereas German says, **" Ich habe ihn heute gesehen "** and **" ich habe ihn gestern gesehen "**, using the same Tense in both cases. In fact, in spoken German, and especially in the South, the Perfect has ousted the Imperfect, which has become a literary Tense, the Tense for narration in books and newspapers. This is what Sütterlin and Waag say on this point in their *Deutsche Sprachlehre*: **In den Mundarten ist das Präteritum—im Süden ganz—untergegangen und das Perfekt an seine Stelle getreten, so dass " iche habe gesehen " gleichzeitig schriftdeutschem " ich sah " und " ich habe gesehen " entspricht,** in the dialects the Preterite (Imperfect) has disappeared—

entirely in the South—and the Perfect has taken its place, so that **ich habe gesehen** corresponds at one and the same time to the literary German **ich habe gesehen** and **ich sah.** Now, **Mundarten** covers much more than the English " dialects ", and means practically " the spoken language ", so that we can say that in spoken German the Perfect **ich habe gesehen** has replaced **ich sah,** which is reserved for the written language, except in certain cases, e.g. when a repeated or usual action in the Past is expressed. Here is an example out of *Immensee* by Theodor Storm in a letter: **Die schönen Zuckerbuchstaben können Dir wohl erzählen, wer bei den Kuchen mitgeholfen hat; dieselbe Person hat die Manschetten für Dich gestickt. . . . Nun ist vorigen Sonntag der Hänfling gestorben, den Du mir geschenkt hattest; ich habe sehr geweint, aber ich hab' ihn doch immer gut gewartet. Der sang noch immer nachmittags, wenn die Sonne auf sein Bauer schien,** the beautiful sugar-letters can no doubt tell you who helped with the cakes; the same person embroidered the cuffs for you. And now the linnet that you had given me has died; I cried a lot, but I always looked after it well, all the same. He used always to sing in the afternoon, when the sun shone on his cage. In the same letter the Imperfect is also frequently used where a Perfect would have done.

To sum up: the English Perfect " I have seen " has always a Present idea behind it; the German Perfect **ich habe gesehen** has also a Present idea behind it; but it is also used where English uses the Imperfect " I saw ", and in spoken German the Perfect replaces the Imperfect, which is the Tense of narration in the written language.

The Perfect is commonly used instead of the Future Perfect, which is found only in the written language: **in einem Jahr hat man das Haus gebaut,** in one year the house will have been built (one will have built the house); **wenn ich ihn besucht habe, komme ich zu Ihnen,** when I have called on him (shall have called on him), I shall come to you.

THE IMPERFECT TENSE

The Imperfect (or Preterite) is, as I have said, the Tense of narration : **Nun las Reinhard auch den Brief seiner Mutter, und als er beide Briefe gelesen hatte, überfiel ihn ein unerbittliches Heimweh. Er ging eine Zeitlang in seinem Zimmer auf und nieder; er sprach leise zu sich selbst. Dann trat er an sein Pult, nahm einiges Geld heraus und ging wieder auf die Strasse hinab. Hier war es stiller geworden. Der Wind fegte durch die einsamen Strassen; Alte und Junge sassen in ihren Häusern zusammen,** now R. also read a letter from his mother, and when he had read both letters, an inexorable home-sickness overcame him. For a time he walked up and down his room; he spoke softly to himself. Then he went to his desk, took some money out and went down to the street again. It had grown quieter here. The wind swept through the deserted streets; old and young were sitting in their houses together. Note that German has no special form for our " they were sitting ", just as it has none for " I am writing ", so that **ich schrieb** has to do duty for both " I was writing " and " I wrote ".

The Imperfect is used for two contemporaneous actions in the Past : **er schrieb, als ich eintrat,** he was writing when I entered; **er stand auf, sobald ich eintrat,** he stood up as soon as I entered. It is also used for a repeated or usual action : **als ich noch jung war, spielte ich oft Fussball,** when I was still young, I often used to play football; the verb **pflegen** can, however, be used to express this idea : **ich pflegte Fussball zu spielen.**

THE FUTURE AND FUTURE PERFECT

The formal Future with **werden** is, as I have already pointed out, a literary form, and the Future Perfect is even more so. Thus : **wenn du morgen kommen wirst, werde ich die Arbeit gemacht haben,** when you come (shall come) tomorrow, I shall have done the work, is only to be found in books, and in daily life is replaced by : **wenn du morgen kommst, habe ich die Arbeit gemacht.**

This is what Sütterlin and Waag say about the Future in their *Deutsche Sprachlehre* : **Die Zukunft wird in der Regel jedenfalls von der Umgangssprache und von den Mundarten nicht besonders ausgedrückt. Dass eine Handlung in die Zukunft falle, ergibt sich meist aus dem Zusammenhang, so z.B. in Sätzen wie ; ich komme morgen ; ich reise nächsten Donnerstag. . . . Die Schriftsprache wendet in diesen Fällen freilich eine andere Ausdrucksweise an, eine Zusammensetzung der Gegenwart von w e r d e n mit dem Infinitiv : ich werde kommen.** The Future is generally not specially expressed, at any rate in everyday speech and dialect. The fact that an action takes place in the Future is mostly shown by the context, as, for instance, in sentences like **ich komme morgen ; ich reise nächsten Donnerstag. . . .** The written language, to be sure, uses another way of expressing it : a combination of the Present of **werden** and the Infinitive : **ich werde kommen.**

The Future is often expressed in the spoken language by the verb **wollen,** to want to, will : **wir wollen morgen kommen,** we will come tomorrow, especially if the Present Tense would be ambiguous.

The Future with **werden** can be used as an Imperative : **du wirst hier bleiben !,** you will (shall) remain here ! It is also used like the English Future to express a doubt : **er wird wohl krank sein,** he will no doubt be ill ; **er wird zu spät gekommen sein,** he will have come too late.

THE PLUPERFECT

One action in the Past may precede another action in the Past : **So traten sie ihren Rückweg an ; das Erdbeersuchen hatten sie aufgegeben, denn Elisabeth war müde geworden,** So they started on their way back ; they had given up looking for strawberries, for Elizabeth had grown tired ; **als**

er nach Hause gekommen war, wusste er sich einen kleinen Pergamentband zu verschaffen, when he had got home, he managed to procure a small book bound in vellum (parchment); **kaum hatte er das Frühstück eingenommen, als das Dienstmädchen eintrat,** scarcely had he had his breakfast when the maid entered.

The compound Tenses formed with **haben** and **sein** sometimes drop the auxiliary in a subordinate sentence, i.e. when it falls to the end, as the meaning is clear without it. This takes place in literary language, as in: **Als es Ostern geworden (war), reiste Reinhard in die Heimat,** when Easter had come Reinhard went home; **Wenn ich das Haus verlassen (habe), werde ich ganz froh sein,** when I have left the house I shall be quite pleased. It is most common with the Pluperfect: **als er die Manschetten angeknüpft (hatte), stand er auf,** when he had buttoned on the cuffs, he stood up.

CHAPTER XI

THE SUBJUNCTIVE MOOD

English has lost nearly all its Subjunctive verbal endings, the one remaining being only the dropping of the -s in the 3rd person singular of the Present Tense: he goes home, but: lest he go home. The verb "to be" has a Present and Past Subjunctive: I be, you be, he be, etc.; I were, you were, he were, etc.

Even these scanty forms are little used in modern English, but are quite common in American English, which has, I think, been influenced by the great influx of German immigrants. Here are a few examples I have met with in some American thrillers I have been reading:

American.	English.
It was imperative that he be present.	It was imperative for him to be present, or: it was imperative that he should be present.
He requested that the officer go at once.	He requested that the officer should go.
She suggested that they stop at the hotel.	She suggested that they should stop at the hotel.
He ordered that the men remain there.	He ordered that the men should remain there.

English prefers to use a special Mood auxiliary—should, may, shall—whereas American prefers a Subjunctive verbal form. Note that in the American the verb in the principal clause is in the Past Tense, but the Subjunctive in the subordinate clause is always in the Present. Why is this? Because if the Past Tense were used—was, went, stopped, remained—the meaning would be ruined, and because Tense has no time value in the Subjunctive.

Consider the following sentences, the first in the Past Indicative, the second in the Past Subjunctive:

1. A fire was then burning and I felt warmer.
2. Were a fire now burning I should feel warmer.

In the Indicative a real fire was actually burning at some past time, and I actually felt warmer, the Past Time being shown by the adverb "then" and by the Past Tenses "was burning" and "felt".

In the Subjunctive the time is given by the adverb "now", and is the Present Time; the meaning, too, is entirely present—viz. "a fire is not burning and I do not feel warmer, so I imagine a fire burning and myself as feeling warmer". But the Tenses are Past: "were burning" and "should feel"! Why? Because the Past Tense in the Subjunctive does not indicate remoteness in Time but remoteness in Probability.

The Present Subjunctive indicates a mere doubt, a wavering of the mind between this and that, as in: be he alive or be he dead; come weal, come woe; the Past Subjunctive indicates a much greater degree of doubt as to the event; indeed, it often amounts to a rejection of the possibility of the event, as in: were he my own son I should still blame him (i.e. he is not my own son); if "ifs" and "ans" were pots and pans (i.e. they are not pots and pans).

In the inner world of our mind—the spiritual world, the world of our imagination—time no longer exists, and our time mechanism (Tense) is no longer used to mark Time, but Probability.

We shall find this loss of time-value very marked in the German Subjunctive, which is used by the speaker with the sole object of throwing into high relief his mental attitude to an event, marking it as imaginary, as doubtful, or even as not being guaranteed by him as true. Thus in German all reported speech is in the Subjunctive, because the speaker wants to impress on his hearer that what he reports is something which may or may not be factual, and therefore he refuses to be responsible for the statements. For instance, a man says: "I am ill". We report that in English as: "He said he was ill"; German reports "**ich bin krank**" as: **er sagte, er sei krank,** or **er sagte, er wäre krank,** and the two mean exactly the same thing. We shall deal with this more fully below.

Just a little more patience whilst we think over the following Subjunctives before we plunge headlong into the German Subjunctive:

1. He speaks loudly in order that she hear him clearly.
2. He speaks loudly in order that she hears him clearly.
3. He speaks loudly in order that she may hear him clearly.
4. He speaks loudly in order that she shall hear him clearly.
5. He spoke loudly in order that she hear him clearly.
6. He spoke loudly in order that she might hear him clearly.
7. He spoke loudly in order that she should hear him clearly.

Nos. 1 and 5 are American (and German). No. 2 could be English, which, depending on common sense, expects the hearer to understand that "she" may or may not hear him, although the Indicative is used. Nos. 3, 4, 6, 7 are the usual English paraphrases for the Subjunctive. And why should the Subjunctive be necessary? Because, of course, her "hearing him" is presented as being doubtful: she may not hear him!

The German would be:

1. **Er spricht laut, damit sie ihn deutlich höre.**
5. **Er sprach laut, damit sie ihn deutlich höre.**

In No. 5 we should not say: **er sprach laut, damit sie ihn deutlich hörte,** because **hörte** is not a distinctive Subjunctive form, the Past Tense of the Weak verbs being the same for the Indicative and the Subjunctive. It would mean: he spoke loudly so that she (actually) did hear him.

Let us now run through the uses of the Subjunctive in German.

In Principal Clauses

It is used, as in English, to express a wish:

Gott sei dank!	Thank God!
Gott segne dich!	God bless you!
Es lebe die Freiheit!	Long live Liberty!
O hätte ich Flügel wie Tauben!	O had I wings like a dove.

Or a command:

Es werde Licht!	Let there be light!
Geheiligt werde dein Name!	Hallowed be Thy name!
Man beachte die Anweisungen!	Pay attention to the instructions.

Or a concession:

Es koste, was es wolle.	Let it cost what it may.
(Es) komme, was kommen mag!	Come what may.
So sei es!	Let it be so.

Or a qualified statement when the speaker does not want to be assertive or wishes to soften his statement in a polite way:

Nicht dass ich wüsste.	Not so far as I know.
Das dürfte wohl wahr sein.	That might well be true.
Das wäre alles.	That'll be all, I think.

In Subordinate Clauses

I. In conditional clauses—clauses of rejected condition when the speaker sets up an imaginary condition and draws from it an imaginary conclusion—the Subjunctive is used in the Past Tense, but not in the Present, as in English is also the case :

Wenn er kommt, werde ich froh sein.	If he comes I shall be glad.

The Past Tense is seen in :

Wenn er käme, würde ich froh sein, or	If he came I should be glad.
Wenn er käme, (so) wäre ich froh, or	
Käme er, so wäre ich froh.	

You will also find : **wenn er kommen würde,** but it is frowned upon.

Going a step back into the Past we get :

Wenn er gekommen wäre, so würde ich froh gewesen sein, or	If he had come I should have been glad.
Wenn er gekommen wäre, wäre ich froh gewesen.	

Here are a few more examples of these conditional clauses :

Wenn ich nicht Alexander wäre, möchte ich Diogenes sein.	If I were not Alexander I should like to be Diogenes.
Wenn alle so gedacht hätten, stände es noch schlimmer um die Wissenschaft.	If everybody had thought thus things would be still worse with science (or knowledge).
Wäre ich an seiner Stelle, Sie hätten nicht so lange warten müssen.	If I were in his place you would not have had to wait so long.
Man müsste ein Herz von Stein haben, wenn man nicht Wort hielte.	One would have to have a heart of stone if one did not keep one's word.

I think you have enough there for the conditional. Learn the examples by heart: **lernen Sie die Beispiele auswendig!**

II. In unreal comparisons—e.g. he looks as if he were ill. The comparison is unreal because he may not be ill in fact. Here are some examples:

er tut, als ob er krank sei, he acts as if he is ill.

er tat, als ob er krank wäre, he acted as if he were ill.

sie stand da, als ob sie jemanden erwarte, she stood there as if she were expecting somebody.

es war ihm, er habe ihr etwas mitzuteilen, it seemed to him as if he had something to communicate to her.

es war fast, als hätte er jetzt das Ziel seiner Reise erreicht, it was almost as if he had reached the object of his journey.

III. After expressions of wishing, advising, requesting, urging, purposing, doubting, believing, ordering:

ich wollte, mein Vater käme bald, I wish my father would come soon.

es wäre wünschenswert, dass Sie unsere Studien nicht unterbrächen, it would be desirable if you did not interrupt our studies.

wenn der Arme doch einen Diener fände, der ihm gefiele, if only the poor man should find a servant who should (might) please him.

(Note the subjunctive **gefiele**; this " servant " is imaginary, and hence the relative clause which qualifies this non-existent " **Diener** " has the verb in the subjunctive.)

gebe Gott, dass er noch lebe, God grant that he be still alive.

Man bestraft ein Kind, damit es sich bessere, one punishes a child in order that it shall mend its ways (improve itself).

(Note that the purpose here is expressed not by the verb but by the conjunction **damit.**)

Man isst, damit man lebe, we eat in order that we may live.

er glaubte, es sei Elisabeth, he believed (thought) it was Elizabeth.

er zweifelte, ob sie es gewesen sei, he doubted whether it had been she.

du glaubtest, dass es dein Schatz wäre, you believed it was your sweetheart.

er befahl, dass Heinrich sofort nach Hause gehe, he ordered that Henry should go home at once.

IV. After a negative or a question :

ich kenne niemand, der so etwas täte, I know nobody who would do such a thing.

wo ist der Mann, der es aussprechen könnte?, where is the man who could pronounce it?

da war keiner, der ihn nicht gegrüsst hätte, there was nobody who did not greet him.

er tut nichts, ohne dass er sich befehlen liesse, he does nothing without getting himself ordered (without being ordered).

er sprach nie, ohne dass er gefragt worden wäre, he never spoke unless he had been asked (without having been asked).

V. In Indirect Speech.

The Subjunctive is used in reported speech in German, as it was in Latin, as a precautionary warning to the hearer that the reporter is not guaranteeing the truth of the statements made. In English, when we report another person's statement, we are satisfied that by prefacing it with " He says " or " He said " we have given adequate warning to the hearer that it is not our own statement.

The rules for the use of the Tenses in Reported Speech are rather fluid. In more old-fashioned German a Present Tense in the Direct Speech was treated as follows :

" Ich bin müde und habe Kopfweh ", I am tired and have a headache, became, when introduced by a Present Tense :

Er sagt, er sei müde und habe Kopfweh.

When introduced by a Past Tense it became:

Er sagte, er wäre müde und hätte Kopfweh.

In modern Germany the tendency is to use a Present Subjunctive in both cases:

A. **Er sagt, er sei müde und habe Kopfweh,** and
B. **Er sagte, er sei müde und habe Kopfweh.**

The Past Tense, however, is frequently used, and it is true to say that you can use either the Present or the Past Subjunctive without any difference of meaning.

Thus our first rule is: if the original statement is in the Present Tense, then the Reported Speech may be in the Present Tense or in the Past Tense of the Subjunctive.

If the original statement contains a Future, then the Reported Speech has a Future Subjunctive: **Ich werde müde sein und Kopfweh haben,** becomes **Er sagt** (or **sagte**), **er werde müde sein und Kopfweh haben.**

If the original statement contains (*a*) Imperfect or (*b*) Perfect or (*c*) Pluperfect, then the Reported Speech has for all three a Perfect Subjunctive:

Direct.	Indirect.
(*a*) **Ich war müde und hatte Kopfweh.**	**Er sagt** or **sagte, er sei müde gewesen und habe Kopfweh gehabt.**
(*b*) **Ich bin müde gewesen und habe Kopfweh gehabt.**	
(*c*) **Ich war müde gewesen und hatte Kopfweh gehabt.**	

If the Direct Speech contains a question, it is introduced by **ob,** *whether*, or by the original interrogative word:

Direct.	Indirect.
Er fragte: "Kommt er?"	**Er fragte, ob er komme.**
Er fragte: "Wo wohnt der Mann?"	**Er fragte, wo der Mann wohne.**

If the Direct Speech contains a command, the Indirect Speech has a paraphrase with **müssen** or **sollen** or, more politely, **mögen**:

Er sagte: "Gehen Sie weg!"	**Er sagte, dass ich weggehen müsse (solle).**
	(Er sagte, ich soll(t)e weggehen).

If the Present Subjunctive of the verb is the same as the Present Indicative, then the Past Subjunctive must be used to replace it, as the reporter wants at all costs to stress the subjunctive:

Direct.	Indirect.
Er fragte: "Kommen Sie?"	**Er fragte, ob ich käme.**

ich komme being both Indicative and Subjunctive.

Er sagte: "Wir haben fleissig gearbeitet.	**Er sagte, sie hätten fleissig gearbeitet.**

sie hätten because **sie haben** is both Indicative and Subjunctive.

Here are some examples of Indirect Speech, which includes any statement which is not the personal opinion of the speaker, but merely something reported by him. The introductory clause: **er sagt, etc.**, need not be expressed.

Er sagte ihr eines Tages, er werde Märchen für sie aufschreiben; er wolle sie ihr mit den Briefen an seine Mutter schicken; sie müsse ihm dann wieder schreiben, wie sie ihr gefallen hätten, he told her (said to her) one day he would write fairy-tales for her; he would send them to her with the letters to his mother; she must then write back (to say) how she had liked them (how they had pleased her).

Sie sagt immer, du habest jetzt mehr zu tun als solche Kindereien, she always says you have more to do now than such childish things.

Sie meint, du seiest nicht mehr so gut, wie du gewesen, she thinks you are no longer as nice as you were.

Die Sage geht, dass das Dorf alle hundert Jahre an einem bestimmten Tage wieder ans Licht gehoben würde, the legend runs that the village was again raised up to the light (of day) every hundred years on a certain day.

Du sagtest einmal, er sähe seinem braunen Überrock ähnlich, you once said that he looked like his brown overcoat.

Er fragte, ob es das Werk seines Freundes sei, he asked if it were the work of his friend.

Er meldet mir, er wäre krank, he announces to me that he is ill. Note the Past Tense **wäre** instead of the Present **sei** as would be expected after the Present **er meldet.**

Mein Bruder wünscht dich zu sehen, weil er dich viel zu fragen habe, my brother wishes to see you because, he says, he has much to ask you. Note that the German has no "he says" because the Subjunctive **habe** sufficiently implies the Indirect Speech.

Note that we can say either : **er sagte, dass er müde sei,** with the verb at the end of the subordinate clause, or : **er sagte, er sei müde,** omitting the **dass.**

This has been a rather difficult chapter, but you must not allow yourself to be discouraged by the Subjunctive, which, in North Germany, is tending to be less used in subordinate clauses. The best way to master the Subjunctive is to take a good modern German text and to note down all the Subjunctives you come across and to study them. Think over your examples, and remember that the Subjunctive reports only what is "in the mind's eye, Horatio".

CHAPTER XII

REFLEXIVE, IMPERSONAL, SEPARABLE, INSEPARABLE, AND VARIABLE VERBS

There is little difficulty with the reflexive verbs, as they are only ordinary verbs conjugated with the reflexive pronouns, as in English: he washes himself; he sees himself. As some German verbs govern a Dative or a Genitive, we must take care with such verbs that the reflexive pronoun is in the Dative (or Genitive) case.

Here is the Present Indicative of **sich waschen**, to wash oneself, and **sich schmeicheln**, to flatter oneself, the latter taking the Dative case:

ich wasche mich	**ich schmeichle mir**
du wäschst dich	**du schmeichelst dir**
er wäscht sich	**er schmeichelt sich**
sie wäscht sich	**sie schmeichelt sich**
es wäscht sich	**es schmeichelt sich**
wir waschen uns	**wir schmeicheln uns**
ihr wascht euch	**ihr schmeichelt euch**
sie waschen sich	**sie schmeicheln sich**

and of course **Sie waschen sich** and **Sie schmeicheln sich** for the polite form of the 2nd person.

German uses the reflexive much more than we do in English, where it is limited to verbs where the action starts from the subject and returns to the subject: he reveals himself; he shot himself. Here are a number of examples of German reflexives which are not to be translated by English reflexives:

Ich ärgerte mich über ihn.	I was annoyed at him.
Wie befinden Sie sich?	How are you?

Er beklagte sich über mich.	He complained of me.
Sie betrugen sich schlecht.	They behaved badly.
Ich erinnere mich seiner (Gen.).	I remember him.
Sie hat sich erkältet.	She has caught a cold.
Ich freue mich über seinen Erfolg.	I rejoice at his success.
Bitte, setzen Sie sich !	Please sit down.
Ich sehne mich nach der Heimat.	I long for home.
Sie können sich auf mich verlassen.	You can rely on me.
Er weigerte sich zu kommen.	He refused to come.

In both English and German we often use a verb both transitively and intransitively : I cut the meat with the knife ; the knife cuts badly ; I tear the cloth ; the cloth tears ; I boil the water ; the water boils. In German : **ich schneide das Fleisch mit dem Messer ; das Messer schneidet schlecht ; ich zerreisse das Tuch ; das Tuch zerreisst ; ich koche das Wasser ; das Wasser kocht.** German, however, uses these verbs more sparingly and generally prefers a reflexive :

Die Tür öffnet sich.	The door opens.
Die Erde bewegt sich.	The earth moves.
Der Rock trägt sich gut.	The coat wears well.
Das Wetter ändert sich.	The weather is changing.
Ich muss mich waschen.	I must wash.
Er kleidete sich an.	He dressed.

Finally I must mention verbs which are intransitive but which nevertheless are used reflexively in German ; many of these are common in everyday life.

Sie irren sich.	You are wrong ; making a mistake.
Sie müssen sich eilen.	You must hurry.

Diese Leute streiten sich den ganzen Tag.	These people quarrel the whole day.
Ich sah mich um.	I looked around.
Sie können sich satt sehen.	You can look your fill (till you're tired of it).
Er lief sich wund.	He walked (till) his feet (were) sore.
Er verlief sich.	He lost his way.
Er versprach sich.	He made a slip in speaking.

Again I advise you to spend some time on your texts, noting down the reflexives you come across and thinking them over. You will reap a rich harvest.

IMPERSONAL VERBS

These are verbs which are used only in the 3rd person singular, like: it rains; it is ten o'clock. They are conjugated like any other verbs. This " it " has no meaning, but is merely a trick whereby a verb is given a grammatical subject when the speaker cannot or will not define more precisely the reason for the verbal action. In German the es is used as follows:

A. Mainly with the verbs **sein** and **werden** when the subject has not yet been named: **Was ist das? Es ist ein Hund,** What is that? It is a dog. **Es gibt Leute, die Sprachen leicht lernen,** there are people who learn languages easily. We shall discuss below the difference in usage between **es ist** and **es gibt.**

B. When the subject is vague as in: **es klopft,** there is a knock, somebody is knocking; **es klingelt,** there is a ring, somebody is ringing the bell; **es riecht hier nach Gas,** there is a smell of gas here; **es ruft,** somebody is calling. These personal verbs thus become used impersonally. We can include the impersonal passive here: **es wird getanzt,** there is dancing; **es lässt sich machen,** it can be done.

C. The impersonal verbs proper generally indicate some

natural phenomenon or a sensation: **regnen,** to rain, **es regnet,** it is raining; **donnern,** to thunder, **es donnerte,** it was thundering; **schneien,** to snow, **es schneit,** it is snowing; **tauen,** to thaw, **es taut,** it is thawing; **frieren, es friert,** it is freezing; **es wird kalt,** it is getting cold; **es wird Nacht,** night is falling. Some of these have a personal pronoun: **es friert mich,** I am cold; **es ekelt mich,** it disgusts me; **es graut mir, wenn ich daran denke,** I shudder to think of it; **es fehlte ihm an Mut,** he was lacking in courage; **es wird mir übel,** I am feeling sick. This **es** disappears, except in the impersonals indicating some natural phenomenon, when it does not introduce the statement: **es ekelt mich,** but **mich ekelt**; **es graute mir vor ihm,** I had a horror of him, but **vor ihm graute mir.**

D. In the following cases the **es** is merely a prop-word, a mere introductory gesture, like the English "there" in: There came to the beach a poor exile of Erin. Here are some examples of this usage of **es**:

Es starb der Held.	The hero died.
Es braust ein Ruf wie Donnerhall.	There roars out a call like a thunder-clap.
Es sticht mich eine Biene.	A bee stings me.
Es schmerzt mich meine Wunde.	My wound hurts (smarts).

This **es** is kept even when the subject is in the plural: **es wohnen viele Leute in dem Haus,** there live a number of people in the house; **es sind schöne Bücher in der Bibliothek,** there are beautiful books in the library.

Although we can say: **es kam ein alter Mann,** there came an old man, we cannot use the construction with the personal pronouns, we cannot say **es kam er.** "It is I" is in German: **ich bin es,** and similarly **Sie sind es,** it is you, etc.

The difference between **es ist** and **es gibt,** there is, there are, is that **es gibt** is used for stating a general truth, a general law; **es ist** and **es sind** state a particular fact at a particular time or place. **Es gibt,** and all the other Tenses: **es gab, es hat gegeben, es wird geben,** etc., are always in the singular and they all take the Accusative case; **es ist, es sind,** and all the other Tenses, **es war, es ist gewesen,** etc., are singular or plural, according to the number of the real subject, and of course take the Nominative. Here are some typical examples:

Es gibt Bücher, die man nicht lesen kann.	There are books that one cannot read.
Es ist hier ein Buch, das ich mit Vergnügen gelesen habe.	There is a book here that I have read with pleasure.
Es gibt wunderbare Fische.	There are wonderful fishes.
Es sind Fische in diesem Teich.	There are fishes in this pond.
Es gibt Menschen, die zu viel rauchen.	There are people who smoke too much.
Es sind Menschen im Garten.	There are people in the garden.
Es gibt einen Gott.	There is a God.
Das gibt's nicht.	That is not possible; that is not done.

INSEPARABLE AND SEPARABLE VERBS

In English we have verbs like: undergo, upset, withstand, which are inseparable, and others like: to go under, to set up, to stand with, which are separable. The separable verbs keep the meaning of each part literally, the inseparable have taken on new, specialized meanings: he went under twice; he underwent an operation; he set up his tent; they upset his plans; he stood with them; he withstood them.

Now, German has a great number of such separables and

inseparables, which are, indeed, characteristic of the language. We can divide them into three classes: Inseparable, Separable, Variable, according as the prefix is indissolubly attached to the verbal stem, is loosely attached and splits off in certain conditions, or is separable in one meaning and inseparable in another.

Inseparable Verbs

The following prefixes are always inseparable: **be-**, **emp-**, **ent-**, **er-**, **ge-**, **miss-**, **ver-**, **zer-**, ***hinter-**, **wider-**. These prefixes are never stressed, they are never separated from the verb, and the **ge-** of the Past Participle is never added to them. Here are some examples of them.

From **stehen**, to stand, **ich stehe**, **ich stand**, **ich bin** (or **habe**) **gestanden** we can create:

bestehen, to pass (an examination), **ich bestehe**, **ich bestand**, **ich habe bestanden**;

entstehen, to arise, **ich entstehe**, **ich enstand**, **ich bin entstanden**;

erstehen, to arise, to buy, **ich erstehe**, **ich erstand**, **ich habe erstanden** (or in the sense of "arise" **ich bin erstanden**);

gestehen, to confess; **ich gestehe**, **ich gestand**, **ich habe gestanden**;

verstehen, to understand, **ich verstehe**, **ich verstand**, **ich habe verstanden**;

widerstehen, to resist, withstand; **ich widerstehe**, **ich widerstand**, **ich habe widerstanden**.

Note that the auxiliary is **haben** or **sein**, according to the meaning of the derived inseparable verb. **Missverstehen**, to misunderstand, gives **ich missverstehe**, **ich missverstand**, **ich habe missverstanden**.

Other examples are: **fangen**, to catch, **ich fange**, **ich fing**,

* **Hinter** is separable in colloquial language only: **er bringt kein Bissen hinter**, he can't eat a bite.

ich habe gefangen; **empfangen**, to receive, **ich empfange, ich empfing, ich habe empfangen. Brechen**, to break, **ich breche, ich brach, ich habe gebrochen**; **zerbrechen**, to smash to pieces, **ich zerbreche, ich zerbrach, ich habe zerbrochen. Bleiben**, to remain, **ich bleibe, ich blieb, ich bin geblieben**; **hinterbleiben**, to remain behind, **ich hinterbleibe, ich hinterblieb, ich bin hinterblieben.**

See p. 153 for meaning of these prefixes.

Separable Verbs

The separable prefixes are very numerous indeed. In fact they include all the prepositions and adverbs not included under the Inseparable and Variable verbs, together with some adjectives and nouns. Here are some examples:

Prefix.	Meaning.	Example.
ab-	off	**abbrechen**, to break off; **absetzen**, to set down, deposit
an-	at, on	**ansehen**, to look at, respect; **ankommen**, to arrive
bei-	by, near	**beistehen**, to stand by, help; **beiwohnen**, to be present at, attend
bevor-	before	**bevorstehen**, to be imminent
hin-	hence	**hingehen**, to go hence
her-	hither	**herkommen**, to come hither, approach
ein-	into	**einschenken**, to pour in; **einschiffen**, to embark, ship
empor-	up	**emporsteigen**, to ascend
fort-	onward, away	**fortfahren**, to drive away, depart, to continue
entgegen-	towards, against	**entgegenkommen**, to advance, to meet; **entgegenstehen**, to oppose
nach-	after	**nachsagen**, to repeat after; **nachfragen**, to ask about, enquire

Prefix.	Meaning.	Example.
nieder-	down	**niederbrennen**, to burn down
vor-	before	**vorbedeuten**, to forebode, presage
weg-	away	**wegwerfen**, to throw away
wieder-	again	**wiederkommen**, to come back again
weiter-	further	**weitergeben**, to pass on; **weiterschreiben**, to go on writing
zurück-	back	**zurückkommen**, to return, come back; **zurückkaufen**, to buy back
zu-	to, in addition	**zubringen**, to take to, carry to; **zubauen**, to block up by building, to add to by building
zusammen-	together	**zusammenrufen**, to convoke, call together; **zusammenfallen**, to collapse

The following are formed from adjectives and nouns:

tot-	dead	sich **totlachen**, to split one's sides
frei-	free	**freisprechen**, to acquit
los-	loose, away	**losbinden**, to untie
preis-	price, prize	**preisgeben**, to give up, surrender
statt-	place	**stattfinden**, to take place
acht-	heed	**achtgeben**, to pay attention to

These Separable verbs are stressed on the prefix: **AUSsprechen**, to pronounce; **ANfangen**, to begin; **PREISgeben**, to surrender.

When the verb in the simple tenses occupies its normal place in a principal sentence, the prefix splits off and falls to the end: **ich spreche das Wort aus**; **er fängt die Arbeit um 8 Uhr an**, he begins the work at 8 o'clock; **er gab seinen Freund der Schande preis**, he exposed his friend to shame; **sprich das Wort aus !**, pronounce the word !; **fange jetz an !**, begin now !

When the Infinitive or the Past Participle falls to the end of the sentence, the prefix joins up again with the verb, as follows :

ich muss das Wort aussprechen, I must pronounce the word.

ich hoffe, die Arbeit anzufangen, I hope to begin the work.

ich habe das Wort ausgesprochen, I have pronounced the word.

ich habe die Arbeit angefangen, I have begun the work.

Similarly in a subordinate sentence when the inflected verb falls to the end the prefix joins up again :

weil ich das Wort ausspreche, because I pronounce the word.

da ich die Arbeit anfange, as I begin the work.

wenn ich ihn preisgebe, if I betray him.

Of course in Reported Speech if **dass** is omitted the order is :

er sagt, er spreche das Wort aus

but if **dass** is used it is :

er sagt, dass er das Wort ausspreche.

VARIABLES

The prefixes **durch, über, um, unter, voll** are sometimes Separable, sometimes Inseparable, the two resulting verbs being different in meaning. In most cases the Inseparable verb has a specialized meaning, the Separable keeps the literal meaning of the verb plus the prefix.

Hinter and **wieder** are sometimes put under the head of Variables, but **hinter** is overwhelmingly Inseparable, and there is only one Inseparable verb with **wieder**—viz. **wiederholen,** to repeat : **ich wiederhole, was ich sagte,** I repeat what I said, but **ich hole ihn wieder,** I fetch him back.

Remember that the Separable Prefix is stressed, the Inseparable unstressed. Here are some examples of the Variable verbs :

Inseparable.	Separable.
durchREISEN	**DURCHreisen**
er durchreiste Deutschland, he travelled all over Germany.	**er reiste durch,** he travelled through (without stopping).
durchSETZEN, to permeate.	**DURCHsetzen,** to carry through.
er durchsetze das Heer mit Spionen, he permeated the army with spies.	**er setzte seinen Plan durch,** he carried through his plan.
überSETZEN, to translate.	**ÜBERsetzen,** to ferry across.
ich habe das Buch übersetzt, I have translated the book.	**ich habe ihn übergesetzt,** I have ferried him over.
überSEHEN, to overlook.	**ÜBERsehen,** to see too much of.
ich übersah den Fehler, I overlooked the error.	**ich sah mich an ihm über,** I saw more than enough of him.
überTRETEN, to violate.	**ÜBERtreten,** to overflow.
er übertrat die Vorschrift, he violated the regulation.	**der Fluss trat über,** the river overflowed.
umGEHEN, to elude.	**UMgehen,** to go round.
er has das Gesetz umgangen, he has eluded the law.	**er ist umgegangen,** he has gone a round-about way.
umZIEHEN, to cloud over.	**UMziehen,** to move (from one's house.
der Himmel hat sich umzogen, the sky is overcast.	**er ist umgezogen,** he has removed.
unterSTELLEN, to impute to.	**UNTERstellen,** to put under.
das darf man ihm nicht unterstellen, one must not impute that to him.	**er hat den Eimer untergestellt,** he has put the bucket under.

Inseparable.	Separable.
unterHALTEN, to entertain.	**UNTERhalten**, to hold under.
ich unterhielt ihn, I entertained him.	**er hielt das Gefäss unter**, he held the vessel under.
vollENDEN, to complete.	**VOLLgiessen**, to pour full, to fill.
er vollendete die Arbeit, he completed the work.	**er goss das Glas voll**, he filled the glass.

There are some verbs with double prefixes : Separable + Inseparable, **ANvertrauen**, to entrust, **ich vertraue an, ich habe anvertraut**; Separable + Separable, the second prefix being stressed, **herUNTERgehen**, to go down, **ich ging herunter, ich bin heruntergegangen.**

CHAPTER XIII

THE PASSIVE VOICE

I can present an action to my hearer in two ways. I can put in the forefront the agent performing the action on an object, or I can put in the forefront the object suffering the action at the hands of the agent: the woodman fells the tree; the tree is felled by the woodman. The former is the Active Voice, the latter the Passive Voice.

Let us examine a little more closely our model Passive: the tree is felled by the woodman; the tree has been felled by the woodman; the tree was felled by the woodman. In English we use the verb "to be" as the auxiliary to form the Passive, and at the same time we use the same verb "to be" when we are not thinking at all of something or somebody suffering an action, but merely to describe a state, as in: this tree is lofty; that tree is scarred; those trees are diseased. None of those is a Passive, and since German does not use the verb **sein**, but the verb **werden** to form the Passive, you will have to learn to distinguish a mere description of a state from a true Passive.

Consider these two statements:

A.	B.
My windows are broken, I must get them mended.	My windows are frequently broken by my neighbour's boys.

In A the windows are actually broken windows; in B the windows are not broken at all, but they get broken by the boys; somebody breaks them. A is a description, B is a true Passive. The German would be:

A.	B.
Meine Fenster sind zerbrochen.	**Meine Fenster werden von den Jungen zerbrochen.**

Again, think over these examples:

A.	B.
After the storm I saw some trees that were uprooted.	Some trees were uprooted by the storm.

In A the trees had already suffered the action of uprooting—they were simply uprooted trees; in B the trees suffered the uprooting by the storm—we could say: the trees got uprooted by the storm. In German we should have:

A.	B.
Die Bäume waren entwurzelt.	**Die Bäume wurden durch den Sturm entwurzelt.**

Again ponder on the following:

A.	B.
The park was closed, I could not enter.	The park was closed at 8 o'clock.

In A it was a closed park; in B the park got closed by somebody. The German would be:

Die Anlage war geschlossen.	**Die Anlage wurde um acht Uhr geschlossen.**

Which is Passive of these two sentences: "The tea is made" or "The tea is being made"? In the former the action is over and we are dealing with "made" tea; in the latter the tea is suffering the action. The German is: **der Tee ist gemacht; der Tee wird gemacht.**

Just one more example. I look at an umbrella and see it has a tear in it which has been mended; I say: "This umbrella is mended." It is, in fact, a mended umbrella. I pass a shop which has a notice saying: "Umbrellas are mended here." This does not mean that the umbrellas I see are mended umbrellas, but that umbrellas get mended; it is a true Passive. The German is: **Dieser Regenschirm ist repariert** and **Regenschirme werden hier repariert.**

We can now give a few useful rules which will enable you to distinguish the true Passive from the mere description:

A. If we can replace "is" by "is being" or "gets" or "was" by "got" or "was being", it is a Passive: the books were sold when I arrived is: **die Bücher wurden verkauft, als ich ankam,** if the meaning is: "the books were being sold"; it is: **die Bücher waren verkauft, als ich ankam,** if the books were already sold. Note that if you can insert "already" without changing the meaning, you are not dealing with a Passive.

B. If the agent or the instrument is mentioned or implied, you are dealing with a Passive: he was wounded by his enemy; he was wounded by a bullet. In German: **er wurde von seinem Feind verwundet: er wurde durch eine Kugel verwundet.** Note that the agent is governed by **von,** the instrument by **durch.**

C. And, overruling everything else: if the state is described, it is not a Passive, and **sein** must be used; if the performing of an action is implied, and not merely the state resulting from an action, then we have the Passive, and **werden** must be used; **er war verwundet,** he was wounded, the wounding already having taken place and leaving merely a wounded state; **er wurde verwundet,** he got wounded, he suffered the action of being wounded, somebody and something wounded him at a particular time and place.

English has a peculiar trick which allows us to make both the direct and the indirect object the subject of the

Passive sentence. Thus there are two possible Passives to:

George gave Mary the book,

namely,

(1) The book was given to Mary by George.
(2) Mary was given the book by George.

Now, in (1) "The book was given" means what it says—viz. the book was given to somebody. In No. (2) "Mary was given" does not mean what it says, for Mary was not given to anybody; the book, not Mary, was the gift. In German only the direct object can be the subject of the Passive.

Now German has a number of verbs which govern the Dative or the Genitive cases, such as: **glauben,** to believe, **er glaubt mir,** he believes me; **folgen,** to follow, **ich folgte dem Mann**; **spotten,** to mock at (with the Gen.), **er spottete seines Feindes,** he mocked at his enemy. In order to use these in the Passive we must resort to an impersonal form:

I am believed.	**es wird mir geglaubt** or **mir wird geglaubt.**
The man was followed.	**es wurde dem Mann gefolgt** or **dem Mann wurde gefolgt.**
The enemy was mocked.	**es wurde des Feindes gespottet** or **des Feindes wurde gespottet.**

German is not quite so fond of the Passive as English, and frequently prefers to use the impersonal pronoun **man,** one, with the Active: it is believed, **man glaubt**; it was said, **man sagte**; children are punished to improve them, **man straft Kinder, damit sie sich bessern**; an overcoat is worn in winter, **man trägt einen Überrock im Winter.**

Another idiomatic way of turning the Passive is by means

of a reflexive verb, often with **lassen**: that can be imagined, **das lässt sich denken**; that can't be seen from here, **das lässt sich von hier aus nicht sehen**; that can be done, **das lässt sich machen**; **das Tor öffnete sich**, the gate was opened; **das versteht sich**, that is understood.

An idiomatic use of the Passive is found in impersonal phrases such as: **es wurde die ganze Nacht gespielt**, there was gambling the whole night; **es wurde viel gebrummt**, there was a deal of grumbling; **es wurde die ganze Nacht getanzt**, dancing went on all night.

The verb **werden** used as the Passive auxiliary is conjugated like **werden** on p. 100, with the exception that the Past Participle is **worden** and not **geworden**: **ich bin gelobt worden**, I have been praised, but **ich bin alt geworden**, I have grown old. Here are the first persons of the various Tenses of the Passive Indicative of **loben**.

Present:	**ich werde gelobt**, I am praised.
Past:	**ich wurde gelobt**, I was praised.
Perfect:	**ich bin gelobt worden**, I have been praised.
Pluper.:	**ich war gelobt worden**, I had been praised.
Future:	**ich werde gelobt werden**, I shall be praised.
Fut. Per.:	**ich werde gelobt worden sein**, I shall have been praised.
Cond.:	**ich würde gelobt werden**, I should be praised.
Past Con.:	**ich würde gelobt worden sein**, I should have been praised.

The Future Perfect and the Past Conditional are little used, being replaced by ich **werde gelobt sein**, I shall be praised, and **ich würde gelobt sein**, I should be praised.

The Infinitive is: **gelobt werden** and **gelobt zu werden**, to be praised.

Of course the Subjunctive forms are used, but you have them on p. 100 where **werden** is conjugated. Now, do not let yourself be worried by all these Passive forms; in practical life you will need only the following: the Present

Tense, **ich werde gelobt**; the Imperfect, **ich wurde gelobt**; the Perfect, **ich bin gelobt worden.** You will meet the other forms only in books.

Grammars are bound to put in all the forms and give all the rules, but life does not worry about grammars and grammarians, and manages to rub along in the jog-trot of existence on quite an austere allowance of forms and rules. Remember that whenever you find me piling up the grammar!

CHAPTER XIV

THE AUXILIARIES OF MOOD

This chapter-heading looks very highbrow and forbidding, but in practice it is concerned only with the bread-and-butter ideas expressed by means of can, must, shall, will, may. Then why, you may ask, call them Auxiliaries of Mood? For the very good reason that these verbs do not designate an action or state, like " to work " or " to believe ", but express the attitude of the speaker to an action or state.

When I say " he works " I merely report a fact; when I say " he can work " I regard his working not as a fact but as a possibility; in " he goes tomorrow " I am dealing with the fact of his going, in " he may go tomorrow " I am dealing with the probability of his going; in " they yield " I am concerned with the fact of their yielding, in " they must yield " I am concerned with the obligation of their yielding. These verbs deal with abstract ideas, not with concrete realities. Since abstract ideas are not clear-cut and definite, you must not be surprised if these Auxiliaries tend to overlap each other in meaning. What I mean is that nobody would confuse " to smoke " with " to run ", but it is easy to confuse " I may go " with " I can go "; " thou shalt not kill " is very close to " thou must not kill "; " you should be grateful " is very like " you ought to be grateful ". You will find these ideas sliding into each other when we get to the German uses, and you will be inclined to think the Germans are unreasonable people to make their language so difficult. As a matter of fact, however, the German Auxiliaries of Mood are easier than the English.

The German verbs are all normal: they have an Infinitive, a Past Participle, all the Tenses and the two Moods. Compare that fullness with the defective English verbs, e.g. must, which exists only in the Present Tense: I must, you must, he must, etc. For the Infinitive we have to resort to a trick: to be obliged to, to have to and similarly with the Participles. Why, we cannot even use must in the Past Tense and say " Last week I must go to London " but we dodge and say: " Last week I had to go to London ", whereas the German is straightforward: **Vorige Woche musste ich nach London reisen.**

The conjugation of the German Auxiliaries of Mood is abnormal in that (*a*) the Past Participle is formed normally with **ge-** plus **-t** when they are used as full verbs: **ich habe gekonnt, gemusst,** etc., but when there is a dependent verb the Infinitive is used as the Past Participle: **ich habe schreiben können,** I have been able to write; **ich habe bleiben müssen,** I have had to remain; (*b*) the Present Participles are rarely used; (*c*) the Imperatives are lacking.

These Auxiliaries are also called Past-Present verbs because the modern Present Tense was, in the old language, a Past Tense, and it still bears the forms of that old Past. **Wissen,** to know, is also a Past-Present Verb, and for that reason we include it in this chapter.

Let us first of all set down the conjugation of these Auxiliaries.

Infinitive

dürfen	**können**	**mögen**	**müssen**	**sollen**	**wollen**	**wissen**

Present Indicative

ich darf	**kann**	**mag**	**muss**	**soll**	**will**	**weiss**
du darfst	**kannst**	**magst**	**musst**	**sollst**	**willst**	**weisst**
er darf	**kann**	**mag**	**muss**	**soll**	**will**	**weiss**
wir dürfen	**können**	**mögen**	**müssen**	**sollen**	**wollen**	**wissen**
ihr dürft	**könnt**	**mögt**	**müsst**	**sollt**	**wollt**	**wisst**
sie dürfen	**können**	**mögen**	**müssen**	**sollen**	**wollen**	**wissen**

Present Subjunctive

ich	dürfe	könne	möge	müsse	solle	wolle	wisse
du	dürfest	könnest	mögest	müssest	sollest	wollest	wissest
er	dürfe	könne	möge	müsse	solle	wolle	wisse
wir	dürfen	können	mögen	müssen	sollen	wollen	wissen
ihr	dürfet	könnet	möget	müsset	sollet	wollet	wisset
sie	dürfen	können	mögen	müssen	sollen	wollen	wissen

Past Indicative

ich durfte, etc.	konnte	mochte	musste	sollte	wollte	wusste

Past Subjunctive

ich dürfte etc.	könnte	möchte	müsste	sollte	wollte	wüsste

Past Participle

gedurft	gekonnt	gemocht	gemusst	gesollt	gewollt	gewusst
			or			
dürfen	können	mögen	müssen	sollen	wollen	—

The compound tenses are regularly formed as follows :

Perfect : **ich habe gedurft, gekonnt,** etc. or, with a dependent infinitive,
ich habe schreiben dürfen, können, etc.

Pluperf. : **ich hatte gedurft, gekonnt,** etc., or
ich hatte schreiben dürfen, können, etc.

Future: **ich werde dürfen, können,** etc.

Condit. : **ich würde dürfen, können,** etc.

Wissen has **wissend** as its Present Participle, but those of the other verbs, e.g. **könnend,** etc., are very rarely to be met with. Only **wissen** and **wollen** possess an Imperative : **wisse, wisst** and **wolle, wollt.**

USES OF THE AUXILIARIES OF MOOD

Dürfen

Dürfen has the meaning of " to be permitted to do something " : **ich darf meinen Hund mitnehmen,** I am allowed to take my dog along ; **ich darf nicht ausgehen,** I may not go out, I can't go out, I'm not allowed to go out. **Kinder, ihr dürft nicht so viel essen !,** children, you must not eat so much! **Darf ich um eine Tasse Tee bitten?**, may I ask for a cup of tea?; **Kriegsgefangene durften Briefe empfangen,** prisoners of war were permitted to receive letters; **gestern haben wir früh nach Hause gehen dürfen,** yesterday we were allowed to go home early.

With **nur**, only, **dürfen** is used with the meaning of "to need": **Sie dürfen es ihm nur sagen, so wird er es tun,** you only need to tell him and he will do it; **Sie dürfen nur fragen,** you only need to ask (a question).

The Past Subjunctive, as usual, expresses a modest assertion: **Sie dürften sich irren,** you are making a mistake, I think; **das dürfte so sein,** that is probably so; **es dürfte sich erübrigen, ihn zu erwähnen,** it is probably unnecessary to mention him.

The Pluperfect Subjunctive takes on the meaning of "ought to": **das hätten Sie nicht sagen dürfen,** you ought not to have said that.

Können

Können expresses the idea of being able, of having the power to do something: **ich kann gut schwimmen,** I can swim well; **er kann das nicht tragen, es ist zu schwer,** he can't carry it, it is too heavy; **können Sie mir sagen, wo Bertha ist?**, can you tell me where Bertha is? With **umhin** it translates our idiom "cannot help" as in: **ich konnte nicht umhin zu zittern,** I could not help trembling.

As in English, it expresses possibility: **es kann noch regnen,** it may (can) still rain; **er kann um 8 Uhr hier sein,** he may be here by 8; **das kann sein,** that may be so; **ich kann mich irren,** I may be wrong.

Note the difference between: **ich habe ihn sprechen können,** I have been able to speak with him, and **ich kann ihn gesprochen haben,** I may have spoken with him; **er hat es tun können,** he has been able to do it, and **er kann es getan haben,** he may have done it.

The Past Indicative must be distinguished from the Past

Subjunctive: **als ich noch jung war, konnte ich schön singen,** when I was young I could (= was able to) sing beautifully; **wenn ich jung wäre, könnte ich schön singen,** if I were young I could (= should be able to) sing beautifully.

The Pluperfect Subjunctive is very useful: **ich hätte ihm helfen können, wenn ich ihn getroffen hätte,** I could have helped him (= should have been able to help him) if I had met him.

The original meaning of **können** was "To know (how to)" and it is still used with this meaning: **er kann nichts,** he knows nothing; **laufe was du kannst,** run as fast as you can (know how to); **er kann das Buch auswendig,** he knows the book by heart.

Mögen

Mögen states a probability: **das mag wohl wahr sein,** that may be true; **es mag zu spät sein,** it may be too late; **der arme Junge mag krank sein,** the poor boy may be sick; **er mochte 80 Jahre alt sein,** he may have been 80 years old; **es möchte besser sein, die Wahrheit zu sagen,** it might be better to tell the truth.

Mögen has also the meaning of "to like": **ich mag nicht ausgehen,** I don't care (want) to go out. **Magst du keinen Wein?,** don't you care for any wine?; **Sie mag heute nicht spielen,** she does not want to play today.

This idea of liking is frequently reinforced by **gern,** willingly: **sie mochte uns gern necken,** she liked to tease us: **ich möchte gern eine Tasse Tee trinken,** I should like (to drink) a cup of tea; **ich hätte gern mitgehen mögen,** I should have liked to go along.

Mögen has also the meaning of permitting or "not preventing": **meinetwegen mag er bleiben,** for my part (for all I care) he may stay. It is also used in concessive clauses: **er mag so stark sein, wie er will, er kann es doch nicht tragen,** he may be as strong as he likes, he can't carry it;

was ich auch sagen mag (mochte), man glaubt (glaubte) mir nicht, whatever I may (might) say, I am (was) not believed.

It is used instead of the simple Subjunctive in clauses of wishing: **Gott segne dich !,** God bless you !, or **Möge Gott dich segnen** ; **Möge er glücklich sein !,** may he be happy ! ; **ich wünsche, dass er kommen möge,** I wish he would come.

The Past Subjunctive is used in a modest assertion : **Sie möchten sich wohl irren,** you may perhaps be mistaken ; **es möchte wohl besser sein, wenn sie hier blieben,** it might be better if they remained here.

Müssen

Müssen indicates compulsion not dependent on the will of a person, but which arises from the nature of things, from the circumstances : **der Mensch muss sterben,** human beings must die ; **diese Leute müssen Sommer und Winter arbeiten, um ihr Leben zu erhalten,** these people must work summer and winter to keep alive ; **sie sieht bleich aus, sie muss krank sein,** she looks pale, she must be ill ; **das Gras ist jetzt ganz grün, es muss geregnet haben,** the grass is now quite green, it must have rained ; **wir mussten lachen,** we had to (were obliged to) laugh. **Ich habe spät arbeiten müssen,** I had to work late; **das müssen Sie nicht tun,** you need not do that. **Und gerade an diesem Tage musste ich den Zug versäumen !,** and just on this very day I had to miss the train !

In **das müssten Sie nicht sagen,** you ought not to say that ; **das hätten Sie nicht sagen müssen,** you ought not to have said that, **müssen** comes in meaning near to **sollen.** Note the difference between : **er muss es getan haben,** he must have done it, and **er hat es tun müssen,** he has had to do it.

Sollen

Sollen expresses a moral compulsion emanating from outside the speaker : **du sollst nicht stehlen,** thou shalt not steal ; **Kinder, ihr sollt fleissig studieren,** children, you must study diligently ; **er soll hier bleiben,** he is to remain here, I want him to remain here.

It expresses a promise in: **Sie sollen einen Brief von mir bekommen,** you shall get a letter from me; **der Finder soll belohnt werden,** the finder will be rewarded.

It is frequently used for reporting a rumour: **der Junge soll krank sein,** the boy is said to be ill; **er soll gestern die Stadt verlassen haben,** he is reported to have left the town yesterday.

Doubt is expressed by **sollen** in: **wer soll das gesagt haben?** who is supposed to have said that?; **sollte er doch gegangen sein?,** has he really gone?; **ich sollte meinen, Sie hätten genug gearbeitet,** I should think you had worked enough; **sollte er vielleicht abwesend sein?** is he perhaps absent?

There is a sort of predestined futurity in: **ich denke, es soll ihm doch gelingen,** I think he will nevertheless succeed; **er sollte sie nicht mehr sehen,** he was to see her no more.

Possibility is expressed in: **wenn er kommen sollte, werde ich mich freuen,** if he should come I shall be glad.

Moral obligation is expressed by the Subjunctive in: **die Regierung sollte für die Armen sorgen,** the Government ought to look after the poor; **man hätte ihn warnen sollen,** one ought to have warned him, he ought to have been warned; **das hätten Sie nicht sagen sollen,** you ought not to have said that.

Wollen

Wollen expresses the will of the subject of the sentence: **ich will auf ihn warten,** I will wait for him; **wir wollten gestern einen Ausflug machen,** we wanted to go on an excursion yesterday.

It is often equivalent to a future: **ich will es Ihnen gleich sagen,** I'll tell you immediately; **es wollte Abend werden,** evening was about to fall; **es will regnen,** it is going to rain; **ich wollte eben ausgehen, als er ankam,** I was just about to go out when he arrived.

Wollen makes a claim in: **sie will ihn gestern gesehen**

haben, she claims to have seen him yesterday. Note the difference between this and: **sie hat ihn gestern sehen wollen,** she wanted to see him yesterday.

It is frequently used without a dependent Infinitive in the sense of wanting, desiring: **wollen Sie Bier oder Wein ?,** will you have beer or wine ? ; **wollen Sie eine Tasse Kaffee ?,** will you have a cup of coffee ?

Wir wollen can also have the sense of " *Let us . . .*" Thus " **wir wollen gehen** " : " Let us go : " **(Gehen wir !)**

OMISSION OF VERBS OF MOTION

As in older English usage, e.g. " Farewell, my dear, I must away, 'tis death to go, 'tis life to stay ", the verb of motion is often omitted after the auxiliaries of mood in German: **ich muss jetzt nach Hause,** I must go home now; **wohin wollen Sie?,** where do you want to go to?

Lassen

Though not a Modal Auxiliary, **lassen** can be conveniently included here.

It is equivalent to the English " let " or " leave " : **lassen Sie mich zufrieden !,** let me alone ! ; **lass das !,** leave that alone, stop it ! ; **wir liessen ihn in das Haus,** we let him into the house, but : **wir liessen ihn in dem Haus,** we left him in the house.

It has the meaning of " to get something done " : **der König hat die Minister kommen lassen,** the King sent for the Ministers ; **er liess sich die Haare schneiden,** he had (got) his hair cut ; **Sie müssen sich einen Anzug machen lassen,** you must get a suit made. Note that the past participle with a dependent infinitive takes on the form of the infinitive, as is the case with the Modal Auxiliaries.

The Imperative of **lassen** is used, as the English let, to form the Imperative of other verbs : **lass uns gehen !, lasst uns gehen !, lassen Sie uns gehen!,** let us go.

Wissen

Wissen means to know, to be informed of, to have knowledge of, to know how to, like the French *savoir*, and must be distinguished from **kennen**, to be acquainted with, like the French *connaître*: **ich weiss, wo er wohnt,** I know where he lives; **ich kenne seinen Vater,** I know his father.

Wissen takes **zu** with a dependent infinitive only in the sense of " to know how to ": **ich weiss mich zu verteidigen,** I know how to defend myself.

I know what to say, where to go, etc. must be translated as: **ich weiss, was ich sagen (wohin ich gehen) soll.**

The Past Subjunctive is used as a modest assertion: **nicht dass ich wüsste,** not so far as I know.

Fühlen, Heissen, Helfen, Hören, Lassen, Lehren, Lernen, Machen, Sehen

The above verbs use two forms of the Past Participle, a regular form and one identical with the Infinitive. When used with a dependent Infinitive, **fühlen,** to feel, and **lehren,** to teach, generally prefer the regular Past Participle, whilst **heissen, lassen, sehen, hören** have the Infinitive form.

Examples are: **ich habe ihn kommen hören,** I heard him come; **ich habe ihn singen hören,** I heard him sing; **hast du das kommen sehen?,** did you see it come?; **ich habe ihm arbeiten helfen,** I helped him to work; **man hat ihn kommen heissen,** they bid him come; **sie haben die Schuld auf sich lasten fühlen** (or **gefühlt**), they felt the blame rest on them; **er hat mich singen lehren** (or **gelehrt**), he taught me singing.

The German grammarian Sütterlin insists that the Infinitive form is almost always used when the Participle comes directly after the dependent Infinitive. He gives as an example: **ich habe ihm suchen helfen,** I helped him to look (for it), but **ich habe ihm geholfen, das Verlorene zu suchen,** I helped him to seek for what was lost. Thus, when used independently, or when **zu** occurs with the infinitive, the past participle with **ge=** is used.

CHAPTER XV

CASES GOVERNED BY VERBS

In general, Transitive verbs govern the Accusative, but there are verbs which govern two Accusatives, others the Dative and others the Genitive. The most useful of these are given below.

VERBS GOVERNING TWO ACCUSATIVES

heissen, to call, to name: **man heisst ihn den schönen Wilhelm,** he is called handsome William; **nennen,** to call, to name: **er nannte mich seinen Freund,** he called me his friend; **schelten** and **schimpfen,** scold, call a bad name: **man schalt ihn einen Lump,** they called him a scamp; **fragen** takes two objects when one is a person and the other a pronoun referring to a thing: **er fragte es seinen Vater;** but "He asked me the way" is: **er fragte mich nach dem Weg. Lehren,** to teach, takes two Accusatives: **er lehrte mich die deutsche Sprache,** he taught me the German language.

VERBS GOVERNING THE DATIVE

A number of Transitive verbs naturally take the indirect object in the Dative, such as: **antworten** and its synonyms **entgegnen, erwidern, versetzen,** to reply, answer: **er antwortete mir wie zu Hofe,** he replied evasively (lit. as if at Court); **bieten,** to offer; **bringen,** to bring; **leihen,** to lend; **reichen,** to pass, to hand to; **sagen,** to say; **schenken,** to make a present to; **zeigen,** to show, etc. **Erlauben,** to allow: **erlauben Sie mir!,** allow me; **glauben,** to believe: **ich glaube ihm nicht,** I don't believe him; **raten,** to advise:

andern rät er, selbst kann er sich nicht helfen, he advises others but cannot help himself; **verbieten,** to forbid; **borgen,** to borrow; **stehlen,** to steal (from) also take the dative.

The following verbs, which often correspond to English Transitives, also take the Dative: **begegnen,** to meet; **danken,** to thank; **drohen,** to threaten; **folgen,** to follow; **gratulieren,** to congratulate; **helfen,** to help; **nahen,** to approach; **passen,** to fit, to suit; **schaden,** to harm; **schmeicheln,** to flatter; **trauen,** to trust; **trotzen,** to defy; **ziemen,** to befit.

Many verbs take the Dative when compounded with the particles **ab, an, auf, bei, ein, mit, nach, ob, unter, vor, zu, wider** and **ent,** e.g. **beiwohnen,** to attend: **er wohnte der Versammlung bei,** he attended the meeting; **nachkommen: er kam seiner Pflicht nach,** he fulfilled his duty; **unterliegen: das unterliegt keinem Zweifel,** there is no doubt about that; **entsprechen,** to correspond to: **das hat meinen Erwartungen nicht entsprochen,** that has not come up to my expectations; **widersprechen,** to contradict: **er widersprach seinem Lehrer,** he contradicted his teacher.

Some Impersonal verbs: **ahnen,** to have a presentiment: **es ahnt mir nichts Gutes,** I have a foreboding of evil; **bangen,** to be afraid: **mir bangt vor der Zukunft,** I am afraid of the future; **fehlen, gebrechen, mangeln,** to lack: **es fehlt ihm nichts,** he lacks nothing (also: he is quite well); **ekeln,** to be disgusted: **mir ekelt davor,** I loathe it; **sein: es ist mir wohl, kalt, warm, bange,** I am cold, warm, afraid.

Note that the above verbs cannot be used in the Passive (see p. 137): I was followed is: **mir wurde gefolgt.**

VERBS GOVERNING THE GENITIVE

A large number of verbs govern the Genitive in literary German, but nowadays most of them are constructed with a preposition or take the Accusative. Here are the most commonly used:

Transitive verbs: **berauben,** to rob, deprive: **der Krieg hat das Vaterland seiner Söhne beraubt,** the war has robbed the country of its sons; **beschuldigen,** to accuse of: **man beschuldigte ihn des Verrats,** he was accused of treason; **entheben,** to relieve of: **er wurde seines Amtes enthoben,** he was dismissed from his office; **würdigen,** to vouchsafe: **er würdigte mich keiner Antwort,** he vouchsafed me no answer.

Intransitive verbs: **bedürfen,** to need: **der Alte bedarf der Pflege,** the old man needs care (nursing); **harren,** to await anxiously: **er harrte des Feindes,** he awaited the enemy, but **auf** with the Accusative is now more usual; **spotten,** to mock, laugh at: **er spottete seiner Ketten,** he mocked at his chains, also with **über: sie spotten über ihn,** they ridicule him; **walten,** to rule, govern, found in: **seines Amtes walten,** to perform the duties of one's office, otherwise **walten über** with Dative in the meaning of "rule over"; **Hungers sterben,** to die of hunger, more usually **vor Hunger sterben.**

Reflexive verbs: **sich annehmen,** to interest oneself in, assist: **er nahm sich der Kranken an,** he befriended the sick; **sich bedienen,** to use: **er bediente sich eines Hammers,** he used a hammer; **sich bemächtigen,** to seize: **er bemächtigte sich des Thrones,** he seized the throne; **sich enthalten,** to abstain from: **ich kann mich des Weinens nicht enthalten,** I cannot refrain from crying, I cannot help crying; **sich erbarmen,** to have mercy on: **erbarme dich meiner !,** have mercy on me, used also with **über** and the Accusative; **sich erfreuen,** to enjoy: **er erfreut sich eines guten Rufes,** he enjoys a good reputation, also with **an** and Dative, to take pleasure in: **er erfreut sich an dem Jungen; sich erinnern,** to remember: **ich erinnere mich jenes Tages,** I remember that day, also with **an** and the Accusative: **ich erinnere mich an diesen Unfall,** I remember this accident; **sich freuen,** to be delighted, rejoice: **ich freue mich deines Glücks,** I rejoice at your happiness; **auf** with Accusative is used for a future happening : **ich freue mich auf die Ferien,** I am looking forward to the holidays ; **an** with the Dative for something past : **der Vater freut sich an den Fortschritten seines Sohnes,** the father rejoices at his son's progress ; **über** with Accusative : **er freut sich über sein neues Buch,** he takes pleasure in his new book ; **sich schämen,** to be ashamed of : **er schämt sich seiner Arbeit,** he is ashamed of his work, or : **über seine Arbeit** ; **sich versehen,** to expect : **ehe er sich dessen versah,** before he expected it, in the twinkling of an eye ; **sich wehren,** to defend oneself : **er wehrte sich seines Lebens,** he defended his life.

CHAPTER XVI

FORMATION OF VERBS

A number of intransitive verbs are turned into " factitive " verbs by modification of the stem vowel, as in English: to fall, from which we derive the factitive " to fell ", i.e. to cause to fall; to lie, which gives " to lay ", to cause to lie. Here are the most important:

dringen, to throng, to crowd, **drängen,** to press; **erkalten,** to grow cold, **erkälten,** to cool, chill, **sich erkälten,** to catch a cold; **fallen,** to fall, **fällen,** to fell; **lernen,** to learn, **lehren,** to teach; **liegen,** to lie, **legen,** to lay; **sitzen,** to sit, **setzen,** to set; **sinken,** to sink, **senken,** to cause to sink; **schwimmen,** to swim, float, **schwemmen,** to set afloat; **trinken,** to drink, **tränken,** to give to drink, suckle; **hangen,** to hang, **hängen,** to cause to hang: **ich hänge es an die Wand**; **verschwinden,** to disappear, **verschwenden,** to waste.

A number of verbs are formed from adjectives by modification of the vowel: **rot,** red, **röten,** to redden, colour red; **schwach,** weak, **schwächen,** weaken; **kurz,** short, **kürzen,** to shorten; others are formed with **be-**: **reicher,** richer, **bereichern,** to enrich; **erweitern,** to broaden; also **ver-** is used: **besser,** better, **verbessern,** to improve, correct; **grösser,** bigger, **vergrössern,** to enlarge. Similarly from nouns by modification: **der Hammer,** hammer, **hämmern**; **der Pflug,** plough, **pflügen,** to plough; **der Sturm,** storm, **stürmen,** to storm.

The following inseparable prefixes form a large number of verbs (see also under Separable and Inseparable Verbs, p. 127):

be- turns Intransitive into Transitive verbs: **sprechen,** to speak, **besprechen,** to discuss; **kommen,** to come,

bekommen, to get, to come by ; **arbeiten,** to work, **bearbeiten,** to till (land), to work up (a subject). It also intensifies an action : **bauen,** to build, **bebauen,** to cover with buildings ; **sehen,** to see, **besehen,** to examine ; it forms verbs from nouns and adjectives : **ruhig,** calm, quiet, **beruhigen,** to calm ; **die Seele,** soul, **beseelen,** to animate.

ent- and **emp-** (the latter in only three verbs : **empfangen,** to receive, **empfehlen,** to recommend, **empfinden,** to feel) mean to pass into a state or begin an action : **entzünden,** to inflame, kindle ; **entstehen,** arise ; they also mean " away from " : **enthaupten,** to behead ; **entkommen,** to escape ; **entführen,** to abduct ; and finally they may reverse the meaning of the original verb : **ehren,** to honour, **entehren,** to dishonour ; **binden,** to bind, tie, **entbinden,** to free, release ; **wickeln,** to wrap, twist, **entwickeln,** to unravel, develop.

er- has the idea of becoming, entering into a state : **grünen,** to be green, **ergrünen,** to grow green ; **erröten,** to blush ; **erbleichen,** to grow pale ; **erwachen,** to wake up ; it is frequently used with the idea of obtaining something by an action : **bitten,** to ask for, **erbitten,** to obtain by asking ; **denken,** to think, **erdenken,** to invent, devise ; **fechten,** to fight, **erfechten,** to obtain by fighting. Finally it has the meaning of " to do to death by " : **erdolchen,** to stab to death ; **erschiessen,** to shoot dead ; **erschlagen,** to strike down dead ; **ertrinken,** to drown ; **ermorden,** to murder.

ge- is difficult to analyse, and its original collective meaning has faded ; in a few verbs it contains the idea of " clotting " : **gerinnen,** to coagulate ; **gefrieren,** to freeze.

hinter-, behind, gives : **hinterbleiben,** to remain behind, survive ; **hinterbringen,** to inform secretly ; **hintergehen,** to deceive ; **hinterlassen,** to leave behind, bequeath.

miss- is like the English mis- in mistake, misunderstand : **missdeuten,** misinterpret ; **missbrauchen,** misuse, abuse (past participle **missbraucht**) ; **missfallen,** to displease.

ver- has the idea of away : **verlaufen,** to pass away ;

verreisen, to go away; **versprechen,** to promise (speak away); **verhallen,** to die away (of sound). It also means "to make a slip in doing something": **sich versprechen,** to make a slip in speaking; **sich verrechnen,** to miscalculate; it is pejorative in: **verraten,** to betray; **verrufen,** to speak ill of.

zer- means "in pieces": **zerbrechen,** to smash; **zerstreuen,** to scatter; **zerreissen,** to tear to pieces; **zerschmettern,** to shatter; **zerstören,** to destroy.

The suffixes **-ieren** and **-eien** are added to foreign words: **spazieren,** to take a walk: **prophezeien,** to prophesy.

CHAPTER XVI

THE ADVERB

Adjectives qualify nouns; adverbs, as the name indicates, qualify verbs, but they also qualify adjectives and other adverbs: he speaks fluently; he speaks very fluently; his speech is extremely fluent. The German name for "adverb" is **das Umstandswort** = circumstance-word.

Now, adverbs are kittle cattle, and are often grouped together with prepositions and conjunctions (and interjections) as particles; they all have one thing in common—namely, that they are uninflected. Moreover, an adverb is liable to change its function and to be used as a preposition or a conjunction: I have seen him before (adverb); I saw him before sunrise (preposition); I saw him before the sun rose (conjunction).

I will first of all deal with the adverb derived from the adjective, e.g. slow, slowly. In English we add -ly (= like) to the adjective in order to form the adverb, and we compare it by means of "more" and "most": more slowly, most slowly. In German the adverb has the same form as the positive of the adjective: **langsam**, slow or slowly. Thus **die Postkutsche ist langsam** means "The mail-coach is slow"; **sie geht langsam**, means "It goes slowly"; **die schöne Frau singt schön** means "The beautiful lady sings beautifully".

In a few cases the adverbial form may add **-e**: **lang** or **lange**: **ich bin schon lange hier,** I have been here a long time (already); **fern** or **ferne,** far: **ich sah ihn von ferne,** I saw him from afar; **gern** or **gerne,** willingly, with pleasure: **ich trinke gern Tee,** I like (drinking) tea; **Wollen Sie mitkommen? Gerne!,** will you come along? With pleasure, willingly; **ich möchte gern nach Haus gehen,** I should like to go home. This **gern** is very much used, especially to translate our " like to ".

COMPARISON OF THE ADVERBS

The comparative is formed like the adjective by adding **-er** to the positive: **lange, länger; langsam, langsamer; schnell,** quickly, **schneller,** more quickly: **er ging schnell ans Fenster,** he quickly went to the window; **er läuft schneller als ich,** he walks (runs) more quickly than I; **er schreibt eben so schnell wie ich,** he writes as quickly as I.

There are two forms for the Superlative: **am schnellsten** and **aufs schnellste.** The form in **am -sten** is called the Relative Superlative, and is used when different objects are compared or the same object is compared with itself in different circumstances: **Heinrich bleibt hier am längsten,** Henry remains here longest, i.e. he remains longer than anybody else; **er bleibt im Sommer am längsten,** he remains longest in summer, i.e. he remains longer in summer than in the other seasons.

The form in **aufs -ste** is called the Absolute Superlative, and is used to describe a quality in its highest degree without any comparison being intended: **Marie sang aufs schönste,** Mary sang most beautifully, i.e. very beautifully indeed; **er empfing mich aufs höflichste,** he received me most courteously, in a most courteous manner.

The following Superlatives are also used without the **am** or **aufs: bald,** soon, makes **baldigst: ich bitte Sie, die Waren baldigst zu schicken,** I beg you to send the goods as soon as possible; **gefällig,** obligingly, kindly, is a word in frequent daily use: **was ist Ihnen gefällig,** means " what can I do for you? what can I get you? "; the Superlative **gefälligst** is equally common: **wollen Sie gefälligst Platz nehmen?** will you please take a seat? will you be so kind as to be seated? **Hoch,** high, makes **höchst,** most highly:

ich war höchst empört, I was most indignant, very highly indignant.

Here are some examples of adverbs regularly compared:

schnell, quickly	**schneller**	**am schnellsten**	**aufs schnellste**
arm, poorly	**ärmer**	**am ärmsten**	**aufs ärmste**
edel, nobly	**edler**	**am edelsten**	**aufs edelste**

The following are irregular:

bald, soon	**eher,** sooner, rather	**am baldigsten aufs baldigste**
gern, willingly	**lieber,** rather	**am liebsten,** etc.
gut, well	**besser**	**am besten**
oft, often	**öfter** (also adj.)	**am häufigsten**
viel, much	**mehr**	**am meisten**
wenig, little	**weniger** or **minder**	**am wenigsten** or **am mindesten**

A series of adverbs is formed by adding **-s** to the Superlative, as for example: **meistens,** mostly, usually, generally: **er kommt meistens um 2 Uhr,** he generally comes at two; **wenigstens,** at least, at all events: **das hat wenigstens (mindestens) 10 Mark gekostet,** that cost at least 10 marks; **höchstens,** at most: **das Dorf hat höchstens hundert Einwohner,** the village has at most a hundred inhabitants; **nächstens,** very soon, shortly: **ich fahre nächstens nach Berlin,** I am going to Berlin shortly.

A number of adverbs are formed from the Genitive of nouns: **tags,** from **Tag,** day: **tags darauf,** next day; **morgens,** in the morning, every morning: **morgens trinke ich eine Tasse Kaffee,** in the mornings I drink a cup of coffee; **abends,** in the evening: **abends lese ich die Zeitung,** in the evenings I read the paper; **nachts,** at night: **ich kann nachts nicht schlafen,** I can't sleep at night; **anfangs,** at first: **anfangs konnte ich den Mann nicht leiden,** at first I couldn't bear the man; **keineswegs,** by no means: **er ist keineswegs reich,** he is by no means rich; **vorwärts,** forwards; **rückwärts,** backwards; **seitwärts,** sideways.

A few end in **-lich**: **neulich,** recently; **gänzlich,** entirely; **freilich,** certainly, by all means; others are formed from a present participle : **bedeutend,** considerably : **das ist bedeutend schöner,** that is considerably nicer ; others end in **-lings** (cf. our headlong) : **blindlings,** blindly.

We must now tackle the adverbs of place, time, etc., the number of which is so great that we can deal only with the most important. We will start with the adverbs of place.

ADVERBS OF PLACE

German makes a distinction between " rest at " a place and " motion towards " a place. With certain prepositions (see p. 181) " rest at " requires the Dative, " motion towards " the Accusative.

When " rest at " is meant the interrogative adverb is **wo ?** where ? : **wo ist mein Buch ?,** where is my book ? The answer may be : **Ihr Buch ist hier,** i.e. near the speaker, or : **Ihr Buch ist dort,** your book is there, i.e. far from the speaker. **Da,** which also means " there ", indicates neither nearness nor distance : **Da hast du dein Buch,** there's your book for you ; **da bin ich,** here I am.

Da and **wo** combine with prepositions, inserting **-r-** before a vowel, to form a very useful series : **an,** at, gives **woran,** whereat ; **daran,** thereat ; **aus,** out of, gives **woraus,** whereout, and **daraus,** thereout ; **von,** of, from, gives **wovon,** wherefrom, whereof, and **davon,** therefrom. **Warum,** why ? wherefore ? corresponds to **darum,** therefore. We have met these words already on pp. 63, 72, 73.

The following adverbs of place are useful : **oben,** up above, upstairs (corresponding to the preposition **über**) ; **unten,** down below, downstairs (corresponding to **unter**) ; **aussen,** outside (corresponding to **ausser**) : **innen,** within, inside ; **vorn(e),** in front ; **hinten,** behind (preposition **hinter**) ; **neben,** near (preposition also **neben**).

If " motion towards " a place is intended, as in " Where are you going (to) ? " the Germans use **wohin ?,** whither ? : **Wohin gehen Sie ?,** or **Wo gehen Sie hin ?** **Hin** is used to indicate direction away from the speaker, **her** to indicate direction towards the speaker. Thus if I am sitting at an upstairs window speaking to somebody below me in the garden, I will say to him when inviting him to come up to me: **Kommen Sie herauf!** He will say as he passes my wife: **ich gehe hinauf,** I am going upstairs, meaning that he is going away from the place he was at. When he knocks at my study door I will say: **kommen Sie herein,** or more usually just **herein!,** or even: **'rein!,** because the movement is towards me, the speaker. When looking for my book I say: **Wohin habe ich das Buch gelegt?,** where did I put the book? or **wo habe ich das Buch hingelegt?** **Hin** and **her** combine with **ab,** down, **aus,** out of, **ein,** in, etc. to make **hinab, herab; hinaus, heraus; hinein, herein,** etc., indicating motion towards the speaker with **her,** from the speaker with **hin.** Corresponding to **wohin?,** whither?, we have **dorthin,** thither, **dahin,** thither; corresponding to **woher?,** whence?, we have **dorther, daher,** thence. I know it sounds a little complicated, but you will soon get this " rest at " or " motion towards " feeling.

ADVERBS OF TIME

Adverbs of Time are numerous and important, but you will have to go to the dictionary for most of them. The Interrogative is **wann?,** when?, e.g.: **wann darf ich Sie anrufen?,** when may I ring you up?, which we shall discuss again on p. 169. Some common adverbs of time which demand a little care are:

jetzt, now, at the present moment: **es ist jetzt Zeit,** it's time now. **Nun,** now, is used in relation to a past time and corresponds to " thereupon ": **er ging nun fort,** he thereupon went off, he then went off, he now went off. **Nun** has behind it the idea of continuity: **nun geht's los,** now things are going to happen, the balloon's going up. **Jetzt** here would simply mean: look, at this moment of time, the balloon is going up; **nun** directs the attention to the events following. **Nun** is used exclamatively: **nun, was machen**

Sie da?, well, what are you doing there? **Nun, und?** is equivalent to our (or rather the American) so what?, what about it?

Noch, still, yet, again, is useful: **er ist noch sehr schwach**, he is still very weak. "Not yet" is **noch nicht**: **der Brief ist noch nicht angekommen**, the letter has not yet arrived. It may mean "only": **noch gestern habe ich ihn getroffen**, I met him only yesterday. In **sagen Sie das noch einmal!**, say that again, once more; **er ist immer noch krank**, he is still sick; **noch etwas gefällig?**, anything more you would like?; **Kinder noch so artig**, children however good (well-behaved), it is intensive. **Noch** is used in German where we say "another": **Kellner, geben Sie mir noch ein Brötchen!**, Waiter, give me another roll; **ein andres Brötchen** would mean "another roll" in the sense of a different roll, not the same roll as this one, and the waiter would take it away.

Schon, already, is straightforward in: **es ist schon spät**, it is late already. In **das ist schon wahr**, that is indeed true; **das ist schon genug**, that will do; **schon den nächsten Tag war er fort**, he had gone the very next morning; **er wird schon kommen**, he will come all right, sure enough, **schon** has idiomatic meanings; keep your eye on **schon** as you read or hear German and note when it does **not** mean "already".

The answer to **wann?**, when? is **dann**, then; **damals**, then, at that time; **sofort, sogleich**, at once, immediately; **vorher**, before; **nachher**, afterwards.

ADVERBS OF DEGREE

Adverbs of degree need not detain us very long: **sehr**, very (our English "sore", as in "sore afraid"); **äusserst, höchst**, etc. already discussed; **zu**, too: **das ist zu heiss**, that is too hot; **zu spät** may mean either "too late" or simply "late"; **ziemlich**, pretty, fairly: **er ist ziemlich reich**, he is pretty (tolerably), rich; **fast**, almost; **ungefähr**, about: **ich habe ungefähr zwei Dutzend,** I have about two dozen; **genug,** enough: **er hat Geld genug,** he has enough money (note the order in German). **Nur,** only, is used with a sense of finality: **das kostet nur zehn Mark,** that costs only ten marks; **ich habe nur eine Schwester,** I have only one sister. In **er ist erst sechs Jahre alt,** he is only six years old, the idea underlying the statement is that he has only reached the age of six and there are more to follow. **Erst** is generally used of time: **ich habe ihn erst gestern gesehen,** I saw him only yesterday; **ich habe ihn nur gestern gesehen,** would mean I saw him yesterday only (and not any other day).

AFFIRMATIVE AND NEGATIVE ADVERBS

Adverbs which qualify the whole sentence are the Affirmative **ja,** yes, and its emphatic form **jawohl**: **kommt er?,** is he coming?, **ja!, er kommt,** yes, he is; **jawohl!, er kommt,** yes, he certainly is. In reply to a negative question the emphatic **doch** is used: **Sie sind kein Engländer? Doch!,** you are not English? Yes, I am.

Ja is used in a number of idiomatic ways, unstressed, e.g. **er kommt ja jeden Abend,** you see he comes every evening; **er sieht ja krank aus,** he looks quite ill. It is emphatic and stressed in: **Sie müssen ja Berlin besuchen,** you really must visit Berlin.

Doch is emphatic in: **Sie glauben es nicht? Ist es doch wahr,** you don't believe it? It *is* true; **komm doch!,** do come. **Wenn ich doch Geld hätte!,** if only I had money!

The negatives are: **nein,** no, nay, **nicht,** not: **kommt er?,** is he coming?, **Nein!, er kommt nicht.** Emphatic is **nein doch!** We shall have a word to say about **nicht** under Word Order, p. 197. **Nicht wahr?,** is it not true?, is useful for questions: **Sie sind müde, nicht wahr?,** you are tired, aren't you?; **Sie sprechen Deutsch, nicht wahr?,** You speak German, don't you?

Useful words which modify or temper a statement are:

allerdings, to be sure, of course; **vielleicht,** perhaps; **natürlich,** of course, naturally; **hoffentlich,** it is to be hoped, as in: **hoffentlich bleibt er die ganze Nacht,** it is to be hoped he will stay the whole night.

This ends our chapter on the adverbs, which has perhaps proved a trifle heavy, although grammatically the adverb is very simple. The difficulties are mainly idiomatic.

CHAPTER XVIII

THE CONJUNCTION

The conjunction is a particle used to link up words, phrases and sentences: time and tide; the ships already manned and those not yet ready; the ships hoisted sail and left the port. We shall deal mainly with the linking of sentences here.

We can classify conjunctions into co-ordinating, i.e. those which link up ideas of equal importance, such as "and", "but", etc.; and subordinating, i.e. those which join up a main idea—a principal sentence—with a subsidiary idea or subordinate clause, such as "because", "when", etc. In German the former have no effect on the position of the verb; in the latter the verb is thrown to the end of the subordinate sentence.

CO-ORDINATING CONJUNCTIONS

We will divide these into two classes: pure conjunctions, such as **und, aber, denn,** etc., and adverbial conjunctions, such as **doch, sonst, daher,** etc. The difference is important, since the pure conjunction does not affect the position of the verb, whereas the adverbial, being an adverb, will cause inversion of the verb and subject if it commences the sentence. Here are a couple of examples which will make that clear:

A. **Ich suchte das Buch, aber ich fand es nicht,** I looked for the book but I did not find it.

B. **Ich suchte das Buch, doch fand ich es nicht,** I looked for the book, nevertheless I did not find it.

In A **aber** causes no change in the position of the verb; in B **doch**, which is an emphatic " but ", inverts the verb order: **fand ich.** I ought perhaps to add that with **doch** there need not be inversion, and it would be perfectly good German to write: **doch ich fand es nicht.**

THE PURE CO-ORDINATING CONJUNCTIONS

These are: **und,** and; **aber, allein,** but, however; **oder,** or; **denn** and **nämlich,** for; **sondern,** but (after a negative). We will run through them in alphabetical order. Note that these conjunctions—except **und** and **oder,** which see below—are always preceded by a comma.

ABER, but, like the English " however ", can be inserted later on in the sentence, and need not head it: **die Lampen an den Wänden waren angezündet, aber es waren wenige Gäste,** the lamps on the walls were lit but there were few guests, or: **die Lampen an den Wänden waren angezündet, es waren aber wenige Gäste. Aber** is also used as an adverb in: **tausend und aber tausend,** thousands and thousands.

ALLEIN, but, is more emphatic than **aber,** and is always at the head of the sentence: **ich wollte gern mitgehen, allein ich konnte nicht,** I wanted to go along but I could not (or: only I could not).

SONDERN, but, is found only after a negative, which it emphasizes: **er ist nicht reich, sondern arm,** he is not rich but poor; **er ist nicht nur reich, sondern sogar ein Millionär,** he is not only rich but even a millionaire. Note that the element of emphasizing the negative idea must be present; thus in: *he is not rich but he lives in a large house,* the meaning is: he is not rich although he lives in a large house; his living in a large house does not contradict the idea of his being poor nor make his being poor more emphatic as was the case with: he is not rich but poor. Hence: he is not rich but lives in a large house is in German: **er ist nicht reich, aber er wohnt in einem grossen Hause.** Similarly: I do not smoke but I have cigarettes in my pocket, is: **ich rauche nicht, aber ich habe Zigaretten in der Tasche**; he is not rich but nevertheless happy, is: **er ist zwar nicht reich, aber er ist doch glücklich.** You must not automatically put **sondern** after every negative but think out the meaning first.

DENN, for (in the meaning of because), as in: **er kommt nicht, denn er ist krank,** he is not coming, for he is ill. **Denn** is also an adverb and will be found below.

NÄMLICH, as, since, need not introduce the sentence, but can stand after the verb: **ich konnte es nicht kaufen, ich hatte nämlich kein Geld,** I could not buy it, as I had not any money.

ODER, or, is straightforward: **Sie müssen arbeiten oder hungern,** you must work or starve; **kommen Sie sofort, oder Sie werden zu spät kommen,** come at once or you will be too late. The comma is dropped with **oder** (and **und**) if the two clauses have the same subject: **er kann hier bleiben oder nach Berlin fahren,** he can remain here or go to Berlin.

UND, and: **er ging auf sein Zimmer und kam gleich mit einer Papierrolle zurück,** he went to his room and came back at once with a roll of paper; no comma because **er** is the subject of both **ging** and **kam**; **mein Vater hatte sich erkältet, und wir mussten den Arzt holen lassen,** my father had caught cold and we had to send for a doctor; a comma because the two clauses have not the same subject. **Und** is equivalent to " even if " in e.g.: **ich muss es tun, und koste es mein Leben,** I must do it even if it should cost my life.

We may add to the above the following useful conjunctions in double harness:

Entweder . . . oder, either . . . or: **entweder Sie bezahlen die Hälfte, oder ich kaufe es nicht,** either you pay half or I do not buy it.

Weder . . . noch, neither . . . nor: **ich will dich weder verlassen, noch vernachlässigen,** I will neither leave you nor neglect you.

Sowohl . . . als, both . . . and: **er war sowohl ein**

grosser Dichter als auch ein hervorragender Staatsman, he was both a great poet and a prominent statesman.

Ebenso . . . wie, as . . . as: **er ist ein ebenso guter Mensch wie du,** he is just as good a man as you; **sie arbeitet ebenso fleissig, wie ich spiele,** she works as hard as I play.

"Nor" requires care as there is no German word for it: I cannot see him nor can I hear him: **ich kann ihn nicht sehen, auch kann ich ihn nicht hören;** he is not happy. Neither am I, **er ist nicht glücklich. Ich auch nicht.**

ADVERBIAL CONJUNCTIONS

There are many adverbs of this type which show the relationship of one idea to another, and since they are adverbs, they invert the subject and the verb when the adverb commences the clause. Here are the most commonly used amongst them: **also,** therefore; **da,** then, there; **dann,** then; **denn,** then; **dennoch,** however; **deshalb,** therefore; **doch,** but, nevertheless; **so,** thus, so; **sonst,** else; **trotzdem,** nevertheless; **übrigens,** moreover, for that matter; **wohl,** no doubt, presumably; **zwar, allerdings,** it is true, indeed, to be sure.

ALSO, thus, therefore, so, one of the words most heard in German conversation: **also muss ich gehen.,** so I must go; **Sie kommen also um zwei Uhr?,** you are coming at two o'clock then?

DA: when, then: **als ich erwachte, da war es schon heller Tag,** when I awoke, (then) it was full daylight; **im Jahre 1936 befand ich mich in Köln, da traf ich einen alten Freund,** in 1936 I was in Cologne when I met an old friend. **Da** is also a subordinating conjunction, for which see below.

DANN, then: **wenn Sie noch lange warten, dann versäumen Sie den Zug,** if you wait any longer, (then) you will miss the train.

DENN, so, well then, after all: **was ist denn los?** what *is* the matter?; **es ist ihm denn doch gelungen,** he has succeeded after all; **so mag es denn dabei bleiben!,** then let it be so. This is not to be confused with denn, the subordinating conjunction, which see below.

DAHER, hence, therefore: **ich war müde, daher ging ich nicht aus,** I was tired, therefore (so) I did not go out.

DARUM, therefore: **das Wetter ist schön, darum wollen wir einen Ausflug machen,** the weather is fine, therefore (so) we will make a trip.

DENNOCH, yet, nevertheless: **es ist unglaublich, dennoch ist es wahr,** it is incredible, nevertheless it is true.

DESSENUNGEACHTET, nevertheless, notwithstanding (stronger than **dennoch**): **er wurde gewarnt; dessenungeachtet kaufte er das Haus,** he was warned, nevertheless he bought the house.

DOCH, yet, still: **ich lud ihn ein, doch er wollte nicht kommen,** I invited him, yet he would not come. Inversion can take place: **es ist möglich, doch glaube ich es nicht,** it is possible but (yet) I do not believe it.

ENTWEDER . . . ODER, either . . . or: **entweder Sie bleiben hier, oder Sie kommen mit,** either you remain here or you come along. Note the idiomatic: **entweder oder!** either one thing or the other, e.g. take it or leave it!

INDESSEN, nevertheless: **der Verlust ist gross, indessen ist er nicht unersetzlich,** the loss is great, nevertheless it is not irreplaceable.

JE . . . DESTO (UM SO), the . . . the: **je mehr ich ihn lobe, desto (um so) mehr strengt er sich an,** the more I praise him, the more he strives. In set expressions and short clauses: **JE . . . JE, Je mehr man hat, je mehr man will,** the more one has, the more one wants. **Je länger, je lieber,** the longer the better.

TROTZDEM, nevertheless: **er ist reich, trotzdem gibt er wenig aus,** he is rich, nevertheless he spends little.

ZWAR, indeed, it is true, to be sure: **zwar kam er, doch war es zu spät,** he came, to be sure, but it was too late.

SUBORDINATING CONJUNCTIONS

These are numerous, the most used being : **als**, as, when, than ; **bis**, until ; **da**, as, since ; **damit**, in order that ; **dass**, that ; **ehe** or **bevor**, before ; **falls**, in case, if ; **indem**, while ; **je nachdem**, according as ; **nachdem**, after ; **ob**, whether ; **obgleich**, although ; **seit**, since ; **sobald**, as soon as ; **während**, while ; **weil**, because ; **wenn**, if, when, whenever ; **wie**, as ; **wo**, where. Let us run through them with examples :

Als, as : **sie ist schöner, als man sagt**, she is more beautiful than they say ; **er tut nichts als arbeiten**, he does nothing but work.

We will take **als**, when, together with **wenn**, whenever, when, if, and **wann ?**, when ?, so as to show the difference between them :

Als, when, is used for a single action in the past : **ich sah ihn vor einem Jahr, als er nach Rom abreiste**, I saw him a year ago when he set out for Rome ; **als er mich sah, kam er auf mich zu**, when he saw me he came up to me.

Wenn, when, whenever, is used with a Present or Future : **wenn der Sommer kommt, machen wir immer Ausflüge aufs Land**, when summer comes we always make trips into the country. With a Past tense it indicates a repeated, habitual action : **wenn der Sommer kam, machten wir Ausflüge aufs Land**, when summer came we used to make trips into the country. This same **wenn** is our " if " : **wenn man ihn erwischt, wird er bestraft**, if he is caught he will be punished ; **wenn er käme, würde ich froh sein**, if he came I should be glad.

Wann ?, when ?, is used for questions : **Wann kommt er ?**, when is he coming ? ; **ich weiss nicht, wann er kommt**, I do not know when he is coming.

Bis, until : **warten Sie, bis ich zurückkomme**, wait until I return.

Da, as, since, whereas: **da er alt war, musste man ihn schonen**, as he was old he had to be taken good care of.

Damit, in order that: **ich spreche laut, damit man mich höre**, I speak loudly in order that I shall be heard.

Dass, that, in order that: **ich sage es Ihnen, dass Sie es wissen**, I tell you in order that you know it; **es war so kalt, dass mich fror**, it was so cold that I was chilled. In the principal sentence with verbs which are constructed with a preposition, such as **bestehen auf**, to insist on, **sich verlassen auf**, to rely on, **erinnern an**, to remind of, the preposition must be combined with **da** (or **dar**), as it cannot govern a whole sentence, as in English. Thus we can say: I insist that he remains here, but German cannot say: **ich bestehe auf, dass er hier bleibt**; instead we get: **ich bestehe darauf, dass er hier bleibt**; similarly: **er erinnerte mich daran, dass ich sie nicht eingeladen hatte**, he reminded me that I had not invited her; in the same way the prepositions **ohne**, without, **statt** (or **anstatt**), instead, **ausser**, except that, are tricky to use: **ich blieb da, ohne dass er ein einziges Wort sagte**, I remained there without his saying a single word; **er spielt, statt dass er arbeitet**, he plays instead of working; **ich weiss nichts Gutes von ihm, ausser dass er freigebig ist**, I know nothing good about him except that he is generous.

Ehe, bevor, before: **bevor er abreiste, küsste er seine Frau**, before he departed he kissed his wife; **ehe er mich sah, war ich verschwunden**, before he saw me I had disappeared.

Falls, in the event that: **machen Sie alles fertig, falls er kommen sollte**, make everything ready in case he comes.

Indem, while, as: **"Guten Tag," sagte er, indem er die Tür aufmachte**, "Good day," he said as he opened the door (opening the door); **er konnte es nur ertragen, indem er es vergass**, he could bear it only by forgetting it. **Indem** refers to an action of short duration, unlike **während**, during, which is used for actions of longer duration as below.

Je nachdem, according as: **man erhält viel oder wenig, je nachdem man arbeitet,** one receives much or little according as one works.

Nachdem, after: **nachdem ich geschlafen hatte, kleidete ich mich an,** after I had slept, I dressed, or: after sleeping I dressed.

Ob, whether: **ich weiss nicht, ob wir morgen kommen,** I don't know whether we are coming tomorrow.

Obgleich and **obschon,** although: **obgleich wir fleissig arbeiten, verdienen wir wenig,** although we work hard we earn little. Both **obgleich** and **obschon** can be used in two words: **ob wir gleich fleissig arbeiten. . . .**

Seit or **seitdem,** since: **ich habe viele Freunde gesehen, seitdem ich hier bin,** I have seen many friends since I have been here.

Sobald, as soon as: **ich werde Ihnen schreiben, sobald ich ankomme,** I shall write to you as soon as I arrive.

Während, while: **er sprach kein Wort, während er im Zimmer auf und ab ging,** he did not speak a word while he walked up and down in the room. See also under **indem.**

Weil, because: **er kann nicht reisen, weil er krank ist,** he cannot travel because he is sick.

Wie, as, how, when: **er ist schon weg, wie ich sehe,** he has already gone, as I see; **wie dumm sie auch ist, muss sie es doch begreifen,** however stupid she is, she must understand it; **wie er seinen Vater sah, ging er auf ihn zu,** when (as soon as) he saw his father he went up to him.

Wo, where, when: **ich weiss, wo er wohnt,** I know where he lives; **am Tage, wo der Krieg ausbrach,** on the day when the war broke out.

CHAPTER XIX

THE PREPOSITION

The German for " preposition ", **Verhältniswort** (= relation or liaison word), explains exactly what job the preposition (= placed-before-word) does : it is a word that links other words together so that their relationship is revealed : in " the tree in the garden ", " in " shows the relationship of the tree to the garden ; in " the cows of the farmer ", " of " shows in what relationship the farmer stands to the cows and the cows to the farmer.

In English all prepositions take the Accusative case : with him ; for me ; by us ; without them, etc. In German they have to be divided into four classes : those taking the Genitive ; those taking the Dative ; those taking the Accusative ; those taking either the Accusative or the Dative, according as they indicate movement towards or rest at a place. Let us deal with them in that order.

PREPOSITIONS GOVERNING THE GENITIVE

In German Grammars for German schoolchildren they generally give little rhymes for memorizing the various prepositions and their cases. In the case of the prepositions governing the Genitive it would not be practical to include all the prepositions, as they are too numerous, and many of them not much used. Here is a rhyme from *Lyons Handbuch der Deutschen Sprache* (Manual of the German Language) which gives the most useful ones :

Unweit, mittels, kraft und während,
Laut, vermöge, ungeachtet,
Oberhalb und unterhalb,
Diesseit, jenseit, halber, wegen,

Statt, auch längs, zufolge, trotz
Stehen mit dem Genitiv.
Doch ist hier nicht zu vergessen,
Dass bei diesen letzten drei
Auch der Dativ richtig sei.

The last three lines tell you not to forget that **längs, zufolge** and **trotz** may also take the Dative. Let us go through these prepositions in the order in which they occur in our mnemonic rhyme :

UNWEIT, not far from, with which we may couple **unfern,** which has the same meaning : **wir wohnen unweit des Meeres,** we live not far from the sea ; **unfern des Dorfes steht ein altes Schloss,** not far from the village there stands an old castle.

MITTELS or **MITTELST**, by means of : **mittels vieler Streiche fällt auch die stärkste Eiche,** by means of many blows (strokes) even the strongest oak falls.

KRAFT, by virtue of : **kraft seines Amtes hat der Bürgermeister den Verdächtigten einsperren lassen,** by virtue of his office the Mayor has had the suspect gaoled.

WÄHREND, during (the Present Participle of the verb **währen,** to last) : **während des Sommers ist der Aufenthalt auf dem Lande angenehm,** during the summer a sojourn in the country is pleasant.

LAUT, according to : **laut seines Briefes geht es ihm gut,** according to his letter he is well.

VERMÖGE, by virtue of, through, owing to : **vermöge seiner geringeren Schwere schwimmt has Holz auf dem Wasser,** owing to its smaller specific gravity wood floats on water.

UNGEACHTET, in spite of, notwithstanding : **ungeachtet meines Befehls blieb er zu Hause,** in spite of my order(s) he remained at home.

OBERHALB, above ; **unterhalb,** below ; **innerhalb,** within, inside of ; **ausserhalb,** outside of : **Düsseldorf, Köln**

und Bonn liegen an dem Rhein : Düsseldorf liegt unterhalb Kölns, Bonn liegt oberhalb Kölns, Dusseldorf, Cologne and Bonn are on the Rhine ; Dusseldorf is below Cologne, Bonn is above Cologne. **Ausserhalb des Dorfes liegen grosse Wälder,** outside the village there lie large forests ; **innerhalb des Hauses,** inside the house ; **innerhalb eines Jahres,** within a year.

DIESSEIT, this side of, **jenseit,** the other side of : **mancher, der sich diesseit des Ozeans nicht glücklich fühlt, glaubt jenseit des Ozeans sein Glück zu machen,** many a one who does not feel happy on this side of the ocean, thinks he will be successful on the other side of the ocean.

HALBER, on account of : **er ist seiner Unzuverlässigkeit halber aus dem Dienst entlassen worden,** he has been dismissed the service on account of his unreliability. Note that **halber** follows the noun it governs. Note also **halben** in **meinethalben,** for my sake.

WEGEN, on account of, owing to : **wegen des Festes** (or **des Festes wegen) konnte er nicht hier sein,** owing to the festival he could not be here. Note **meinetwegen,** on my account.

STATT or **ANSTATT,** instead of : **anstatt** (**statt**) **des Sohnes kam der Vater,** the father came instead of the son.

LÄNGS, along : **längs des Weges sind Bäume angepflanzt worden,** trees have been planted along the road. **Entlang,** which has the same meaning, also takes the Genitive : **entlang des Weges,** but it generally takes the Accusative and follows the noun : **den Weg entlang,** along the road.

ZUFOLGE, according to, in consequence of : **zufolge Ihres Versprechens habe ich Sie den ganzen Tag erwartet,** in consequence of your promise I have waited the whole day for you. **Zufolge** takes the Dative when it follows its noun : **dem Urteil der Sachverständigen zufolge,** according to the judgment (opinion) of the experts. It generally is found with the Dative.

TROTZ, in spite of : **trotz des Verbotes** (or **dem Verbote**)

blieb er sitzen, in spite of the prohibition he remained seated.

Here are a few more prepositions governing the Genitive which are frequently met with: **um . . . willen,** for the sake of: **um Gottes willen,** for God's sake; **betreffs,** in reference to, concerning, with regard to: **betreffs Ihres Briefes,** in reference to your letter; **namens,** in the name of: **namens des Kaisers,** in the name of the Emperor.

PREPOSITIONS GOVERNING THE DATIVE

Our rhyme is:

Schreib mit, nach, nächst, nebst, samt,
Bei, seit, von, zu, zuwider,
Entgegen, gegenüber, ausser, aus
Stets mit dem Dativ nieder!

Schreib . . . stets mit dem Dativ nieder! means "write down . . . always with the Dative". Let us go over these in alphabetical order with examples:

AUS, out of; **der Regen kommt aus den Wolken,** rain comes out of the clouds; **das Standbild stammt aus der Zeit Hadrians,** the statue dates from the time of Hadrian; **dieser Tisch ist aus Marmor,** this table is of marble; **was soll aus mir werden?,** what is to become of me?; **er starb aus Bekümmernis,** he died of grief.

AUSSER, besides, out of, except: **er verlangt ausser dem Lohn auch eine gute Behandlung,** he demands besides the wages good treatment too; **alle meine Freunde waren zugegen ausser Ihnen,** all my friends were present except you; **der Landmann bringt die meiste Zeit seines Lebens ausser dem Hause zu,** the countryman spends the greater part of his life outside his house.

BEI, at, by, about, amongst, during, near, in: **bei der Kirche stehen Bäume,** trees stand near the church; **er war bei guter Laune,** he was in a good temper; **wir sassen bei Tische,** we were sitting at table (i.e. having a meal; **wir**

sassen am Tische, we were sitting at the table); **beim Frühstück,** at breakfast; **bei deiner Klugheit hättest du diesen Fehler leicht vermeiden können,** with your cleverness you could easily have avoided this mistake; **beim ersten Anblick,** at first sight; **er wohnt bei seinem Onkel,** he lives at his uncle's; **man kauft es beim Buchhändler,** you buy it at the bookseller's; **bei Tage,** by day; **ich habe kein Geld bei mir,** I have no money on me; **bei den Römern,** amongst the Romans; **bei weitem besser,** better by far; **bei Zeiten,** in good time; **die Schlacht bei Sedan,** the battle of Sedan; **bei Todesstrafe,** on pain of death.

BINNEN, within, is not in the rhyme, but is useful: **binnen einem Jahre werde ich zurückkehren,** within a year I shall return.

DANK, thanks to, also not in the rhyme, is worth learning: **dank seinem Geld kam er zu Ehre,** he was honoured thanks to his money.

ENTGEGEN, against, in face of, opposed to, towards: **entgegen meinen Wünschen,** against my wishes. It is generally found adverbially, as in: **er kam mir entgegen,** he came towards me; **er ruderte dem Strom entgegen,** he rowed against the current.

GEGENÜBER, opposite, face to face: **er wohnt gegenüber dem Bahnhof** (or **dem Bahnhof gegenüber**), he lives opposite the station. It is generally to be found following the noun or pronoun: **er sitzt mir gegenüber,** he is sitting opposite me.

GEMÄSS, according to, conformably to: **das war nicht meinem Wunsche gemäss,** that was not according to my desire; **gemäss seinem Charakter** (or **seinem Charakter gemäss**), conformably to his character. It can precede or follow its noun. It is not in our rhyme.

MIT, with, by, at: **mit dir will ich durchs Leben wandern,** I will travel through life along with you; **ich redete mit ihm,** I spoke to him; **mit einem Male,** suddenly, all at once; **ich reiste mit der Eisenbahn,** I travelled by rail; **was ist mit Ihnen?,** what's the matter with you?; **mit Tagesanbruch,**

at daybreak; **mit dem ersten Januar tritt die Verfügung in Kraft,** on the first of January the decree comes into force; **er öffnete die Tür mit dem Schlüssel,** he opened the door with the key; **zwei Fliegen mit einer Klappe schlagen,** to hit two flies with one flap, i.e. to kill two birds with one stone.

NACH, after, behind, toward, later, according to, after the manner of, etc.: **nach uns die Sintflut,** after us the deluge; **eine Stunde nach seiner Abreise war er schon angekommen,** an hour after his departure he had already arrived; **nach dem Gesetze ist er unschuldig,** according to the law he is innocent (not guilty); **nach meiner Meinung** or **meiner Meinung nach,** in my opinion; **nach der Natur malen,** to paint from nature; **ich kenne ihn nur dem Namen nach,** I know him only by name; **nach meiner Uhr ist es Mittag,** by my watch it is noon; **nach Goethe,** after Goethe (i.e. in imitation of); **immer der Reihe nach, wie beim Gänsemarsch,** always in turn, as in follow-my-leader (**Gänsemarsch** is also "goose-step"); **man verkauft es nach dem Gewicht,** it is sold by weight; **er spielt nach Noten,** he plays at sight (i.e. from music).

NÄCHST or **ZUNÄCHST,** next to, close to: **nächst meinem Vater liebe ich dich,** I love you next to my father; **er stand zunächst dem Fenster** or **dem Fenster zunächst,** he stood next to, close to, the window.

NEBST, SAMT, with, together with, along with, besides: **er kam nebst Frau und Kindern,** he came together with wife and children; **Leonidas starb samt seinen Spartanern bei Thermopylä,** Leonidas died along with his Spartans at the pass of Thermopylae.

SEIT, since: **ich bin seit einem Jahre hier,** I have been here one year; **es regnet seit Tagen,** it has been raining for days; **seit undenklicher Zeit,** from time out of mind.

VON, of, from, by, in, on, according to: **ein Freund von mir,** a friend of mine; **ein Bewohner von Berlin,** an inhabitant of Berlin; **vom Morgen bis zum Abend,** from morning to evening; **von Zeit zu Zeit,** from time to time;

ein Standbild von Marmor, a statue of marble; **von diesem Tage an,** from this day forward; **ich kenne ihn von klein auf,** I know him from his childhood; **er ist von Sinnen,** he is out of his mind; **dieses Buch handelt von dem Krieg,** this book treats of the war; **er wurde von seinem Feinde getötet,** he was killed by his enemy.

ZU, to, at, in, on, by, etc.: with the names of persons: **er geht zu seinem Vater,** he goes to his father; with place-names **zu** equals "at": **er studierte zu Heidelberg,** he studied at Heidelberg; **zu Hause,** at home; **zur See,** at sea; **zu Bett,** in bed: **zur Kirche gehen,** to go to church; **zur Schule gehen,** to go to school; **zur Welt bringen,** to bring into the world; **zu Bett gehen,** to go to bed; **zu Anfang,** at the beginning; **zum Ende der Woche,** at the end of the week; **zum Frühstück,** for breakfast; **zum Fenster hinaussehen,** to look out of the window; **Brot zum Fleisch essen,** to eat bread with one's meat; **zur Hand sein,** to be at hand; **zum letzten Male,** for the last time; **der König ernannte ihn zum General,** the King made him general; **nehmen Sie Zucker zum Kaffee?,** do you take sugar in your coffee?; **eine Freimarke zu fünfzig Pfennig,** a 50 Pfennig stamp; **zu Ostern,** at Easter; **er ging auf seinen Vater zu,** he went up to his father.

ZUWIDER, contrary to, against: **das Schicksal ist mir zuwider,** fate is against me; **er handelte dem Befehl zuwider,** he acted contrary to the order(s); **dieser Mensch is mir zuwider,** this man is repugnant to me. Note that **zuwider** always follows its noun.

PREPOSITIONS GOVERNING THE ACCUSATIVE

Our rhyme runs:

Bei durch, für, ohne, um,
Auch sonder, gegen, wider,
Schreib stets den Akkusativ
Und nie den Dativ nieder!

Bei . . . schreib stets den Akkusativ und nie den Dativ

nieder ! means : with . . . always write down the Accusative and never the Dative. That is an easy short list to remember.

Let us take them in alphabetical order, commencing with one that is not in the rhyme :

BIS, until, up to, is generally used together with other prepositions, as in : **sie waren bis an die Zähne bewaffnet,** they are armed to the teeth ; **ich habe alles gesehen, bis auf das Stadthaus,** I have seen everything except the Town Hall. It is used alone in : **bis nächsten Freitag,** until next Friday ; **bis jetzt,** up to now ; **von Berlin bis Köln,** from Berlin to Cologne ; **es ist von A bis Z falsch,** it is wrong from the beginning to the end, from A to Z ; **warten Sie bis 4 Uhr !,** wait until 4 o'clock.

DURCH, through, by, by means of, across : **er ging durch den Park,** he went through (across) the park ; **ich schickte es durch die Post,** I sent it by post ; **durch das ganze Jahr,** throughout the whole year ; **die Stadt wurde durch ein Erdbeben zerstört,** the town was destroyed by (by means of) an earthquake ; **die Entdeckung Amerikas durch Kolumbus,** the discovery of America by Columbus.

FÜR, for, instead of, as : **dieses Geschenk ist für dich,** this present is for you ; **das können Sie für eine Mark bekommen,** you can get that for one Mark ; **für seine Jahre ist er noch sehr rüstig,** for his age he is still very vigorous ; **ich für meine Person,** I for my part ; **ich erachte es für überflüssig,** I consider it (as) superfluous ; **Schritt für Schritt,** step by step ; **Tag für Tag,** day by day ; **er sprach für sich hin,** he spoke to himself ; **ich tue es für mein Leben gern,** I like doing it above all things ; **nichts für ungut !,** no offence meant.

GEGEN, towards, to, about, against, opposed to, compared with, in exchange for, etc. : **gegen die Natur kann man nichts tun,** nothing can be done against nature ; **der Wurf war gegen die Regel,** the throw was against (contrary to) the rule ; **er starrte gegen die Decke,** he stared at the ceiling ; **er warf den Stein gegen die Wand,** he threw the stone against the wall ; **er war freundlich gegen mich,** he was friendly (kind) to me; **es waren gegen 100 Personen da**, there were about 100 people there; **gegen den Weltkrieg sind alle früheren Kriege klein**, as compared with the World War all former wars are small; **er kam gegen drei Uhr**, he came at about three o'clock.

OHNE, without: **ohne seine Hilfe hätten Sie nicht diesen Erfolg gehabt**, without his help you would not have had this success; **das ist nicht ohne**, there is a good deal to be said for it; **ohne weiteres**, without more ado.

SONDER, without, is found only in set expressions and poetry: **sonder Zweifel**, without doubt.

UM, about, around, for: **wir gingen um die Stadt (herum)**, we went round the town; **er kommt um 8 Uhr**, he comes at 8 o'clock; **er kommt um Pfingsten**, he is coming round about Whitsuntide; **er kam um das Leben**, he lost his life; **man betrog ihn um sein Geld**, he was cheated out of his money; **Aug' um Auge**, an eye for an eye; **er ist um zwei Jahre älter als ich**, he is older than I by two years; **wie steht es um ihn?**, how is it with him?; **einen Tag um den andern**, every other day; **sie sangen einer um den anderen**, they sang one after the other (in turn); **er schickte nach Hause um Hilfe**, he sent home for help.

WIDER, against: **wer nicht für mich ist, der ist wider mich**, he who is not for me is against me; **wider Willen**, against one's will. **Wider** has always the meaning of being opposed to, whereas **gegen** can be used without the idea of opposition: **er ist freundlich gegen mich**, he is kind to me.

PREPOSITIONS GOVERNING THE ACCUSATIVE OR DATIVE

The rhyme runs:

An, auf, hinter, neben, in,
Über, unter, vor und zwischen
Stehn mit dem Akkusativ,
Wenn man fragen kann: Wohin?
Mit dem Dativ stehn sie so,
Dass man nur kann fragen: Wo?

The last four lines mean : . . . stand with the Accusative when one can ask " Whither ? " They stand with the Dative when one can only ask " Where ? "

If there is motion towards a place—and hence a reply to the question " Whither ? "—the Accusative is used ; if there is rest at a place—and hence a reply to the question " Where ? "—the Dative must be used. This needs careful watching, as the following examples will show : **er kniet auf dem Boden,** he is kneeling on the ground ; **er kniet auf den Boden,** he kneels down onto the ground. In the first case there is no movement towards the ground—he is already kneeling—in the second case there is movement. **Ich schreibe am Fenster,** I am writing at the window, by the window ; **ich schreibe ans Fenster,** I write on the window ; only in the second sentence—since you put your writing onto the window—is there movement ; **ich ging im Garten auf und ab,** I walked to and fro in the garden ; **ich ging in den Garten,** I went into the garden. In the first sentence your movement is not towards the garden, but inside it ; in the second the movement is from outside towards the garden ; **ich schwamm unter die Brücke,** I swam (from above or below the bridge) under the bridge ; **ich schwamm unter der Brücke,** I swam (about) under the bridge. **Ich sitze auf dem Stuhl,** I am sitting on the chair, but **ich setze mich auf den Stuhl,** I sit down on the chair ; **ich lege das Buch auf den Tisch,** I put (lay) the book on the table, but **das Buch liegt auf dem Tisch,** the book is (lies) on the table.

Even if there is no question of place involved, the distinction still holds good, the Dative being used if the meaning is a continuation of an activity or condition already existing, the Accusative being used if the objective or direction of an activity is intended. Thus **er stürzte seinen Freund ins Unglück,** he plunged his friend into misfortune, does not refer to any actual movement but nevertheless the Accusative is used, as it is the objective of the " plunging " ; **er denkt an die Zukunft,** he thinks of the future, the future being the direction of his thoughts; **er freut sich auf ein Fest,** he looks forward to a festival (holiday), literally: he rejoices (in anticipation of) at a holiday, but **sie freut sich am Glück ihrer Kinder,** she rejoices at the happiness of her children; the Accusative shows the direction of his "rejoicing", the Dative is static, for the happiness is already in being and she rejoices at it. Similarly: **er wartet auf das Schiff** means he waits for the ship; **er wartet auf dem Schiff** means he waits on the ship; in the first case the ship is the objective of his waiting, in the second the ship is the place where he finds himself.

Let us now run through our list:

AN, at, on, by, against, to, etc.

With Dative.	With Accusative.
Er lehnt an der Wand, he leans (is leaning) against the wall (also **an die Wand** is to be found).	**Er lehnt sich an die Wand,** he leans (starts to lean) against the wall.
Ich sitze am Fenster, I am sitting at the window.	**Ich gehe ans Fenster,** I go to the window.
Ich ging an dem Hause vorbei, I went past the house. (As I walked past I happened to be by the house.)	**Ich ging an das Haus,** I went to the house.
Das Bild hängt an der Wand, the picture is hanging on the wall.	**Ich hänge das Bild an die Wand,** I hang the picture on the wall.
Mein Freund geht an meiner Seite, my friend walks at my side (his movement is not towards my side).	**Er setzte sich an meine Seite,** he sat down at my side.
Sie führte das Kind an der Hand, she led the child by the hand.	**Das Kind geht der Mutter an die Hand,** the child gives the mother a helping hand.

Dative.	Accusative.
Ich bin an der Reihe, it is my turn.	**Ich komme an die Reihe,** my turn is coming.
Am Morgen, am Abend, am Mittwoch, in the morning, in the evening, on Wednesday.	**Er arbeitet vom Morgen bis an den Abend,** he works from morning to evening.
	An die 600 Menschen waren anwesend, about 600 people were present (i.e. going on for 600 people).

AUF, on, in, at, of, by :

Dative.	Accusative.
Wir wohnen auf dem Lande, we live in the country.	**Wir gehen auf das Land,** we are going into the country.
Die Kinder spielen auf der Strasse, the children are playing in the street.	**Wir gehen auf die Strasse hinunter,** we go down into the street.
Er trägt viel auf dem Rücken, he carries much on his back.	**Auf meinen Rücken geht viel,** I have a broad back (much goes on to my back).
Er hat die Sache auf dem Herzen, he has the matter at heart.	**Die Sache fällt ihm auf das Herz,** the matter weighs on him.
Sie begegneten sich auf einem Ball, they met at a ball.	**Sie gehen oft auf Bälle,** they often go to dances.
Er befindet sich auf der Reise, he is on a journey.	**Er begibt sich auf eine Reise,** he is going on a journey.
Ich kaufte es auf dem Markt, I bought it at the market.	**Er brachte seine Waren auf den Markt,** he took his goods to the market.
	Auf diese Weise, in this way.

When it is a question of time, **auf** indicates duration or a point of time, as in: **leihen Sie mir das Buch nur auf einen Tag !**, lend me the book for a day only; **ich bin auf den Abend eingeladen,** I am invited for the evening. We could include the proverb: **auf (den) Regen folgt Sonnenschein,** sunshine follows rain. **Auf** is also used in the sense of "at", as in: **das Heer wird auf 100 000 Mann geschätzt,** the army is estimated at 100,000 men. All the above are Accusative, and in general **auf** takes the Accusative when there is no direction expressed: **ich rechne auf Sie,** I count on you; **ich verlasse mich auf ihn,** I rely on him; **ich bin neugierig auf den Ausgang,** I am curious as to the outcome; **auf die Bibel schwören,** to swear on the Bible; **er versprach auf sein Ehrenwort,** he promised on his word of honour; **auf jeden Fall,** in any case.

HINTER, behind:

Dative.	Accusative.
Der Knecht geht hinter dem Pfluge, the farm-hand walks behind the plough (his walking is not towards the plough).	**Dann trat er hinter meinen Bruder,** then he stepped behind my brother.
Er ist noch nicht trocken hinter den Ohren, he is not yet dry behind the ears, i.e. he is a greenhorn.	**Er schrieb es sich hinter die Ohren,** he wrote it behind his ears, i.e. he made a note of it, took it to heart.
Ich sah hinter mir eine verdächtige Person, I saw a suspicious individual behind me.	**Ich sah hinter mich,** I looked behind me.
Wir fanden ihn hinter der Tür, we found him behind the door.	**Er lief hinter die Tür,** he ran behind the door.

NEBEN, beside, by the side of, close to, besides :

Dative.	Accusative.
Er sass neben mir, he sat beside me.	**Er setzte sich neben mich,** he sat down beside me.
Du sollst keine andern Götter haben neben mir, thou shalt have no other gods but (besides) me.	

IN, in, into, at :

Dative.	Accusative.
Er geht im Garten, he walks (about) in the garden.	**Er geht in den Garten,** he goes into the garden.
Wir schwimmen in der See, we swim in the sea.	**Wir rudern in die See hinaus,** we row out to sea.
In aller Frühe, very early.	**Er arbeitete bis in die Nacht hinein,** he worked late into the night.
Im Herzen ist Himmel und Hölle, Heaven and Hell are in one's heart.	**Wer kann einem jeden ins Herz sehen?** who can see into everybody's heart?
Er hielt den Hut in der Hand, he held his hat in his hand.	**Er nahm das Schwert in die Hand,** he took his sword in his hand.
In einer Stunde bin ich fertig, I'll be finished (ready) in an hour.	
Er reist in der Schweiz, he is travelling in Switzerland.	**Er reist in die Alpen,** he is travelling to the Alps.
Im voraus bezahlen, to pay in advance.	**Der Krieg dauert schon in die sechzehn Jahre,** the war has lasted some sixteen years already.
	Er lebt in den Tag hinein, he lives from hand to mouth.

ÜBER, over, above, higher than :

Dative.	Accusative.
Der Vogel schwebt über dem Dach, the bird hovers over the roof (it remains above the roof as it hovers).	**Der Vogel schwebt über das Dach**, the bird (flying from elsewhere) hovers over the roof.
Über der Stadt liegt ein dichter Nebel, a dense fog lies over the town.	**der Adler erhebt sich über die Wolken**, the eagle rises above the clouds.
Er war über dem Lesen eingeschlafen, he had fallen asleep while reading.	**Er schreibt mir Briefe über Briefe**, he writes me letters after letters.
	Ich habe über einen Gulden ausgegeben, I have spent over (more than) a guilder.
	Über acht Tage werde ich zurückkommen, I will return a week hence.
	Er herrscht über das Volk, he rules over the people.
	Das geht über meine Kräfte, that is beyond my strength.
	Sie machten sich lustig über mich, they made fun of me.
	Über kurz oder lang, sooner or later.

UNTER, under, amongst, below, beneath, during :

Dative.	Accusative.
Unter diesen Umständen ist es nicht möglich, in these circumstances it is not possible.	**Er verteilte das Geld unter die Armen**, he divided the money amongst the poor.

Dative.	Accusative.
Der Hund kroch unter dem Ofen hervor, the dog crawled from under the stove.	**Der Hund kroch unter den Ofen,** the dog crawled under the stove.
Unter dieser Bedingung tue ich es nicht, I won't do it on this condition.	**Ich rechne ihn unter meine Freunde,** I count him among my friends.
Es entstand ein Streit unter ihnen, a quarrel arose amongst them.	**Er geriet unter die Räuber,** he fell amongst thieves.
Der Papierkorb steht unter dem Tisch, the waste-paper basket is under the table.	**Er schob den Korb unter den Tisch,** he pushed (shoved) the basket under the table.
Wir schliefen unter freiem Himmel, we slept out in the open.	**Wer will unter die Soldaten (gehen), der muss haben ein Gewehr** (proverb), Who wants to enlist must have a gun.

VOR, before, in front of, for, on account of, because of, etc.:

Dative.	Accusative.
Er stand vor der Tür, he stood in front of the door.	**Er trat vor die Tür,** he stepped in front of the door.
Er starb vor seinem Vater, he died before his father.	
Ich war vor drei Jahren in Berlin, I was in Berlin three years ago.	**Ich pfiff vor mich hin,** I whistled to myself.
Er flieht vor dem Feinde, he flees before the enemy.	
Er fürchtet sich vor dem Gewitter, he is afraid of the thunderstorm.	

Dative.	Accusative.
Sie konnte vor Herzklopfen nicht einschlafen, she could not get to sleep owing to palpitation of the heart.	
Sie vergeht vor Liebe, she is dying of love.	
Er sieht den Wald vor Bäumen nicht, he can't see the wood for the trees.	

ZWISCHEN, between, betwixt, among:

Er stand zwischen mir und ihm, he stood between me and him.	**Er trat zwischen mich und ihn,** he stepped between me and him.
Es ist Unkraut zwischen dem Weizen, there are tares amongst the wheat.	**Er sät Unkraut zwischen den Weizen,** he sows tares amongst the wheat.
Es ist kein Unterschied zwischen dem Bruder und der Schwester, there is no difference between the brother and the sister.	
Er sitzt zwischen zwei Stühlen, he sits between two stools.	
Er ging zwischen den Häusern hindurch, he went through between the houses (cf. **am Hause vorbeigehen**).	

That ends the prepositions; all that remains for you to do is to learn the examples by heart!

CHAPTER XX

THE INTERJECTION

Interjections—**Empfindungswörter**, sensation-words, or **Ausrufwörter**, outcall-words, exclamations—scarcely enter into the province of grammar proper, but belong rather to the dictionary. They are used to express various emotions, to attract attention, or to imitate a natural sound (like " bang ! "). Here are some of the most used :

Disgust is expressed by : **Pfui !**, shame !, fie ! ; **Pah !**, pshaw, pooh ; surprise by : **Ah !**, ah ! ; **Potztausend !**, well I never, good gracious ! ; pain by : **Ach !**, oh ! ; **Weh !**, alas !, woe ! ; **au Weh !**, that hurts ! ; joy by : **Ach !**, oh ! ; **Juchhe !** hurrah ! ; warning by : **Behüte (bewahre) Gott**, God forbid ; **Pst !**, hush ! (also used to attract somebody's attention, e.g. the waiter's) ; **Ruhig !**, silence !, be quiet ! ; **Kusch !**, lie down ! (to a dog) ; **Achtung !**, look out ! ; **Donnerwetter !**, hang it all ! (may express surprise or annoyance, etc.) ; **Schade !**, what a pity ! ; **Pech !**, hard lines ! **Na** is probably the most used interjection in the German language ; it is equivalent to : well, well then, come now, tut-tut ! ; **nanu** means : there now !, well I never ! **Plumps !** is bang ! wallop ! ; **Husch** indicates some sudden and quick movement or is used to command silence, like our sh ! ; **Bums !** is bang ! ; **bimbam !** is ding-dong !

Some of the interjections can take a Genitive : **Pfui des Verräters !**, shame on the traitor ! ; **Ach der Freude !**, oh ! the delight ! In speech **über** is usually preferred to the Genitive : **Pfui über ihn !**, shame on him !

CHAPTER XXI

WORD ORDER

ORDER OF SUBJECT AND VERB

Let us first of all examine the relative positions of the subject and the finite verb—that is to say, the inflected verb which agrees with the subject. The normal order in all statements is that the subject occupies the first place, and the finite verb the second. We can go farther than this, and say that the finite verb is fixed in the second place and it is on this fixed pivot that all the other grammatical elements of the sentence turn.

If, for the sake of emphasis, the first place is taken by any element other than the subject, then the finite verb keeps its fixed second place and the subject follows it. This is called Inverted Order. The other element which is thus brought into prominence may be an object, whether noun or pronoun, a predicative adjective or noun, an adverb, a past participle, an infinitive, a subordinate clause. Here are examples of: A. Normal Order, B. Inverted Order.

A. Normal Order.	B. Inverted Order.
Das Kind hat einen Hund.	**Einen Hund hat das Kind.**
The child has a dog.	The child has a *dog* (i.e. not a cat).
Ich habe ihn gesehen.	**Ihn habe ich gesehen.**
I have seen him (it).	He is the one I've seen.
Die Frau war kränklich.	**Kränklich war die Frau.**
The woman was sickly.	The woman was *sickly*; it was sickly that the woman was.

A. Normal Order.	B. Inverted Order.
Er erwachte ganz früh.	**Ganz früh erwachte er.**
He woke up quite early.	It was quite early that he woke up.
Ich will nicht spielen.	**Spielen will ich nicht.**
I will not play.	Play I will not.
Ich habe die Tasse zerbrochen.	**Zerbrochen habe ich die Tasse.**
I have broken the cup.	I have *broken* the cup.
Ich musste stehen bleiben, weil kein Platz frei war.	**Weil kein Platz frei war, musste ich stehen bleiben.**
I had to remain standing because there was no seat vacant.	Because there was no seat vacant I had to remain standing.

Note the next two, as in the inverted order the object pronoun (direct or indirect) always precedes the Noun subject, but not the Pronoun subject :

Der König fühlte sich sehr müde.	**Sehr müde fühlte sich der König**
The King felt very tired.	but
	Sehr müde fühlte er sich.
Der Junge folgte mir langsam.	**Langsam folgte mir der Junge,**
The boy followed me slowly.	but
	Langsam folgte er mir.

INVERTED ORDER

Inverted Order is obligatory with verbs of saying, thinking, etc., after a quotation or inserted into it :

"**Das ist meine Mutter,**" **sagte Gertrud ernst,** "That is my mother," said Gertrude seriously ; "**Das ist natürlich,**" **lachte das Mädchen,** "**weil niemand hineingeht.**", "That is natural," laughed the girl, "because nobody goes in." ; "**Aber,**" **setzte sie hinzu,** "**sprecht nicht davon.**", "But," she added, "do not speak of it." This inversion is usual when there is no actual quotation as in : **Wir haben, denke ich, genug zu essen,** we have, I think, enough to eat.

ORDER IN QUESTIONS, COMMANDS, EXCLAMATIONS

The finite verb occupies the first place in questions, commands and exclamations:

Sind Sie fertig?, are you ready?

Will er es annehmen? Is he going to accept it?

Sei ein Mann!, be a man!

Hätte ich nur Zeit genug! If I only had time enough!

War ich entäuscht! Was I disappointed!

Ist sie aber schön! Isn't she lovely!

Behüte Gott!, God forbid!

In exclamations in the 3rd person normal order is also usual: **Gott behüte!** and in the 3rd person of the Subjunctive used as an Imperative it is the natural order: **er komme sofort!**, let him come at once.

THE FINITE VERB AND ITS CLOSE DEPENDENTS

The finite verb, we have seen, normally occupies the second place; let us now see where the elements most intimately bound up with the finite verb go—namely, the past participle, infinitive, separable particle, predicative adjective or noun. Since they are all essential to the meaning, they will be stressed, and will go to the end of the sentence, which is, in German, the most important place. Here are examples of end-position:

Past Participle.

1. **Er hat mir einen Brief geschrieben**, he has written me a letter.

One Infinitive.

2. **Er wird mir einen Brief schreiben**, he will write me a letter.

Two Infinitives.

3. **Er wird mir einen Brief schreiben sollen,** he will have to write me a letter.

Three Infinitives.

4. **Er hätte mir einen Brief schreiben lassen sollen,** he ought to have had a letter written to me.

An Infinitive and Past Participle.

5. **Er soll in Amerika gestorben sein,** he is said to have died in America.

Predicative Adjective or Noun.

6. **Mein Freund war vor einer Woche krank,** my friend was ill a week ago.

Er wurde im Jahre 1939 Soldat, he became a soldier in 1939.

Separable Prefix.

7. **Wir kamen gestern in Hamburg an,** we arrived yesterday at Hamburg.

THE FINITE VERB IN A SUBORDINATE CLAUSE

We have already seen (p. 164) that in subordinate clauses the finite verb falls to the end: **er hat mir einen Brief geschrieben,** but: **weil er mir einen Brief geschrieben hat.** If, however, there are two, or three, infinitives; or an infinitive and a past participle, then the finite verb precedes them, unless it is a modal auxiliary: this still falls to the end. Thus in the examples 3, 4, and 5 above we get:

Principal Clause.	Subordinate Clause.
3. **Er wird mir einen Brief schreiben sollen.**	. . . **weil er mir einen Brief wird schreiben sollen.**
4. **Er hätte mir einen Brief schreiben lassen sollen.**	. . . **weil er mir einen Brief hätte schreiben lassen sollen.**
5. **Er soll in Amerika gestorben sein.**	. . . **weil er in Amerika gestorben sein soll.**

You will, however, frequently find that the finite verb does not fall to the end of the subordinate clause, especially in colloquial German or when a non-essential element of the sentence is added as a sort of after-thought: **als ich ihn dann wiedersah in seinem Elend,** when I saw him again in his misery; **ich entsinne mich, dass ich verlegen wurde über diese Frage,** I remember that I was embarrassed at this question. The laws of grammar are not like those of the Medes and Persians and, besides, it may well be that German is gradually tending to shift the finite verb closer to the subject. Languages are continually in a state of flux, and German is no exception to this rule.

ORDER OF OBJECTS AND ADVERBS

We have seen that the words most closely connected with the finite verb fall to the end of the principal clause. The position immediately before these end-words is taken by the objects (in Accusative or Dative case) and the adverbs. There is, however, a great deal of freedom left to the individual speaker or writer, according as one idea may need to be emphasized over another, so that one cannot lay down absolutely hard-and-fast rules about the word order. The overall rule is that the unimportant word comes before the important word, the unemphatic before the emphatic. Let us examine the relative positions of: Nouns and Pronouns and Adverbs.

Relative Order of Noun and Pronoun Objects

1. If the verb has two Accusatives, like **lehren,** to teach, the person object will precede the thing object: **ich lehre meinen Jungen das Schreiben,** I teach my boy writing.

2. If the thing object is a pronoun it precedes the noun object: **ich lehre es meinen Jungen.**

3. If both objects are pronouns the person comes last: **ich lehre es ihn.**

4. If the verb takes a Dative and an Accusative and both

are nouns, the Dative precedes the Accusative : **ich schrieb meinem Freund einen Brief,** I wrote my friend a letter ; **er schickte seiner Mutter das Geld,** he sent his mother the money.

5. If the Dative is a pronoun and the Accusative a noun, the Dative again precedes the Accusative : **ich schrieb ihm einen Brief; ich schickte ihr das Geld.**

6. If both the Dative and the Accusative are personal pronouns (and I include under personal pronouns those referring to inanimate objects), then the Accusative precedes the Dative : **ich schrieb ihm den Brief** becomes **ich schrieb ihn ihm** (but **ich schrieb ihm denselben**) ; **ich schickte ihr die Rose** becomes **ich schickte sie ihr; ich gab Ihnen die Bücher** becomes **ich gab sie Ihnen.** This order is not rigid, and with short pronouns like **mir, dir,** the order with **es** may be : **er gab es mir** or **er gab mir's.** In fact, the order is pretty loose, and varies with the dialect spoken.

Relative Order of the Adverbs

We had better start with a " don't " rule : do not, as in English, put the adverb between the subject and the finite verb : he always gets up early, **er steht immer früh auf;** she often visits her friends, **sie besucht oft ihre Freundinnen;** they seldom see their son, **sie sehen selten ihren Sohn.** Note that these, and other, short adverbs come generally close behind the finite verb.

The relative order of the adverbs is : (1) adverbs of time, (2) adverbs of place, (3) adverbs of manner, cause, etc. When there are two adverbs of time, the more general precedes the more particular : **ich komme morgen um 8 Uhr; er wird heute abend hier sein.**

Here is an example of the above order : **der Junge wird nächste Woche in der Schule tüchtig arbeiten müssen,** the boy will have to work hard in school next week. Of course this order is pretty fluid, and depends on what idea the speaker wishes to emphasize ; for instance, if he wants to bring out " in the school ", he can start the sentence with it: **in der Schule wird der Junge . . .**; or he can stress it by putting it farther back in the sentence: **der Junge wird nächste Woche tüchtig in der Schule arbeiten müssen.**

Here is another example: **der Dampfer ist gestern in den Hafen wegen des Sturmes eingelaufen,** the steamer put into the harbour yesterday owing to the storm. There you have the order: Time—Place—Cause. But since **in den Hafen** and **eingelaufen** are very intimately connected in sense, it would be more natural to say: **der Dampfer ist gestern wegen des Sturmes in den Hafen eingelaufen.**

Taking it all in all, we can say that adverb order is fluid, but that Time precedes Place, and that emphasis is an overriding factor.

Relative Order of Objects and Adverbs

Since the noun object is, in general, more important to the sense than the adverb, it will come later in the sentence than the latter: **ich mache jeden Abend regelmässig meine Aufgaben,** I do my exercises regularly every evening; **wir besitzen seit zwanzig Jahren ein Haus in der Königstrasse** we have owned a house in King Street for 20 years. Of course, **in der Königstrasse** comes after **ein Haus** because it qualifies it, and has nothing to do with the verb **besitzen.** Again I must warn you that this order is not rigid, and depends on what stress the speaker wishes to put on any particular idea. Thus **ich trinke nach dem Abendessen Tee** is a plain statement of fact: I drink tea after dinner; but if I want to draw attention to the fact that it is tea (not coffee) that I drink, then I juggle with the word-order: **ich trinke Tee nach dem Abendessen.** But, as a pronoun—which of course refers to something already mentioned—is unemphatic, it will precede the adverb: **ich mache sie jeden abend,** I do them every evening; **wir besitzen es seit zwanzig Jahren,** we have owned it for twenty years.

I warned you above about short adverbs; now I have to

give another warning : in short sentences we often find the adverb coming after the noun object : **ich kaufte das Buch gestern,** I bought the book yesterday ; **ich las die Zeitung sehr flüchtig,** I read the paper very hastily.

Place of the Negative

Nicht and other negative adverbs which qualify the verb or the whole clause usually fall to the end of the sentence : **er schickte mir das Geld nicht,** he did not send me the money. Of course the past participle, infinitive, separable prefix, predicative adjective or noun will take their usual place at the end : **er hat mir das Geld nicht geschickt** ; **er wird mir das Geld nicht schicken.** In all other cases **nicht** immediately precedes the word it qualifies : **er kommt nicht heute, sondern morgen, er** comes not today but tomorrow.

Do not get depressed about this word-order business : it sounds very abstruse and complicated but, in fact, it is just plain common sense and rule of thumb, or rather rule of ear. You must not learn the rule by heart, but the example, and thus you will gradually get a feeling for the correct natural position of the various grammatical elements in a sentence. Just think what a frightening description a phonetician would make of all the movements of the tongue, lips, vocal cords, jaws, lungs, etc., needed when you say " How's your father ? " not to mention the delicate rise and fall of the voice, known as " intonation " ! If you were presented with that scientific analysis alone, you would exclaim : " It's impossible for me to execute all those delicate operations, I just can't do it." And yet a little child never hesitates over such a sentence as " How's your father ? " Of course not ; he just doesn't know how difficult it is. He follows the rule of ear. You must learn, as he does, by accumulating in your memory and your muscles the run of the words, the tune of the sentences, the swing of the rhythms, but, as you have a need for the soothing guidance of reason—which he has not—you must study your grammar, which sets out in orderly fashion the phenomena of the language. Let your slogan be: "Practice makes perfect." The Germans have a word for it, indeed they have several: **Übung macht den Meister,** practice makes the master; **Übung bringt Erfahrung, Erfahrung kann's allein,** practice brings experience, experience alone can do it; **Übung bringt Kunst, Kunst bringt Ehren,** practice brings art, art brings honours. Learning a language is exactly like learning an art: you can never paint a picture or compose a piece of music by conning the rules; you can only achieve that by practice—and of course a bit of genius is useful! The difference between the true artist and the linguist is that the former creates new ideas, conceptions, views; the latter is a mere copyist, and anything really original that he creates in a language (especially a foreign language) is *ipso facto* wrong and bad.

APPENDIX A

LIST OF PRINCIPAL GERMAN STRONG AND IRREGULAR VERBS

Verbs marked with an asterisk are conjugated with *sein*.

Infinitive.	3rd Sing. Pres. Indic.	1st and 3rd Sing. Impf. Indic.	Past Participle.	English.
backen	bäckt	buk	gebacken	bake
befehlen	befiehlt	befahl	befohlen	command
beginnen	beginnt	begann	begonnen	begin
beissen	beisst	biss	gebissen	bite
bergen	birgt	barg	geborgen	hide
betrügen	betrügt	betrog	betrogen	deceive
bewegen	bewegt	bewog	bewogen	induce
biegen	biegt	bog	gebogen	bend
bieten	bietet	bot	geboten	offer
binden	bindet	band	gebunden	bind
bitten	bittet	bat	gebeten	request
blasen	bläst	blies	geblasen	blow
*bleiben	bleibt	blieb	geblieben	remain
brechen	bricht	brach	gebrochen	break
brennen	brennt	brannte	gebrannt	burn
bringen	bringt	brachte	gebracht	bring
denken	denkt	dachte	gedacht	think
*dringen	dringt	drang	gedrungen	press
empfehlen	(as befehlen)			recommend
*erlöschen	erlischt	erlosch	erloschen	get extinguished
erschrecken	erschrickt	erschrak	erschrocken	be terrified
essen	isst	ass	gegessen	eat
*fahren	fährt	fuhr	gefahren	go
*fallen	fällt	fiel	gefallen	fall
finden	findet	fand	gefunden	find
*fliegen	fliegt	flog	geflogen	fly
fressen	frisst	frass	gefressen	eat (of animals)

Infinitive.	3rd Sing. Pres. Indic.	1st and 3rd Sing. Impf. Indic.	Past Participle.	English.
frieren	friert	fror	gefroren	freeze
geben	gibt	gab	gegeben	give
*gehen	geht	ging	gegangen	go
*gelingen	gelingt	gelang	gelungen	succeed
gelten	gilt	galt	gegolten	be worth
*genesen	genest	genas	genesen	recover
geniessen	geniesst	genoss	genossen	enjoy
*geschehen	geschieht	geschah	geschehen	happen
gewinnen	gewinnt	gewann	gewonnen	win
giessen	giesst	goss	gegossen	pour
gleichen	gleicht	glich	geglichen	resemble
*gleiten	gleitet	glitt	geglitten	glide
graben	gräbt	grub	gegraben	dig
greifen	greift	griff	gegriffen	grasp
halten	hält	hielt	gehalten	hold
hangen	hängt	hing	gehangen	hang
heben	hebt	hob	gehoben	lift
heissen	heisst	hiess	geheissen	to be named
helfen	hilft	half	geholfen	help
kennen	kennt	kannte	gekannt	know
klingen	klingt	klang	geklungen	sound
*kommen	kommt	kam	gekommen	come
laden	lädt	lud	geladen	load
lassen	lässt	liess	gelassen	let, allow
*laufen	läuft	lief	gelaufen	run
leiden	leidet	litt	gelitten	suffer
leihen	leiht	lieh	geliehen	lend
lesen	liest	las	gelesen	read
liegen	liegt	lag	gelegen	lie
lügen	lügt	log	gelogen	tell a lie
meiden	meidet	mied	gemieden	avoid
messen	misst	mass	gemessen	measure
nehmen	nimmt	nahm	genommen	take
nennen	nennt	nannte	genannt	name
preisen	preist	pries	gepriesen	praise
raten	rät	riet	geraten	advise
reiben	reibt	rieb	gerieben	rub
reissen	reisst	riss	gerissen	tear
*reiten	reitet	ritt	geritten	ride
*rennen	rennt	rannte	gerannt	run

Infinitive.	3rd Sing. Pres. Indic.	1st and 3rd Sing. Impf. Indic.	Past Participle.	English.
riechen	riecht	roch	gerochen	smell
ringen	ringt	rang	gerungen	wrestle
*rinnen	rinnt	rann	geronnen	flow
rufen	ruft	rief	gerufen	call
schaffen	schafft	schuf	geschaffen	create
scheiden	scheidet	schied	geschieden	separate
scheinen	scheint	schien	geschienen	shine, seem
schieben	schiebt	schob	geschoben	push
schiessen	schiesst	schoss	geschossen	shoot
schlafen	schläft	schlief	geschlafen	sleep
schlagen	schlägt	schlug	geschlagen	beat
schliessen	schliesst	schloss	geschlossen	shut
schneiden	schneidet	schnitt	geschnitten	cut
schreiben	schreibt	schrieb	geschrieben	write
schreien	schreit	schrie	geschrieen	cry
*schreiten	schreitet	schritt	geschritten	stride
schweigen	schweigt	schwieg	geschwiegen	be silent
*schwellen	schwillt	schwoll	geschwollen	swell
*schwimmen	schwimmt	schwamm	geschwommen	swim
schwingen	schwingt	schwang	geschwungen	swing
schwören	schwört	schwor	geschworen	swear
sehen	sieht	sah	gesehen	see
senden	sendet	sandte	gesandt	send
singen	singt	sang	gesungen	sing
*sinken	sinkt	sank	gesunken	sink
sitzen	sitzt	sass	gesessen	sit
sprechen	spricht	sprach	gesprochen	speak
*springen	springt	sprang	gesprungen	spring
stehen	steht	stand	gestanden	stand
stehlen	stiehlt	stahl	gestohlen	steal
*steigen	steigt	stieg	gestiegen	ascend
*sterben	stirbt	starb	gestorben	die
stossen	stösst	stiess	gestossen	push
streichen	streicht	strich	gestrichen	stroke
streiten	streitet	stritt	gestritten	quarrel
tragen	trägt	trug	getragen	carry
treffen	trifft	traf	getroffen	hit, meet
treiben	treibt	trieb	getrieben	drive
*treten	tritt	trat	getreten	tread
trinken	trinkt	trank	getrunken	drink

Infinitive.	3rd Sing. Pres. Indic.	1st and 3rd Sing. Impf. Indic.	Past Participle.	English.
tun	tut	tat	getan	do
verderben	verdirbt	verdarb	verdorben	spoil
vergessen	vergisst	vergass	vergessen	forget
verlieren	verliert	verlor	verloren	lose
*verschwinden	verschwindet	verschwand	verschwunden	disappear
verzeihen	verzeiht	verzieh	verziehen	forgive
*wachsen	wächst	wuchs	gewachsen	grow
wägen	wägt	wog	gewogen	weigh
waschen	wäscht	wusch	gewaschen	wash
*weichen	weicht	wich	gewichen	yield
weisen	weist	wies	gewiesen	point
wenden	wendet	wandte	gewandt	turn
werben	wirbt	warb	geworben	woo
werfen	wirft	warf	geworfen	throw
wiegen	wiegt	wog	gewogen	weigh
winden	windet	wand	gewunden	wind
wissen	weiss	wusste	gewusst	know
ziehen	zieht	zog	gezogen	draw
zwingen	zwingt	zwang	gezwungen	force

APPENDIX B

THE GERMAN ALPHABET

English	German Characters	
	Printed	Written
A a (ä)	𝔄 𝔞 (𝔞̈)	A a
B b	𝔅 𝔟	B b
C c	ℭ 𝔠	C c
D d	𝔇 𝔡	D d
E e	𝔈 𝔢	E e
F f	𝔉 𝔣	F f
G g	𝔊 𝔤	G g
H h	ℌ 𝔥	H h
I i	ℑ 𝔦	I i
J j	𝔍 𝔧	J j
K k	𝔎 𝔨	K k
L l	𝔏 𝔩	L l
M m	𝔐 𝔪	M m

English	German Characters	
	Printed	Written
N n	𝔑 𝔫	
O o (ö)	𝔒 𝔬 (𝔬̈)	
P p	𝔓 𝔭	
Q q	𝔔 𝔮	
R r	ℜ 𝔯	
S s	*𝔖 ſ ß 𝔰	
T t	𝔗 𝔱	
U u (ü)	𝔘 𝔲 (𝔲̈)	
V v	𝔙 𝔳	
W w	𝔚 𝔴	
X x	𝔛 𝔵	
Y y	𝔜 𝔶	
Z z	ℨ 𝔷	

* *See Note overleaf.*

* Note.—The capital letter S is, of course, only used initially and is pronounced like our z in zeal.

The ſ is used initially, as in ſonnig, ſehen, and in the interior of a word after vowels or l, m, n, r, as in leſen, weiſe. In both cases it is pronounced like our z. It is also used in the interior of a word after other consonants than l, m, n, r, as in Ochſe, Erbſe, and is then pronounced like our s in soap. It is used in combination with p and t belonging to the stem of the word, and is pronounced shp and sht when initial, as in ſpät, ſtimmen; when in the interior of a word, as in Knoſpe, Kaſten, it is pronounced sp and st as in English.

The s is used at the end of a word or a stem syllable, as in Gans, Hänschen, and in compound words like Vaterlandsliebe, being pronounced like our s in both cases.

The ß is always pronounced like our s; it is used in the interior of a word after a long vowel, as in grüßen, reißen, and at the end of a word or stem syllable and before a t, as in Gruß, Fluß, mußt.

The ſſ is always pronounced as our s in soap and is found only in the interior of a word after a short vowel, as in Flüſſe, Gaſſe, Hinderniſſe.

In our *Grammar* we have printed the German examples in Roman characters and we have used "s" and "ss" instead of the various letters given above.

GERMAN PRONUNCIATION

We give below a short simple guide to German pronunciation, giving the nearest English sound to the German one in order to help the beginner. It should be remembered that this is only an approximation, as no two sounds in different languages are really exactly alike, e.g. the German t is much more "breathy" than the usual English t. The learner should, as advised in Chapter I, study the sounds on gramophone records.

There is one point which must be stressed, namely that

German vowels when initial are pronounced with an explosion of the breath which is suddenly released. This is called the Glottal Stop and is a striking feature of German, giving it a sort of sergeant-major hammer-beat as the explosion bites off the words. In English we run the words together, as in oneandall or oneanall; in German the Glottal Stop separates the words and einundachtzig is pronounced ?ein?und?achtzig, the ? representing the Glottal Stop. This Stop is found in many English and Scottish dialects, e.g. the Glasgow bu.er for butter.

Letters.	*Description.*
a	As *a* in father.
ai, ay	As *i* in fine.
au	As *ow* in fowl.
ä	Short, as *e* in get; long, as *a* in gate.
äu	As *oy* in coy.
b	As in English, but pronounced *p* when final.
c	As *ts* in waits before **i, e, ü, ö, ä**; as *k* elsewhere.
ch	As *ch* in Scottish loch after **a, o, u, au**; as an exaggerated *h* in hue after **i, e, ü, ö, ä**.
d	As in English, but pronounced *t* when final.
e	When short, as *e* in get; when long (also spelt **eh** and **ee**), like the long close *é* in French *passé* or like Northern English and Scottish *a* in cake; when unaccented, like *a* in about.
ei, ey	Same value as **ai** and **ay** above.
eu	Same value as **äu** above.
f	As in English.
g	As *g* in English gape; when final, it is pronounced like the *ch* in Scottish loch after **a, o, u, au** and like *h* in hue elsewhere.
h	Aspirated as the *h* in half.
i	When short, as *i* in fit; when long (also spelt **ih, ie, ieh**), as *i* in machine.
j	As *y* in you.

Letters.	*Description.*
k	As in English. ck = *kk.* In kn the *k* is pronounced.
l	As *l* in long; never as the second *l* in little.
m	As in English.
n	As in English.
o	When short, as *o* in not; when long, as Northern English and Scottish *o* in no.
ö	When short, like *eu* in French *leur*, i.e. the *ir* sound in sir pronounced with the lips pouted; when long, like *eu* in French *feu*, i.e. a close e pronounced with the lips pouted.
p	As in English; in pf both the *p* and the *f* are sounded; ph = *f.*
qu	As *kv.*
r	Rolled on the tongue as in Scotland or on the uvula as in the Northumbrian "burr".
s	See under "Alphabet".
sch	As *sh* in shoot.
sp and st	As *shp* and *sht* (see under "Alphabet") when initial.
t, th, dt	As *t* in English.
tz	As *ts* in waits.
u	When short, as *u* in put; when long (spelt also uh), as *oo* in rood.
ü	As French *u* in *lu*, i.e. pronounce "lee" with the lips well pouted.
v	As *f* in English.
w	As *v* in English.
x	As English *x* in wax.
y	As German ü in words loaned from Greek; as German i in other words.
z	As *ts* in waits.

APPENDIX C

CAPITAL LETTERS

A few short rules on this point will be useful:

1. All nouns or other parts of speech used as nouns have a capital letter: **das Glas; das Aber; der Blinde; das Trinken; etwas Neues.**

2. Adjectives with the definite article used as part of a title need the capital: **Karl der Grosse; Wilhelm der Dritte.**

3. Adjectives in **-er** (which are indeclinable) derived from the names of towns and those in **-sch** or **-isch** derived from the names of persons keep the capital letter: **Berlin, die Berliner Zeitung; Grimm, das Grimmsche Wörterbuch;** but **die britische Flotte; die italienische Armee.**

4. The 2nd person **Sie** in all its cases, together with its possessive adjectives and pronouns, requires the capital.

5. In letters all words used to designate the person addressed take a capital: **Du, Ihr, Euch, Dein,** etc.; also all titles of the person addressed: **Gnädiger Herr,** Sir, My Lord; **Ew. Wohlgeboren,** Your Honour.

DIVISION OF SYLLABLES

In English you divide a word that overflows a line pretty much as you please, so long as you do not destroy the look of the word. Thus you would divide "stocking" into stock-ing, but not into sto-cking, or stoc-king, or stocki-ng. In German you have definite rules to guide you. Here they are:

1. When dividing a word at the end of a line, the syllable carried over must, if possible, begin with a consonant: **tö-ten; Rei-ter; Ret-ter; kämp-fen; ge-ben; Pin-sel.**

2. The following groups of consonants are indivisible: **ch, ph, sch, st, ss, th: Lö-cher; lö-schen; be-ste; sech-ste.**

3. When **ck** is divided it becomes **k-k: Bäcker** becomes **Bäk-ker.**

4. Compounds are broken up into their constituent parts: **gegen-über; her-ein; an-kommen.**

5. It is not considered elegant to divide a word too near its beginning or too close to its end: **Aberglaube** should not become **A-berglaube,** but **Aber-glaube; totmüde** not **totmü-de,** but **tot-müde.**

6. Vowels may be divided only if they are pronounced separately: **Jubilä-um.**

LENGTH OF VOWELS

Perhaps a few rules will be helpful in guiding you on this point, which often puzzles the beginner. There is not much real difficulty.

Long Vowels

1. All vowels, except **-e,** terminating a word are long: **da, wo, so;** all diphthongs are long.

2. Vowels followed by a single consonant are generally long: **Tag, Hut, kamen, Lid** (eyelid), **lügen, haben.** But see 1 below.

3. Length may be shown by an **h** added to the vowel: **Wahl; lehren; Kuh; Sohn; gähnen; Mühe.** Note that this **h** is silent, although you will find it pronounced in words like **gehen** by not very well educated Germans who want to impress people with their culture!

4. A doubled vowel is long: **Aal; Haar; Beere; Heer; Boot; Kaffee.** If modified, the vowel becomes single: **das Härchen,** little hair.

5. The digraph **ie** is always long in an accented syllable: **Lied; lieben; Akademie.** In an unaccented syllable it is pronounced like German **je: Familie** is pronounced as if it were written **famílje,** the acute accent showing the accented syllable.

Short Vowels

1. Vowels are short in monosyllables ending in a single consonant if the word is uninflected: **ab, in, man, mit, ob, um, zum, zur, an, von.** Some inflected words are also in this class: **bin; hat; das; der; des; was; es.**

2. A double consonant shortens the preceding vowel: **Affe; Egge; fallen; still; voll; Hammer; komme; Mann; Sonne; murren; Wasser; besser; Schüssel; glatt; Bett; Stock; nass. Ch** and **sch** generally shorten the vowel: **ich, mich, dich; Sache; Asche; Fisch;** but the vowel is long in **Sprache, bloss, gross.**

3. The vowel is short when followed by a group of two or more consonants: **Halm; alt; Stern; warf; starb; hart; kämpfen; Lust; Rost.**

4. Unaccented vowels are short: **Gárten; Hérrin.**

APPENDIX D

EXERCISES

Exercises in grammar usually take the form of sentences illustrating a particular point to be translated into and out of the language. They are boring, and they usually have a strong flavour of the dear old "pen-of-the-gardener's-aunt" about them, because the sentences have to be invented to illustrate the point of grammar. They are divorced from language which is a means of communication, a source of pleasure, and not a code.

Moreover, these exercises practise much that is useless or unusual. You need to practise, and to practise thoroughly, those forms—declensions, cases, tenses, moods, etc.—which are most frequently met with, and not bother with oddities. How can this be done without boredom?

To solve this problem I have taken a delightful tale by Wilhelm Hauff, "The Story of Caliph Stork", and set it down in two columns: in the left column the German text, but with all the verbs in the infinitive in brackets, and all the nouns, pronouns, adjectives and all other similarly inflected words with a dash instead of the inflexion. Thus automatically we get the grammatical points proportionate to the frequency of their occurrence in the language, and at the same time we have a text worth reading which will keep our attention. In the right-hand column I have given a fairly literal translation into English, so that you can see the meaning of the German, and therefore know what tenses, cases, etc., etc., you must use.

This may sound complicated, but if you will read on you will find an example worked out below, and the matter will become clear.

There are just a few explanations I must give here :

Key: The key is the full text of the German with the brackets and dashes worked out. Consult it when in difficulties.

Verbs: All the verbs are in brackets and are in the infinitive. If they are of the weak conjugation they are followed by *w*, e.g. (**rauchen** *w*). If there is no *w* the verbs are strong or irregular.

Separable verbs have a stroke dividing the prefix from the verb, e.g. (**aus/sprechen**), and it is left to you to put the prefix in its correct place in the sentence.

If the verb is followed by *!* it is either a subjunctive or an imperative, not an indicative, as shown in the examples worked out below.

Nouns: All nouns are followed by *m* for masculine, *f* for feminine, and *n* for neuter if singular and, if plural, by *mp*, *fp*, *np*. In both cases the noun itself is given in the singular, e.g. **mit d- Fuss** *m* = **mit dem Fuss,** but **mit d- Fuss-** *mp !* = **mit den Füssen,** the *!* indicating that the plural either has an umlaut or is otherwise tricky.

All inflexions are replaced by a dash, e.g. **ein alt- Krämer** *m* **stand an d- Tür d- Schloss-** *n* = An old pedlar stood at the door of the castle ; hence the full German text is : **ein altER Krämer stand an dER Tür dES SchlossES.**

One last word : derivatives of strong verbs, e.g. **ergehen,** will not be found in the list of Strong Verbs in this Grammar ; you will have to look up the parent verb, i.e. in this case " **gehen** ".

And now to the task !

Let us first of all work through the verbs in paragraph 1 of Section I, and thus see what our problems are.

Der Kalif von Bagdad (sitzen).	The Caliph of B. was sitting.

Der Kalif von Bagdad sass.

Evidently we must have the Imperfect Tense and the verb must agree with its subject " **Der Kalif** " = " **sass** ".

er (haben) ein wenig (schlafen).	He had slept a little.
er hatte ein wenig geschlafen.	

" **Haben** " must be Imperfect Tense and agree with " **er** " = " **hatte** "; " **schlafen** " must be the Past Participle = " **geschlafen** ".

denn es (sein) ein heiss– Tag.	For it was a hot day.
denn es war ein heiss– Tag.	

" **Sein** " must be Imperfect and agree with " **es** " = " **war** ".

und (aus/sehen) nach sein– Schläfchen heiter.	And looked cheerful after his nap.
und sah nach sein– Schläfchen heiter aus.	

" **Aussehen** " must be Imperfect and agree with " **er** ", but " **aussehen** " is separable and hence the " **aus** " must fall to the end of this principal clause.

Er (rauchen *w*) aus ein– lang– Pfeife.	He smoked out of a long pipe.
Er rauchte aus ein– lang– Pfeife.	

" **Rauchen** " must be Imperfect of the weak conjugation = " **rauchte** ".

(trinken) hie und da ein wenig Kaffee *m*.	Drank now and then a little coffee.
trank hie und da ein wenig Kaffee.	

Again the Imperfect = " **trank** ".

d– ih– ein schwarz– Sklave (ein/schenken *w*).

Which a black slave poured out for him.

d– ih– ein schwarz– Sklave einschenkte.

" **Einschenken** " must be Imperfect and agree with the subject " **Sklave** ", and as it is separable but falls at the end of the subordinate clause it fuses = " **einschenkte** ".

und (streichen) sich vergnügt d– Bart.

And stroked his beard contentedly.

und strich sich vergnügt d– Bart.

Again the Imperfect = " **strich** ".

In paragraph 4 we have a subjunctive :

D– Kalif, d– schon lange gern sein– Grosswesir ein– Freude (machen *w*) (haben *!*).

The Caliph, who for a long time past would-have willingly given (made) his Grand Vizier pleasure.

D– Kalif, d– schon lange gern sein– Grosswesir ein– Freude gemacht hätte.

" **Machen** " is the Past Participle = " **gemacht** ", and " **haben** " must be the Past Subjunctive = " **hätte** ". Note the *!* after " **haben** ".

In paragraph 8 we have an imperative :

(Sagen *!*), was drin (stehen).

Say what is (= stands) in it.

Sage, was drin steht.

Evidently " **sagen** " must be either " **sage !** " (**du**) ; " **sagt** " (**ihr**), or " **sagen Sie !** ". Here it is " **sage !** "; only " **du** " and " **ihr** " are used in this story. " **Stehen** " is Present Tense.

Now let us try the declensions of nouns, adjectives, pronouns, etc.

einmal an ein– schön– Nachmittag *m* behaglich auf sein– Sofa *n*.	Once on a fine afternoon comfortably on his sofa.

" **An** " takes the Dative here as there is no " movement towards " ; **Nachmittag** is masculine. Thus we have the Dative, masculine singular of the mixed declension of the adjective and the Dative masculine singular of the indefinite article " **ein** ".

an einem schönen Nachmittag auf seinem Sofa.

" **Auf** " here takes the Dative and **Sofa** is neuter.

denn es war ein heiss– Tag *m*.	For it was a hot day.
denn es war ein heisser Tag.	

" **Tag** " is masculine and it is the subject. " **Heiss** " is masculine Nominative, mixed declension.

aus ein– lang– Pfeife *f*.	Out of a long pipe.
aus einer langen Pfeife.	

" **Aus** " takes the Dative and " **Pfeife** " is feminine ; it is the mixed declension.

ein wenig Kaffee *m*, d– ih– ein schwarz– Sklave einschenkte.	A little coffee which a black slave poured out for him.
ein wenig Kaffee, den ihm ein schwarzer Sklave einschenkte.	

The relative pronoun " **d–** " is the object and hence Accusative masculine to agree with **Kaffee** = " **den** " ; the personal pronoun " **ih–** " is Dative = **ihm** ; " **Sklave** " is masculine Nominative, so the declension is mixed = " **ein schwarzer Sklave** ".

und strich sich vergnügt d– Bart *m*.	And stroked his beard contentedly.
und strich sich vergnügt den Bart.	

“ **Bart** ” is masculine accusative = “ **den Bart** ”.

You will find that I throw in little problems of all sorts to keep you concentrated on the text and to vary the torture. Remember that you will learn more German grammar by yourself digging it out of texts than by passing hours going over your grammar book. Learn to pick up your grammar as you read : every text contains examples of every grammatical point dealt with in any grammar, and all you have to do is to think about it and worry over it as you enjoy the tale. It spoils the tale? No, it does not. Is a musician's joy in a piece of music spoilt by his noting, as he hears it, all the technical points? No, on the contrary, it is enhanced; so will yours be if you make a hobby of watching the grammar as you read. Good reading !

EXERCISES

Die Geschichte von Kalif Storch.	The Story of Caliph Stork.

I.

1. **Der Kalif von Bagdad (sitzen) einmal an ein– schön– Nachmittag** *m* **behaglich auf sein– Sofa** *n*; **er (haben) ein wenig (schlafen), denn es (sein) ein heiss– Tag** *m*, **und (aus/sehen) nach sein– Schläfchen** *n* **heiter. Er (rauchen** *w*) **aus ein–**	The Caliph of Bagdad once on a fine afternoon was sitting comfortably on his sofa; he had slept a little, for it was a hot day, and looked cheerful after his nap. He smoked (out of) a long pipe, drank now and then a little coffee, which a black

lang– Pfeife *f*, (trinken) hie und da ein wenig Kaffee *m*, d– ih– ein schwarz– Sklave *m* (ein/schenken *w*), und (streichen) sich vergnügt d– Bart *m*.

slave poured out for him, and stroked his beard contentedly.

2. An dies– Nachmittag *m* (kommen) sein Grosswesir Mansor, d– aber sehr nachdenklich (aus/sehen), ganz gegen seine Gewohnheit *f*. D– Kalif (tun) sein– Pfeife *f* ein wenig aus d– Mund *m* und (sprechen): " Warum (machen *w*) du ein so nachdenklich– Gesicht *n*, Grosswesir ? "

On this afternoon came his Grand Vizier Mansor, who however looked very thoughtful, quite contrary to his custom. The Caliph took (= did) his pipe out of his mouth a little and said: " Why dost thou make such a thoughtful face, Grand Vizier ? "

3. D– Grosswesir (schlagen) seine Arm– *mp* kreuzweis über d– Brust *f*, (verneigen *w*) sich vor sein– Herr– *m* und (antworten *w*): " Herr! ob ich ein nachdenklich– Gesicht *n* (machen *w*), (wissen) ich nicht; aber unten an d– Tür *f* (stehen) ein alt– Krämer *m*, d– so schön– Sache– *fp* (haben), dass es mi– (ärgern *w*) nicht viel überflüssig– Geld *n* zu (haben)."

The Grand Vizier crossed his arms over his breast, bowed (himself) before his master, and answered: " Lord ! whether I am making a thoughtful face, I do not know ; but downstairs at the door stands an old pedlar who has such lovely things that it annoys me to have not much superfluous money."

4. D– Kalif, d– sein– Grosswesir schon lange gern ein– Freude *f* (machen *w*) (haben *!*), (schicken *w*) sein– schwarz-Sklave– *m* (hinunter

The Caliph, who for a long time past would-have willingly given (made) pleasure to his Vizier, sent his black slave down in order to fetch

or herunter ?), um d– alt– Krämer *m* (herauf– *or* hin-aufzuholen ?). Bald (zu-rück/kommen) d– Sklave *m* mit d– Krämer *m*. Dies– (tra-gen) ein– Kasten *m*, in welch– er allerhand Ware– *fp* (haben): Perle– *fp*, Ring– *mp*, Pistole– *fp*, Becher *mp* und Kamm– *mp* !

the old pedlar up. Soon the slave came back with the pedlar. The latter carried a box in which he had all sorts of goods : pearls, rings, pis-tols, beakers, and combs.

5. D– Kalif und sein Wesir (durch/mustern *w*) alles, und d– Kalif (kaufen *w*) endlich für sich und Man-sor schön– Pistole– *fp*, für d– Frau *f* d– Wesir– *m* aber ein– Kamm *m*. Als d– Krämer sein– Kasten *m* wieder zu-machen (wollen), (sehen) d– Kalif ein– klein– Schublade *f* und (fragen *w*), ob da auch noch Ware– *fp* (sein *!*) ?

The Caliph and his Vizier examined everything, and the Caliph at last bought for himself and Mansor beautiful pistols, for the Vizier's wife however a comb. When the pedlar was-about-to close his box again, the Caliph saw a little drawer and asked whether there were still more goods there.

6. D– Krämer (heraus- *or* hinaus-ziehen ?) d– Schu-blade *f* und (zeigen *w*) darin ein– klein– Dose *f* mit schwärzlich– Pulver *n* und ein gelb– Papier *n* mit son-derbar– Schrift *f*, d– weder d– Kalif noch Mansor (lesen) (können). D– Kalif, d– in sein– Bibliothek *f* gern alt– Manuskript– *np* (haben), (kaufen *w*) Schrift und Dose und (entlassen) d– alt– Krämer.

The pedlar pulled the drawer out and showed therein a little box with blackish powder and a yellow paper with strange writing which neither the Caliph nor Mansor could (= were able to) read. The Caliph, who liked to have (= had will-ingly) old manuscripts in his library, bought writing and box and dismissed the old pedlar.

7. D– Kalif aber (denken), er (mögen !) gern wissen, was d– Schrift *f* (enthalten *!*), und (fragen *w*) d– Wesir *m*, ob er kein– (kennen *!*), d– sie (entziffern *w*) (können *!*). " Gnädigst– Herr," (antworten *w*) dies–, " an d– gross– Moschee *f* (wohnen *w*) ein Mann, er (heissen) Selim d– Gelehrte, d– all– Sprachen *fp* (verstehen). (Lassen *!*) ih– (kommen), vielleicht (kennen) er dies– geheimnisvoll– Zug– *mp !*."

The Caliph however thought he would-like to know what the writing contained and asked the Vizier if he did not know anybody who could (should-be-able-to) decipher it. "Most gracious Lord," replied the latter, " at the great Mosque lives a man, his name is Selim the Scholar, who understands all languages. Send for him (= let him come), perhaps he knows these mysterious characters."

8. Bald (kommen) d– gelehrt– Selim, (verneigen *w*) sich und (sprechen) : " Dein Wille (geschehen *!*), o Herr ! " Lange (betrachten *w*) er d– Schrift *f*, plötzlich aber (aus/rufen) er: " Das ist Lateinisch, o Herr, oder ich (lassen) mi– (hängen) ! " " (Sagen !), was drin (stehen) ! " (befehlen) d– Kalif.

Soon the learned Selim came, bowed and said : " Thy will be done (= happen), oh Lord ! " Long did he contemplate the writing but suddenly he exclaimed : " That is Latin, oh Lord, or I'll be hanged (= I let myself hang)." " Say what is (= stands) therein," ordered the Caliph.

9. Selim (an/fangen) zu (übersetzen *w*) : " Mensch, d– du dieses (finden), (preisen *w !*) Allah für sein– Gnade *f* ! W– von d– Pulver *n* in dies– klein– Dose *f* (schnupfen *w*) und dazu (sprechen) ' Mutabor ', d– (können) sich in jed– Tier *n* (verwan-

Selim began to translate : " Man, (thou) who findest this, praise Allah for his favour ! He-who snuffs (of) the powder in this little box and besides (thereto) says ' Mutabor ', (he) can transform himself into any (=every) animal and also

deln *w*), und (verstehen) auch d– Sprach– *fp* d– Tiere *np*. (Wollen) er wieder in sein– menschlich– Gestalt *f* (zu-ruck/kehren), so (neigen *w* !) er sich dreimal gen Osten und (sprechen !) jen– Wort *n*. Aber (hüten *w* !) dich, wenn du (verwandeln *w*) (sein), dass du nicht (lachen) *w* !), sonst (verschwinden) d– Zauberwort *n* gänzlich aus dein– Gedächtnis *n*, und du (bleiben) ein Tier."

understands the languages of the animals. If he wants (will) to return into his human shape, so let-him-bow three times towards the East and say the (= that) word. But be-thou-on-thy-guard when thou art transformed that thou dost not laugh, otherwise the magic word disappears entirely out of thy memory, and thou remainest an animal.

10. Als Selim d– Gelehrt– also (lesen) (haben), (sein) d– Kalif über d– Massen *fp* (vergnügen *w*). Er (lassen) d– Gelehrt– *m* (schwören), niemand etwas von d– Geheimnis *n* zu (sagen *w*), (schenken *w*) ih– ein schön– Kleid *n* und (entlassen) ih–. Zu sein– Grosswesir aber (sagen) er: " Morgen früh (kommen) du zu mi–. Wir (gehen) dann miteinander auf– Feld *n*, (schnupfen *w*) etwas Pulver aus mein– Dose *f* und (belauschen *w*) dann, was in d– Luft *f* und i– Wasser *n*, i– Wald *m* und Feld *n* (sprechen) (werden *or* sein ?)."

When Selim the Scholar had thus read, the Caliph was delighted beyond measure. He made (= let) the learned-man swear to tell nobody anything of the secret, presented to him a fine dress and dismissed him. To his Grand Vizier however he said : " Tomorrow morning thou comest to me. We will go (= go) together on to the field, snuff some powder out of my box and then listen-to what is spoken in the air and in the water, in the wood and field."

II.

1. Kaum (haben) a– ander– Morgen *m* d– Kalif (frühstücken *w*) und sich (an/kleiden *w*), als d– Grosswesir (erscheinen). D– Kalif (stecken *w*) d– Dose *f* mit d– Zauberpulver *n* in d– Gürtel *m* und (machen *w*) sich mit d– Grosswesir auf d– Weg *m*. D– Kalif (vor/schlagen), weit (hinaus *or* heraus?) an ein– Teich *m* zu gehen, wo er oft viel– Tier– *np*, namentlich Storch– *mp* !, (sehen) (haben !), d– durch ihr feierlich– Wesen *n* immer sein– Aufmerksamkeit (erregen *w*) (haben !).	Scarcely had the Caliph breakfasted on the next morning and dressed (himself) when the Grand Vizier appeared. The Caliph put (stuck) the box with the magic powder into his belt (girdle) and started on his way with the Grand Vizier. The Caliph proposed to go far out to a pond where he had (he said !) often seen many animals, especially storks, who through their solemn demeanour had (he said !) always attracted his attention.
2. Als sie dort (an/kommen) (haben *or* sein?), (sehen) sie ein– Storch *m* ernsthaft auf– und abgehen und hie und da etwas vor sich (hin/klappern). Zugleich (sehen) sie oben in d– Luft *f* ein– ander– Storch *m* dies– Gegend *f* (zu/fliegen). Schnell (ziehen) d– Kalif sein– Dose *f* aus d– Gürtel *m*, (nehmen) ein– gut– Prise *f*, (dar/bieten) sie d– Wesir, d– gleichfalls (schnupfen *w*), und beid– (rufen): Mutabor !	When they had arrived there they saw a stork gravely walking (walk) up and down and now and then chattering something to himself. At the same time they saw up in the air another stork flying (fly) towards this region. Quickly the Caliph drew his box out of the belt, took a good pinch (of powder), offered it to the Vizier, who also snuffed it, and both called : Mutabor !
3. Da (ein/schrumpfen *w*)	Then their legs shrank and

ihr– Bein– *np*, und (werden) dünn und rot, d– schön– gelb– Pantoffel– *fp* d– Kalif– und sein– Begleiter– (werden) unförmlich– Storchfuss– *mp* !, d– Arm– *mp* (werden) zu Flügel– *mp*, d– Hals *m* (werden) ein– Elle *f* lang. Der Bart (sein *or* haben ?) (verschwinden) und d– Körper *m* (bedecken *w*) weich– Feder– *fp*. Indem (sein *or* haben ?) d– ander– Storch *m* auf d– Erde *f* (an/kommen); er (zu/gehen) auf d– erst– Storch *m*. D– beid– neu– Storch– *mp* ! aber (beeilen *w*) sich, in ih– Nähe *f* zu kommen, und (vernehmen) zu ihr– Erstaunen *n* folgend– Gespräch *n*.

became thin and red, the beautiful yellow slippers of the Caliph and his companion became misshapen stork-feet, the arms became wings, the neck grew (became) an ell long. The beard had disappeared and soft feathers covered the body. Meanwhile the other stork had arrived on the ground (earth); it went up to the first stork. The two (= both) new storks however hastened to come in their neighbourhood (to get near them) and heard to their astonishment the following conversation.

4. " Gut– Morgen *m*, Frau Langbein, so früh schon auf d– Wiese *f*? " " Schön– Dank *m*, liebe Klapperschnabel! Ich (haben) mi– ein klein– Frühstück *n* (holen *w*)." Zugleich (schreiten) d– jung– Störchin *f* in wunderlich– Bewegung– *fp* durch d– Feld *n*. Als sie aber in malerisch– Stellung *f* auf ein– Fuss *m* (stehen) und mit d– Flügel– *mp* anmutig (wedeln *w*), da (können) sich d– beid– nicht mehr (halten);

" Good morning, Mrs. Longleg, already so early on the meadow? " " (I give you my) kindly thanks, dear Chatterbeak! I have fetched myself a little breakfast." At the same time the young she-stork strode in wonderful movements through the field. When she however stood in picturesque attitude on one foot and gracefully waggled (= wagged with) her wings, the two could no longer restrain themselves;

ein unaufhaltsam– Gelächter *n* (hervor/brechen) aus ihr– Schnabel– *mp !*, von d– sie sich erst nach lang– Zeit *f* (erholen *w*).

5. D– Kalif (wieder/fassen *w*) sich zuerst. " Das (sein) einmal ein Spass *m*," (rufen) er, " d– nicht mit Gold zu bezahlen (sein). Schade ! dass d– dumm– Tier– *np* durch unser Gelächter *n* sich (haben) (verscheuchen) (lassen), sonst (haben *!*) sie gewiss auch noch (singen) ! " Aber jetzt (ein/fallen) es d– Grosswesir, dass d– Lachen *n* während d– Verwandlung *f* (verbieten) (sein). Er (mit-teilen *w*) sein– Angst *f* deswegen d– Kalif–.

6. " Das (sein *!*) ein schlecht– Spass *m*, wenn ich ein Storch (bleiben) (müssen *!*). (Besinnen *!*) dich doch auf d– dumm– Wort *n*, ich (heraus/bringen) es nicht." " Dreimal gen Osten (müssen) wir uns (bücken *w*), und dazu (sprechen): ' Mu . . ., Mu . . ., M. . . .' " Sie (stellen *w*) sich gegen Osten und (bücken *w*) sich in einem fort, dass ihr– Schnabel *mp !* beinahe d– Erde *f* (berühren *w*). Aber,

an irresistible burst of laughter broke forth out of their beaks, from which they only (= first) recovered (themselves) after a long time.

The Caliph pulled himself together first. " That was indeed a joke," he called, " which is not to be paid for with gold. A pity that the silly animals have let themselves be scared by our laughter, otherwise they would certainly have sung as well." But now it struck (occurred to) the Grand Vizier that laughing during the metamorphosis was forbidden. He communicated his fear to the Caliph.

" It would be a bad joke if I should-have-to remain a stork. Do think of (remember) the silly word, I can't get it out (= I get it not out)." " Three times we must bow towards the East and at the same time (besides) say ' Mu . . ., Mu . . ., M. . . .' " They placed themselves towards the East and bowed on and on so that their beaks almost touched the earth. But, oh misery, the magic word had escaped

o Jammer! das Zauberwort (sein *or* haben?) ihnen (entfallen), und jed- Erinnerung *f* daran (haben *or* sein?) (verschwinden); d- arm- Kalif und sein Wesir (sein) und (bleiben) Storch- *mp!*

from them (escaped from their memory) and every recollection of it had disappeared; the poor Caliph and his Vizier were and remained storks.

III.

1. Sie (umher/schleichen) mehrer- Tag- *mp* und (ernähren *w*) sich kümmerlich von Feldfrucht- *fp!*, d- sie aber wegen ihr- lang- Schnabel *mp!* nicht gut (verspeisen *w*) (können). Zu Frosch- *mp!* (haben) sie übrigens kein- Appetit *m*, denn sie (befürchten *w*) mit solch- Leckerbissen *mp* sich d- Magen *m* zu (verderben). Ihr einzig- Vergnügen *n* in dies- traurig- Lage *f* (sein), dass sie (fliegen) (können), und so (fliegen) sie oft auf d- Dach- *np!* von Bagdad, um zu sehen, was darin (vor/gehen).

They crept about for several days and fed (themselves) miserably on the produce of the fields (= field fruit), which they could not however eat on account of their long beaks. For frogs they had moreover no appetite, for they feared to ruin (spoil) their stomach with such titbits. Their sole pleasure in this predicament was that they were able to (could) fly and so they often flew on to the roofs of Bagdad in order to see what was going on in it.

2. In d- erst- Tag- *mp* (bemerken *w*) sie gross- Unruhe *f* und Trauer *f* in d- Strasse- *fp*. Aber ungefähr a- viert- Tag *m* nach ihr- Verzauberung *f* (sitzen) sie auf d- Palast *m* d- Kalif-

In the first (few) days they noticed great agitation (unrest) and mourning in the streets. But on about the fourth day after their enchantment they were sitting on the palace of the Caliph

m : da (sehen) sie unten in d– Strasse *f* ein– prächtig– Aufzug *m*. Ein Mann in ein– goldgestickt– Mantel *m* (sitzen) auf ein– schön– Pferd *n*, umgeben von glänzend– Diener– *mp*. Halb Bagdad (nach/springen) ih–, und all– (schreien): " Heil Mizra, d– Herrscher *m* von Bagdad ! "

when they saw below in the street a magnificent procession. A man in a gold-embroidered cloak was sitting on a fine horse surrounded by glittering servants. Half Bagdad ran (sprang) after him and all cried : " Hail to Mizra, the ruler of Bagdad ! "

3. Da (an/sehen) d– beid– Storch– *mp !* auf d– Dache *n* d– Palast– *m* einander, und d– Kalif (sprechen): " (Ahnen *w*) du jetzt, warum ich (verzaubern) (sein), Grosswesir ? Dies– Mizra (sein) d– Sohn *m* mein– Todfeind– *m*, d– mächtig– Zauberer– *m* Kaschnur, d– mi– in ein– bös– Stunde *f* Rache *f* (schwören). Aber ich (auf/geben) d– Hoffnung *f* noch nicht. (Kommen *!*) mit mi–, wir (wollen) zu– Grab *n* d– Prophet– (wandern), vielleicht dass an heilig– Stätte *f* der Zauber (lösen *w*) (werden)."

Then the two storks on the roof of the palace looked at each other and the Caliph said : " Dost thou now suspect why I was bewitched, Grand Vizier ? This Mizra is the son of my deadly enemy, the powerful magician Kaschnur, who swore revenge on me in an evil hour. But I do not yet abandon (give up) hope. Come with me, we will go (wander) to the grave of the Prophet, perhaps (that) at the holy place the spell will be (gets, becomes) broken (dissolved)."

4. Sie (erheben) sich vo– Dach *n* d– Palast– *m* und (zu/fliegen) d– Gegend *f* von Medina. " O Herr ! " (ächzen *w*) nach ein paar Stunde– *fp* der Wesir, " ich (aus/halten) es nicht mehr lange,

They rose from the roof ot the Palace and flew towards the region of Medina. " Oh Lord ! " groaned the Vizier after a couple of hours, " I (can) no longer bear it (hold it out), you fly too quickly.

ihr (fliegen) zu schnell! Auch ist es schon Abend, und wir (tun !) wohl, ein Unterkommen für d– Nacht *f* zu (suchen)." In dies– Augenblick *m* (sehen) sie unten i– Tal– *n* ein– Ruine *f* und (dahin/fliegen) sofort. D– Ruine *f* (scheinen) ehemals ein Schloss *n* (sein) zu (sein). D– Kalif und sein Begleiter (umher/gehen) durch d– Gang– *mp* ! d– Ruine *f*, um sich ein trocken– Plätzchen *n* zu (suchen); plötzlich (bleiben) d– Storch Mansor (stehen).

Also it is already evening and we should-do well to seek a shelter for the night." At this moment they saw below in the valley (dale) a ruin and flew at once thither. The ruin seemed to have formerly been a castle. The Caliph and his companion went about through the corridors of the ruin in order to seek a dry spot (little place); suddenly the stork Mansor stopped (remained standing).

5. "Herr," (flüstern *w*) er leise, "hier neben (haben) ich ein– Seufzer *m* (hören *w*)." D– Kalif (bleiben) nun auch (stehen) und (hören *w*) ganz deutlich ein leis– Weinen *n*, d– eher ein– Mensch– *m*, als ein– Tier *n* anzugehören (scheinen). Er (eilen *w*) in ein– finster– Gang *m* (aufstossen) mit d– Schnabel *m* ein– Tür *f* und (bleiben) überrascht auf d– Schwelle *f* (stehen), denn er (sehen) ein– gross– Nachteule *f* a– Boden *m* (sitzen). Als sie aber d– Kalif– *m* and sein– Wesir (erblicken *w*), (erheben) sie ein laut– Freudenge-

"Lord," whispered he softly, "here next door I have heard a sigh." The Caliph also stopped now and heard quite distinctly a soft weeping which appeared to belong rather to a human-being than to an animal. He hastened into a gloomy corridor, pushed a door open with his beak and stopped surprised on the threshold, for he saw a large screech-owl (night-owl) sitting on the floor. When she however perceived the Caliph and his Vizier she raised a loud cry of joy, and to the great astonishment of the

schrei *n* und zu d– gross– Erstaunen *n* d– beide– *mp* (rufen) sie in gut– menschlich– Arabisch *n*: "Willkommen, ihr (sein) m– ein gut– Zeichen *n* mein– Errettung *f*, denn durch Storch– *mp*! (werden!) mi– ein gross– Glück *n* kommen, (sein) mi– einst (prophezeien *w*) (werden)!"

two, she called in good human Arabic: "Welcome, you are to me a good sign (token) of my rescue, for through storks (there) shall come to me a great happiness (luck), it has once been prophesied to me!"

6. Als sich d– Kalif von sein– Erstaunen *n* (erholen *w*) (haben), (bücken *w*) er sich mit sein– lang– Hals *m*, (bringen) sein– dünn– Fuss– *mp*! in ein– zierlich– Stellung *f* und (sprechen): "Nachteule! Dein– Wort– *np*!! nach (dürfen) ich glauben, ein– Lebensgefährtin *f* in di– zu (sehen). Aber ach! dein– Hoffnung *f*, dass durch uns dein– Rettung *f* (kommen) (werden!), ist vergeblich. Du (werden) unser– Hilflosigkeit *f* selbst (erkennen), wenn du unser– Geschichte *f* (hören *w*)." D– Nachteule (bitten) ih– zu erzählen. D– Kalif (erzählen *w*) ih–, w– wir bereits (wissen).

When the Caliph had recovered from his astonishment he bowed (with) his long neck, brought his thin feet into an elegant position and said: "Screech-owl, according to thy words (spoken words!) I may believe to see in thee a companion through life. But alas, thy hope that through us thy rescue shall come is in vain. Thou wilt recognize our helplessness when thou hearest our story." The night-owl begged him to relate (it). The Caliph told her what we already know.

IV.

1. Als d– Kalif d– Eule *f* sein– Geschichte *f* (vor/tragen) (haben), (danken *w*) sie

When the Caliph had related (delivered) his story to the owl, she thanked him

ih– und (sagen *w*): "Hören!), wie ich nicht weniger unglücklich (sein) als du. Mein Vater (sein) König von Indien, ich, sein– einzig– Tochter *f*, (heissen) Lusa. Jen– Zauberer *m* Kaschnur (kommen) ein– Tag– zu mein– Vater *m* und (begehren *w*) mi– zu– Frau *f* für sein– Sohn *m* Mizra. Mein Vater aber, d– ein hitzig– Mann (sein), (lassen) ih– d– Treppe *f* (hinunter/werfen).

and said: "Listen how I am no less unhappy than thou. My father is the King of India, I his only unhappy daughter am-named Lusa. That magician Kaschnur came one day (= of a day) to my father and solicited my hand in marriage (= desired me to wife) for his son Mizra. My father however, who is a hot-headed man, had him thrown down the stairs.

2. Einig– Zeit *f* später, als ich in mein– Garten *m* Erfrischung– *fp* zu mi– (nehmen) (wollen), (bei/bringen) er mi–, als Sklave verkleidet, ein– Trank *m*, d– mi– in dies– abscheulich– Gestalt *f* (verwandeln *w*). Vor Schrecken ohnmächtig, (bringen) er mi– hieher und (rufen) mi– mit schrecklich– Stimme *f* in d– Ohr– *np*: 'Da (sollen) du (bleiben), hässlich, selbst von d– Tier– *np* (verachten *w*), bis an dein Ende *n*, oder bis einer aus frei– Wille– *m* di–, selbst in dies– schrecklich– Gestalt *f*, zu– Frau *f* (begehren *w*)'."

Some time later when I was taking refreshments (to myself) in my garden, disguised as a slave he administered to me a potion which transformed me into this abominable shape. Unconscious with terror, he brought me hither and shouted in a terrible voice into my ears: 'There shalt thou remain, ugly, despised even by the animals, until thy end or until some-one of his free will asks your hand in marriage even in this abominable shape'."

3. Die Eule (haben) (enden *w*) und (aus/wischen *w*) sich mit d– Flügel *m* d– Auge–

The owl had ended and wiped her eyes with her wing, for the relation of her suffer-

np, denn d– Erzählung *f* ihr–Leiden *np* (haben) ihr Träne–*fp* (entlocken *w*). Der Kalif (sein) bei d– Erzählung *f* d–Prinzessin *f* in tief– Nachdenken *n* (versinken). " Ein geheim– Zusammenhang *m* (statt/finden) zwischen unser- Unglück *n*, aber wo (finden) ich d– Schlüssel *m* zu dies– Rätsel *n*? " Die Eule (antworten *w*) ih–: " O Herr! es ist mi– einst (prophezeien *w*) (werden), dass ein Storch mi– gross– Glück *n* (bringen) (werden !), und ich (wissen !) vielleicht, wie wir uns (retten *w*) (können !)."

ings had drawn tears from her. The Caliph at the tale of the Princess had sunk into deep meditation. " A secret connection exists (takes place) between our misfortune, but where do I find the key to this puzzle?" The owl replied to him: " O Lord, it has once been prophesied to me that a stork should bring to me great happiness, and I might know perhaps how we could (= should be able to) save ourselves."

4. " D– Zauberer *m*, d– uns beid– unglücklich (machen *w*) (haben)," (fort/fahren) sie, " (kommen) all– Monat– *mp* einmal in dies– Ruine *fp*. Nicht weit von dies– Gemach *n* (sein) ein Saal. Dort (pflegen *w*) er dann mit viel– Genosse– *mp* zu (schmausen *w*). Schon oft (haben) ich sie dort (belauschen *w*). Sie (erzählen *w*) dann einander ihr–schändlich– Werk– *np*, vielleicht dass er dann das Zauberwort, d– ihr vergessen (haben), (aus/sprechen).

" The magician who has made both of us unhappy," she went on, " comes once every month into these ruins. Not far from this chamber there is a hall. There he is wont to feast with many comrades. Often already have I listened to them (overheard them). They then tell each other their shameful works; perhaps he will then pronounce (= pronounces) the magic word that you have forgotten."

5. " O teuerest– Prinzessin *f*," (rufen) d– Kalif, (an/sagen !), wann (kommen) er und wo ist d– Saal *m*?" D– Eule *f* (schweigen) ein– Augenblick *m* und (sprechen) dann: " (Nehmen !) es nicht ungünstig, aber nur unter e i n– Bedingung *f* (können) ich eur– Wunsch *m* (erfüllen *w*)." " (Aus/sprechen !), (aus/sprechen !) ! " (schreien) d– Kalif. " Ich (mögen !) auch gern zugleich frei sein, dies (können) aber nur (geschehen), wenn ein– von euch mi– sein– Hand (reichen *w*)," (sagen *w* d– Eule.

" Oh, dearest Princess," cried the Caliph, " say on, when does he come and where is the hall ? " The owl was silent for a moment and then said: " Do not take it amiss (unfavourably), but only on one condition can I fulfil your wish." " Speak, speak," cried the Caliph. " I should also like to be free at the same time ; this can however only happen if one of you offers me his hand," said the owl.

6. D– beid– Storch– *mp !* (scheinen) über d– Antrag *m* etwas (betreffen) zu sein, und d– Kalif (winken *w*) sein– Diener, ein wenig mit ih– (hinauszugehen). " Grosswesir," (sprechen) vor d– Tür *f* d– Kalif, " das (sein) ein dumm– Handel *m*, aber ihr (können) sie schon (nehmen)." " So ? " (antworten *w*) dies–, " dass mi– mein– Frau *f*, wenn ich nach Haus (kommen), d– Auge– *n* (aus/kratzen *w*) ? Auch (sein) ich ein alt– Mann *m*, und ihr (sein) noch jung und unver-

The two storks seemed to be somewhat taken aback at the proposal, and the Caliph beckoned to his servant to go outside a little with him. " Grand Vizier," the Caliph said in front of the door, " that is a silly business but you can take her all right (already)." " Indeed ? " replied the latter, " so that my wife scratches my eyes out when I come home ? Moreover I am an old man and you are young and unmarried and can rather give a beauti-

heiratet und (können) eher ein– schön–, jung– Prinzessin *f* d– Hand *f* (geben)."

ful young Princess your hand."

7. Sie (zu/reden *w*) einander gegenseitig noch lange, aber endlich, als d– Kalif (sehen), dass sein Wesir lieber Storch (bleiben), als die Eule (heiraten *w*) (wollen), (entschliessen) er sich, die Bedingung lieber selbst zu (erfüllen *w*). Die Eule war hocherfreut. Sie (gestehen) ihnen, dass sie zu kein– besser– Zeit *f* (haben *!*) (kommen) (können), weil wahrscheinlich in dies– Nacht die Zauberer sich versammeln) (werden *!*).

They mutually exhorted each other for a long time more, but at last, when the Caliph saw that his Vizier would rather remain a stork than marry the owl, he decided to fulfil the condition himself. The owl was highly delighted. She confessed to them that they could not have come at any better time because the magicians would probably gather in this night.

8. Sie (verlassen) mit d– Störch– *mp !* d– Gemach *n*, um sie in jen– Saal *m* zu (führen *w*); sie (hin/gehen) lange in ein– finster– Gang *m*; endlich (entgegen/strahlen *w*) ihnen aus ein– halbverfallen– Mauer *f* ein hell– Schein *m*. Sie (können) von d– Lücke *f*, an welch– sie (stehen), ein– gross– Saal *m* (übersehen). Rings um ein– Tisch *m* (ziehen) sich ein Sofa, *n*, auf welch– acht Mann– *mp !* (sitzen). In ein– dies– Mann– *mp !* (wieder/erkennen) d– Störch–

She left the chamber with the storks in order to lead them into the (that) hall; they went on for a long time in a dark corridor; at last a bright light (shine) shone towards them out of a half ruined wall. They could from the gap at which they were standing overlook a large hall. Round a table stretched (drew itself) a sofa on which eight men were sitting. In one of these men the storks recognized the pedlar who had sold them the magic word. He was

mp! jen– Krämer *m*, d– ihnen d– Zauberwort *n* (verkaufen *w*) (haben). Er (erzählen *w*) unter ander– d– Geschichte *f* d– Kalif– *m* und sein– Wesir– *m*. " Was für ein Wort (haben) du ihnen denn (auf/geben)? " (fragen *w*) ein ander– Zauberer *m*. " Ein recht schwer–, lateinisch–, es (heissen) Mutabor."

telling, amongst other things, the story of the Caliph and his Vizier. " What kind of a word hast thou proposed (given up) to them? " " A right difficult, Latin one, it is (is called) Mutabor."

V.

1. Als d– Störch– *mp!* an ihr– Mauerlücke *f* dies– (hören *w*), (kommen) sie vor Freude beinahe ausser sich. Sie (zu/laufen) auf ihr– lang– Fuss– *mp!* so schnell d– Tore *n* d– Ruine *f*, dass d– Eule *f* kaum (folgen *w*) (können). Dort (sprechen) d– Kalif gerührt zu d– Eule *f*: " Retterin mein– Leben– *n* und d– Leben– mein– Freund– *m*, (an/nehmen!) zu– ewig– Dank *m* für d–, w– du für uns (tun) (haben) mi– zu– Gemahl *m*."

When the storks at their gap in the wall heard this, they were nearly beside themselves with joy. They ran on their long feet so quickly towards the gate of the ruin that the owl could scarcely follow. There the Caliph said with emotion (touched, moved) to the owl: " Saviour of my life and of the life of my friend, accept me as your husband as eternal gratitude (thank) for what thou hast done for us."

2. Dann aber (wenden) er sich nach Osten. Dreimal (bücken *w*) d– Störch– *mp!* ihr– lang– Hals– *mp!* d– Sonne *f* entgegen, die soeben

Then however he turned to the East. Thrice the storks bowed their long necks towards the sun which was just rising behind the moun-

hinter d– Gebirg– *np* (herauf/steigen); Mutabor (rufen) sie, und im Nu (sein) sie (verwandeln *w*), und in d– hoh– Freude *f* d– neu geschenkt– Leben– *n*, (liegen) Herr und Diener (lachen) *w*) einander in d– Arm– *mp*.

tains; Mutabor, they cried, and in a twinkling they were transformed, and in the great joy at (= of) their newly given life, master and servant lay laughing in each other's arms (each other in the arms).

3. W– (beschreiben) aber ihr Erstaunen, als sie sich (um/sehen)? Ein– schön– Dame *f*, herrlich (schmükken), (stehen) vor ihnen. (Lächeln *w*) (geben) sie d– Kalif– d– Hand *f*. " (Erkennen) ihr eur– Nachteule *f* nicht mehr? " (sagen *w*) sie. Sie (sein) es; d– Kalif (sein) von ihr– Schönheit *f* und Anmut *f* so (entzücken *w*), dass er (aus/rufen): es (sein !) sein grösst– Glück *n*, dass er Storch (werden) (sein !).

Who describes however their astonishment when they looked round? A lovely lady, magnificently attired, was standing in front of them. Smiling she gave the Caliph her hand. " Do you no longer recognize your screech-owl? " she said. It was she; the Caliph was so enchanted with her beauty and grace that he exclaimed: it was (he said) his greatest good fortune that he had (he said !) become a stork.

4. Die drei (zu/ziehen) nun miteinander auf Bagdad. D– Kalif (finden) in sein– Kleid– *np* nicht nur d– Dose *f* mit Zauberpulver, sondern auch sein– Geldbeutel *m*. Er (kaufen *w*) daher i– nächsten Dorfe *n*, was zu ihr– Reise *f* nötig (sein), und so (kommen) sie bald an d– Tor– *np* von Bagdad. Dort aber (erregen *w*) d– Ankunft *f* d– Kalif–

The three now proceeded with each other towards Bagdad. The Caliph found in his clothes not only the box with magic powder but also his purse. He bought therefore in the nearest village what was necessary for their journey and thus they soon came to the gates of Bagdad. There however the Caliph's arrival caused great

gross– Erstaunen *n*. Man (haben) sie für tot (aus/geben), und d– Volk *n* (sein) daher hoch erfreut, sein– geliebt– Herrscher wieder zu haben.

astonishment. They had been given out as dead and the people were therefore greatly delighted to have their beloved ruler back again.

5. Um so mehr aber (entbrennen) ihr Hass gegen d– Betrüger *m* Mizra. Sie (ziehen) in d– Palast *m* und (gefangen/nehmen) d– alt– Zauberer *m* und sein– Sohn *m*. D– Alt– (schicken *w*) d– Kalif in dasselb– Gemach *n* d– Ruine *f*, d– die Prinzessin als Eule (bewohnen *w*) (haben), und (lassen) ih– dort (auf/hängen). D– Sohn *m* aber, welch– nichts von d– Kunst– *fp* d– Vater– (verstehen), (lassen) der Kalif d– Wahl *f*, ob er (sterben) oder (schnupfen *w*) (wollen !).

All the more however did their hatred blaze up against the deceiver Mizra. They marched (drew) into the palace and took the old magician and his son prisoner. The Caliph sent the old one into the same chamber of the ruin which the Princess had inhabited as an owl and had him hanged there. To the son however, who understood nothing of the arts of the father, he left the choice whether he would die or snuff !

6. Als er das letzter– (wählen *w*), (bieten) ih– d– Grosswesir d– Dose *f*. Ein– tüchtig– Prise *f*, und d– Zauberwort *n* d– Kalif– (verwandeln) ih– in ein– Storch *m*. Der Kalif (lassen) ih– in ein– eisern– Käfig *m* sperren *w*) und in sein– Garten *m* (auf/stellen *w*). Lange und vergnügt (leben *w*) d– Kalif mit sein– Frau *f*, d– Prinzessin *f*; sein– vergnügtest–

When he chose the latter the Grand Vizier offered him the box. A hearty pinch (of powder) and the Caliph's magic word transformed him into a stork. The Caliph had him shut up in an iron cage and set up in his garden. Long and happy lived the Caliph with his wife the Princess; his most pleasant hours were those when his Grand Vizier visited him.

Stund- *fp* (sein) immer d–, wenn ih– der Grosswesir (besuchen *w*). Da (sprechen) sie dann oft von ihr– Storchenabenteur *n*, und wenn d– Kalif recht heiter (sein), (herab/lassen) er sich, d– Grosswesir nachzuahmen, wie er als Storch (aus/sehen).

They then often spoke of their stork adventure, and when the Caliph was downright merry he condescended to imitate the Grand Vizier as he looked as a stork.

7. Er (gehen) dann ernsthaft mit steif– Fuss– *mp!* i– Zimmer *n* auf und ab (wedeln *w*) mit d– Arm– *mp* wie mit Flügel– *mp*, und (zeigen *w*), wie jener sich vergeblich nach Osten (neigen *w*) und Mu . . ., Mu . . ., Mu . . . (rufen) (haben *!*). Für d– Frau Kalifin *f* und ihr– Kind– *np* (sein) dies– Vorstellung *f* allemal ein– gross– Freude *f*; wenn aber d– Kalif gar zu lange (nicken) und Mu . . ., Mu . . . (schreien), dann (drohen *w*) ih– der Grosswesir: er (wollen) das, w– vor d– Türe *f* d– Prinzessin *f* Nachteule (verhandeln *w*) (werden) (sein *!*), d– Frau Kalifin (mit/teilen) !

He then walked gravely on his stiff feet up and down the room, waggled with his arms as if with wings and showed how the former bowed in vain to the East and cried Mu . . ., Mu . . ., Mu. . . . For the Lady Caliph and her children this performance was a great delight; when however the Caliph far too long nodded and cried Mu . . ., Mu . . ., then the Grand Vizier threatened him (saying) that he would communicate to the Lady Caliph that which had been negotiated in front of the door of the Princess Screech-owl !

KEY

DIE GESCHICHTE VON KALIF STORCH

I.

1. Der Kalif von Bagdad sass einmal an einem schönen Nachmittag behaglich auf seinem Sofa; er hatte ein wenig geschlafen, denn es war ein heisser Tag, und sah nach seinem Schläfchen heiter aus. Er rauchte aus einer langen Pfeife, trank hie und da ein wenig Kaffee, den ihm ein schwarzer Sklave einschenkte, und strich sich vergnügt den Bart.

2. An diesem Nachmittage kam sein Grosswesir Mansor, der aber sehr nachdenklich aussah, ganz gegen seine Gewohnheit. Der Kalif tat seine Pfeife ein wenig aus dem Mund und sprach: " Warum machst du ein so nachdenkliches Gesicht, Grosswesir? "

3. Der Grosswesir schlug seine Arme kreuzweis über die Brust, verneigte sich vor seinem Herrn und antwortete: " Herr! ob ich ein nachdenkliches Gesicht mache, weiss ich nicht; aber unten an der Tür steht ein alter Krämer, der so schöne Sachen hat, dass es mich ärgert, nicht viel überflüssiges Geld zu haben."

4. Der Kalif, der seinem Grosswesir schon lange gern eine Freude gemacht hätte, schickte seinen schwarzen Sklaven hinunter, um den alten Krämer heraufzuholen. Bald kam der Sklave mit dem Krämer zurück. Dieser trug einen Kasten, in welchem er allerhand Waren hatte: Perlen, Ringe, Pistolen, Becher und Kämme.

5. Der Kalif und sein Wesir musterten alles durch, und der Kalif kaufte endlich für sich und Mansor schöne Pistolen, für die Frau des Wesirs aber einen Kamm. Als der Krämer

seinen Kasten wieder zumachen wollte, sah der Kalif eine kleine Schublade und fragte, ob da auch noch Waren seien?

6. Der Krämer zog die Schublade heraus und zeigte darin eine kleine Dose mit schwärzlichem Pulver und ein gelbes Papier mit sonderbarer Schrift, die weder der Kalif noch Mansor lesen konnten. Der Kalif, der in seiner Bibliothek gern alte Manuskripte hatte, kaufte Schrift und Dose und entliess den alten Krämer.

7. Der Kalif aber dachte, er möchte gern wissen, was die Schrift enthalte, und fragte den Wesir, ob er keinen kenne, der sie entziffern könnte. " Gnädigster Herr," antwortete dieser, " an der grossen Moschee wohnt ein Mann, er heisst Selim der Gelehrte, der alle Sprachen versteht. Lass ihn kommen, vielleicht kennt er diese geheimnisvollen Züge."

8. Bald kam der gelehrte Selim, verneigte sich und sprach: " Dein Wille geschehe, o Herr! " Lange betrachtete er die Schrift, plötzlich aber rief er aus: " Das ist Lateinisch, o Herr, oder ich lasse mich hängen! " " Sag' (*or* sage), was drin steht! " befahl der Kalif.

9. Selim fing an zu übersetzen: " Mensch, der du dieses findest, preise Allah für seine Gnade! Wer von dem Pulver in dieser kleinen Dose schnupft und dazu spricht: ' Mutabor,' der kann sich in jedes Tier verwandeln, und versteht auch die Sprache der Tiere. Will er wieder in seine menschliche Gestalt zurückkehren, so neige er sich dreimal gen (= gegen) Osten und spreche jenes Wort. Aber hüte dich, wenn du verwandelt bist, dass du nicht lachest, sonst verschwindet das Zauberwort gänzlich aus deinem Gedächtnis, und du bleibst ein Tier."

10. Als Selim der Gelehrte also gelesen hatte, war der Kalif über die Massen vergnügt. Er liess den Gelehrten schwören, niemand etwas von dem Geheimnis zu sagen, schenkte ihm ein schönes Kleid und entliess ihn. Zu seinem Grosswesir aber sagte er: " Morgen früh kommst du zu mir. Wir gehen dann miteinander aufs Feld, schnup-

fen etwas Pulver aus meiner Dose und belauschen dann, was in der Luft und im Wasser, im Wald und Feld gesprochen wird!"

II.

1. Kaum hatte am andern Morgen der Kalif gefrühstückt und sich angekleidet, als der Grosswesir erschien. Der Kalif steckte die Dose mit dem Zauberpulver in den Gürtel und machte sich mit dem Grosswesir auf den Weg. Der Kalif schlug vor, weit hinaus an einen Teich zu gehen, wo er oft viele Tiere, namentlich Störche, gesehen habe, die durch ihr feierliches Wesen immer seine Aufmerksamkeit erregt haben.

2. Als sie dort angekommen waren, sahen sie einen Storch ernsthaft auf- und abgehen und hie und da etwas vor sich hinklappernd. Zugleich sahen sie oben in der Luft einen andern Storch dieser Gegend zufliegen. Schnell zog der Kalif seine Dose aus dem Gürtel, nahm eine gute Prise, bot sie dem Wesir dar, der gleichfalls schnupfte, und beide riefen: Mutabor!

3. Da schrumpften ihre Beine ein, und wurden dünn und rot, die schönen gelben Pantoffeln des Kalifen und seines Begleiters wurden unförmliche Storchfüsse, die Arme wurden zu Flügeln, der Hals wurde eine Elle lang. Der Bart war verschwunden und den Körper bedeckten weiche Federn. Indem war der andere Storch auf der Erde angekommen; er ging auf den ersten Storch zu. Die beiden neuen Störche aber beeilten sich, in ihre Nähe zu kommen, und vernahmen zu ihrem Erstaunen folgendes Gespräch:

4. "Guten Morgen, Frau Langbein, so früh schon auf der Wiese?" "Schönen Dank, liebe Klapperschnabel! Ich habe mir ein kleines Frühstück geholt." Zugleich schritt die junge Störchin in wunderlichen Bewegungen durch das Feld. Als sie aber in malerischer Stellung auf einem Fuss stand und mit den Flügeln anmutig dazu wedelte, da konnten sich die beiden nicht mehr halten;

ein unaufhaltsames Gelächter brach aus ihren Schnäbeln hervor, von dem sie sich erst nach langer Zeit erholten.

5. Der Kalif fasste sich zuerst wieder. " Das war einmal ein Spass," rief er, " der nicht mit Gold zu bezahlen ist. Schade! dass die dummen Tiere durch unser Gelächter sich haben verscheuchen lassen, sonst hätten sie gewiss auch noch gesungen!" Aber jetzt fiel es dem Grosswesir ein, dass das Lachen während der Verwandlung verboten war. Er teilte seine Angst deswegen dem Kalifen mit.

6. " Das wäre ein schlechter Spass, wenn ich ein Storch bleiben müsste! Besinne dich doch auf das dumme Wort, ich bring' es nicht heraus." " Dreimal gen Osten müssen wir uns bücken, und dazu sprechen: Mu . . ., Mu . . ., M. . . ." Sie stellten sich gegen Osten und bückten sich in einem fort, dass ihre Schnäbel beinahe die Erde berührten. Aber, o Jammer! Das Zauberwort war ihnen entfallen, und jede Erinnerung daran war verschwunden; der arme Kalif und sein Wesir waren und blieben Störche.

III.

1. Sie schlichen mehrere Tage umher und ernährten sich kümmerlich von Feldfrüchten, die sie aber wegen ihrer langen Schnäbel nicht gut verspeisen konnten. Zu Fröschen hatten sie übrigens keinen Appetit, denn sie befürchteten mit solchen Leckerbissen sich den Magen zu verderben. Ihr einziges Vergnügen in dieser traurigen Lage war, dass sie fliegen konnten, und so flogen sie oft auf die Dächer von Bagdad, um zu sehen, was darin vorging.

2. In den ersten Tagen bemerkten sie grosse Unruhe und Trauer in den Strassen. Aber ungefähr am vierten Tag nach ihrer Verzauberung sassen sie auf dem Palast des Kalifen: da sahen sie unten in der Strasse einen prächtigen Aufzug. Ein Mann in einem goldgestickten Mantel sass auf einem schönen Pferd, umgeben von glänzenden Dienern. Halb Bagdad sprang ihm nach, und alle schrieen: " Heil Mizra, dem Herrscher von Bagdad!"

3. Da sahen die beiden Störche auf dem Dache des Palastes einander an, und der Kalif sprach: "Ahnst du jetzt, warum ich verzaubert bin, Grosswesir? Dieser Mizra ist der Sohn meines Todfeindes, des mächtigen Zauberers Kaschnur, der mir in einer bösen Stunde Rache schwur. Aber ich gebe die Hoffnung noch nicht auf. Komm mit mir, wir wollen zum Grab des Propheten wandern, vielleicht dass an heiliger Stätte der Zauber gelöst wird."

4. Sie erhoben sich vom Dach des Palastes und flogen der Gegend von Medina zu. "O Herr!" ächzte nach ein paar Stunden der Wesir, "ich halte es nicht mehr lange aus, ihr fliegt zu schnell! Auch ist es schon Abend, und wir täten wohl, ein Unterkommen für die Nacht zu suchen." In diesem Augenblick sahen sie unten im Tale eine Ruine und flogen sofort dahin. Die Ruine schien ehemals ein Schloss gewesen zu sein. Der Kalif und sein Begleiter gingen durch die Gänge der Ruine umher, um sich ein trockenes Plätzchen zu suchen; plötzlich blieb der Storch Mansor stehen.

5. "Herr," flüsterte er leise, "hier neben habe ich einen Seufzer gehört." Der Kalif blieb nun auch stehen und hörte ganz deutlich ein leises Weinen, das eher einem Menschen, als einem Tier anzugehören schien. Er eilte in einen finstern Gang, stiess mit dem Schnabel eine Tür auf und blieb überrascht auf der Schwelle stehen, denn er sah eine grosse Nachteule am Boden sitzen. Als sie aber den Kalifen und seinen Wesir erblickte, erhob sie ein lautes Freudengeschrei und zu dem grossen Erstaunen der beiden rief sie in gutem menschlichen Arabisch: "Willkommen, ihr seid mir ein gutes Zeichen meiner Errettung, denn durch Störche werde mir ein grosses Glück kommen, ist mir einst prophezeit worden!"

6. Als sich der Kalif von seinem Erstaunen erholt hatte, bückte er sich mit seinem langen Hals, brachte seine dünnen Füsse in eine zierliche Stellung und sprach: "Nachteule! Deinen Worten nach darf ich glauben, eine Lebensgefährtin in dir zu sehen. Aber ach! deine Hoffnung, dass durch uns

deine Rettung kommen werde, ist vergeblich. Du wirst unsere Hilflosigkeit selbst erkennen, wenn du unsere Geschichte hörst." Die Nachteule bat ihn zu erzählen. Der Kalif erzählte ihr, was wir bereits wissen.

IV.

1. Als der Kalif der Eule seine Geschichte vorgetragen hatte, dankte sie ihm und sagte: " Höre, wie ich nicht weniger unglücklich bin als du. Mein Vater ist der König von Indien, ich, seine einzige unglückliche Tochter, heisse Lusa. Jener Zauberer Kaschnur kam eines Tages zu meinem Vater und begehrte mich zur Frau für seinen Sohn Mizra. Mein Vater aber, der ein hitziger Mann ist, liess ihn die Treppe hinunterwerfen.

2. Einige Zeit später, als ich in meinem Garten Erfrischungen zu mir nehmen wollte, brachte er mir, als Sklave verkleidet, einen Trank bei, der mich in diese abscheuliche Gestalt verwandelte. Vor Schrecken ohnmächtig, brachte er mich hieher und rief mir mit schrecklicher Stimme in die Ohren: Da sollst du bleiben, hässlich, selbst von den Tieren verachtet, bis an dein Ende, oder bis einer aus freiem Willen dich, selbst in dieser schrecklicher Gestalt, zur Frau begehrt."

3. Die Eule hatte geendet und wischte sich mit dem Flügel wieder die Augen aus, denn die Erzählung ihrer Leiden hatte ihr Tränen entlockt. Der Kalif war bei der Erzählung der Prinzessin in tiefes Nachdenken versunken. " Ein geheimer Zusammenhang findet zwischen unserem Unglück statt; aber wo finde ich den Schlüssel zu diesem Rätsel? " Die Eule antwortet ihm: " O Herr! es ist mir einst prophezeit worden, dass ein Storch mir ein grosses Glück bringen werde, und ich wüsste vielleicht, wie wir uns retten könnten."

4. " Der Zauberer, der uns beide unglücklich gemacht hat," fuhr sie fort, " kommt alle Monate einmal in diese Ruinen. Nicht weit von diesem Gemach ist ein Saal.

Dort pflegt er dann mit vielen Genossen zu schmausen. Schon oft habe ich sie dort belauscht. Sie erzählen dann einander ihre schändlichen Werke, vielleicht dass er dann das Zauberwort, das ihr vergessen habt, ausspricht."

5. " O teuereste Prinzessin," rief der Kalif, " sag an, wann kommt er, und wo ist der Saal? " Die Eule schwieg einen Augenblick und sprach dann: " Nehmt es nicht ungünstig, aber nur unter e i n e r Bedingung kann ich euren Wunsch erfüllen." " Sprich aus! Sprich aus! " schrie der Kalif. " Ich möchte auch gern zugleich frei sein, dies kann aber nur geschehen, wenn einer von euch mir seine Hand reicht," sagte die Eule.

6. Die beiden Störche schienen über den Antrag etwas betroffen zu sein, und der Kalif winkte seinem Diener, ein wenig mit ihm hinaus zu gehen. " Grosswesir," sprach vor der Tür der Kalif, " das ist ein dummer Handel, aber ihr könntet sie schon nehmen." " So? " antwortete dieser, " dass mir meine Frau, wenn ich nach Haus komme, die Augen auskratzt? Auch bin ich ein alter Mann, und ihr seid noch jung und unverheiratet, und könnt eher einer schönen, jungen Prinzessin die Hand geben."

7. Sie redeten einander gegenseitig noch lange zu, endlich aber, als der Kalif sah, dass sein Wesir lieber Storch bleiben, als die Eule heiraten wollte, entschloss er sich, die Bedingung lieber selbst zu erfüllen. Die Eule war hocherfreut. Sie gestand ihnen, dass sie zu keiner besseren Zeit hätten kommen können, weil wahrscheinlich in dieser Nacht die Zauberer sich versammeln würden.

8. Sie verliess mit den Störchen das Gemach, um sie in jenen Saal zu führen; sie gingen lange in einem finstern Gang hin; endlich strahlte ihnen aus einer halbverfallenen Mauer ein heller Schein entgegen. Sie konnten von der Lücke, an welcher sie standen, einen grossen Saal übersehen. Rings um einen Tisch zog sich ein Sofa, auf welchem acht Männer sassen. In einem dieser Männer erkannten die Störche jenen Krämer wieder, der ihnen das Zauberpulver

verkauft hatte. Er erzählte unter andern auch die Geschichte des Kalifen und seines Wesirs. " Was für ein Wort hast du ihnen denn aufgegeben?" fragte ihn ein anderer Zauberer. " Ein recht schweres, lateinisches, es heisst Mutabor."

V.

1. Als die Störche an ihrer Mauerlücke dieses hörten, kamen sie vor Freude beinahe ausser sich. Sie liefen auf ihren langen Füssen so schnell dem Tore der Ruine zu, dass die Eule kaum folgen konnte. Dort sprach der Kalif gerührt zu der Eule: " Retterin meines Lebens und des Lebens meines Freundes, nimm zum ewigen Dank für das, was du für uns getan hast, mich zum Gemahl an."

2. Dann aber wandte er sich nach Osten. Dreimal bückten die Störche ihre langen Hälse der Sonne entgegen, die soeben hinter dem Gebirge heraufstieg; MUTABOR riefen sie und im Nu waren sie verwandelt, und in der hohen Freude des neu geschenkten Lebens, lagen Herr und Diener lachend einander in den Armen.

3. Wer beschreibt aber ihr Erstaunen, als sie sich umsahen? Eine schöne Dame, herrlich geschmückt, stand vor ihnen. Lächelnd gab sie dem Kalifen die Hand. " Erkennt ihr eure Nachteule nicht mehr? " sagte sie. Sie war es; der Kalif war von ihrer Schönheit und Anmut so entzückt, dass er ausrief: es sei sein grösstes Glück, dass er Storch geworden sei.

4. Die drei zogen nun miteinander auf Bagdad zu. Der Kalif fand in seinen Kleidern nicht nur die Dose mit Zauberpulver, sondern auch seinen Geldbeutel. Er kaufte daher im nächsten Dorfe, was zu ihrer Reise nötig war, und so kamen sie bald an die Tore von Bagdad. Dort aber erregte die Ankunft des Kalifen grosses Erstaunen. Man hatte sie für tot ausgegeben, und das Volk war daher hoch erfreut, seinen geliebten Herrscher wieder zu haben.

5. Um so mehr aber entbrannte ihr Hass gegen den

Betrüger Mizra. Sie zogen in den Palast und nahmen den alten Zauberer und seinen Sohn gefangen. Den Alten schickte der Kalif in dasselbe Gemach der Ruine, das die Prinzessin als Eule bewohnt hatte, und liess ihn dort aufhängen. Dem Sohn aber, welcher nichts von den Künsten des Vaters verstand, liess der Kalif die Wahl, ob er sterben oder schnupfen wolle.

6. Als er das letztere wählte, bot ihm der Grosswesir die Dose. Eine tüchtige Prise, und das Zauberwort des Kalifen verwandelte ihn in einen Storch. Der Kalif liess ihn in einen eisernen Käfig sperren und in seinem Garten aufstellen. Lange und vergnügt lebte der Kalif mit seiner Frau, der Prinzessin; seine vergnügtesten Stunden waren immer die, wenn ihn der Grosswesir besuchte. Da sprachen sie dann oft von ihrem Storchenabenteur, und wenn der Kalif recht heiter war, liess er sich herab, den Grosswesir nachzuahmen, wie er als Storch aussah.

7. Er ging dann ernsthaft, mit steifen Füssen im Zimmer auf und ab, wedelte mit den Armen, wie mit Flügeln, und zeigte, wie jener sich vergeblich nach Osten geneigt und Mu . . ., Mu . . ., Mu . . ., dazu gerufen habe. Für die Frau Kalifin und ihre Kinder war diese Vorstellung allemal eine grosse Freude; wenn aber der Kalif gar zu lange nickte und Mu . . ., Mu . . ., schrie, dann drohte ihm der Grosswesir: er wollte (*or* wolle) das, was vor der Türe der Prinzessin Nachteule verhandelt worden sei, der Frau Kalifin mitteilen.